I0885426

Implementing Rapid E-Learning Through Interactive Materials Development

Mohammad Issack Santally
University of Mauritius, Mauritius

Yousra Rajabalee
Mauritius Institute of Education, Mauritius

Ravi Rajputh
University of Mauritius, Mauritius

A volume in the Advances in Educational Technologies and Instructional Design (AETID) Book Series

IGI Global
PUBLISHER of TIMELY KNOWLEDGE

Published in the United States of America by
IGI Global
Information Science Reference (an imprint of IGI Global)
701 E. Chocolate Avenue
Hershey PA, USA 17033
Tel: 717-533-8845
Fax: 717-533-8661
E-mail: cust@igi-global.com
Web site: http://www.igi-global.com

Library of Congress Cataloging-in-Publication Data

Names: Santally, Mohammad, 1977- editor. | Rajabalee, Yousra Banoor, 1982- editor. | Rajputh, Ravi, 1990- editor.
Title: Implementing rapid e-learning through interactive materials development / Mohammad Santally, Yousra Banoor Rajabalee, and Ravi Rajputh, Editor.
Description: Hershey, PA : Information Science Reference, [2023] | Includes bibliographical references and index. | Summary: "This research book presents relevant theoretical foundations for the design and development of interactive learning materials using the rapid e-learning method, drawing on research, case studies and/or reports from different contextual applications of the method, the challenges, and learning experiences of students"-- Provided by publisher.
Identifiers: LCCN 2022034163 (print) | LCCN 2022034164 (ebook) | ISBN 9781668449400 (hardcover) | ISBN 9781668449448 (paperback) | ISBN 9781668449417 (ebook)
Subjects: LCSH: Web-based instruction. | Teaching--Aids and devices--Design and construction. | Educational technology. | Curriculum planning.
Classification: LCC LB1028.57 .I47 2023 (print) | LCC LB1028.57 (ebook) | DDC 371.33/44678--dc23/eng/20220825
LC record available at https://lccn.loc.gov/2022034163
LC ebook record available at https://lccn.loc.gov/2022034164

This book is published in the IGI Global book series Advances in Educational Technologies and Instructional Design (AETID) (ISSN: 2326-8905; eISSN: 2326-8913)

British Cataloguing in Publication Data
A Cataloguing in Publication record for this book is available from the British Library.

Advances in Educational Technologies and Instructional Design (AETID) Book Series

ISSN:2326-8905
EISSN:2326-8913

Editor-in-Chief: Lawrence A. Tomei, Robert Morris University, USA

MISSION

Education has undergone, and continues to undergo, immense changes in the way it is enacted and distributed to both child and adult learners. In modern education, the traditional classroom learning experience has evolved to include technological resources and to provide online classroom opportunities to students of all ages regardless of their geographical locations. From distance education, Massive-Open-Online-Courses (MOOCs), and electronic tablets in the classroom, technology is now an integral part of learning and is also affecting the way educators communicate information to students.

The **Advances in Educational Technologies & Instructional Design (AETID) Book Series** explores new research and theories for facilitating learning and improving educational performance utilizing technological processes and resources. The series examines technologies that can be integrated into K-12 classrooms to improve skills and learning abilities in all subjects including STEM education and language learning. Additionally, it studies the emergence of fully online classrooms for young and adult learners alike, and the communication and accountability challenges that can arise. Trending topics that are covered include adaptive learning, game-based learning, virtual school environments, and social media effects. School administrators, educators, academicians, researchers, and students will find this series to be an excellent resource for the effective design and implementation of learning technologies in their classes.

COVERAGE

- Instructional Design
- K-12 Educational Technologies
- Instructional Design Models
- E-Learning
- Bring-Your-Own-Device
- Hybrid Learning
- Collaboration Tools
- Adaptive Learning
- Educational Telecommunications
- Classroom Response Systems

The Advances in Educational Technologies and Instructional Design (AETID) Book Series (ISSN 2326-8905) is published by IGI Global, 701 E. Chocolate Avenue, Hershey, PA 17033-1240, USA, www.igi-global.com. This series is composed of titles available for purchase individually; each title is edited to be contextually exclusive from any other title within the series. For pricing and ordering information please visit http://www.igi-global.com/book-series/advances-educational-technologies-instructional-design/73678. Postmaster: Send all address changes to above address.

Titles in this Series

For a list of additional titles in this series, please visit:
http://www.igi-global.com/book-series/advances-educational-technologies-instructional-design/73678

Fostering Science Teaching and Learning for the Fourth Industrial Revolution and Beyond
Garima Bansal (Australian Council for Educational Research, India) and Umesh Ramnarain (University of Johannesburg, South Africa)
Information Science Reference • copyright 2023 • 290pp • H/C (ISBN: 9781668469323) • US $215.00 (our price)

Phenomenological Studies in Education
Jason D. DeHart (University of Tennessee, Knoxville, USA)
Information Science Reference • copyright 2023 • 328pp • H/C (ISBN: 9781668482766) • US $215.00 (our price)

Practices That Promote Innovation for Talented Students
Julia Nyberg (Purdue University Global, USA) and Jessica Manzone (University of Southern California, USA)
Information Science Reference • copyright 2023 • 300pp • H/C (ISBN: 9781668458068) • US $215.00 (our price)

Cases on Error Analysis in Foreign Language Technical Writing
Nadezhda Anatolievna Lebedeva (Kherson State Agrarian and Economic University, Ukraine)
Information Science Reference • copyright 2023 • 300pp • H/C (ISBN: 9781668462225) • US $215.00 (our price)

Using Assistive Technology for Inclusive Learning in K-12 Classrooms
Jeremy Bell (University of Louisiana at Monroe, USA) and Timothy Gifford (Movia Robotics Inc, USA)
Information Science Reference • copyright 2023 • 300pp • H/C (ISBN: 9781668464243) • US $215.00 (our price)

For an entire list of titles in this series, please visit:
http://www.igi-global.com/book-series/advances-educational-technologies-instructional-design/73678

IGI Global
PUBLISHER of TIMELY KNOWLEDGE

701 East Chocolate Avenue, Hershey, PA 17033, USA
Tel: 717-533-8845 x100 • Fax: 717-533-8661
E-Mail: cust@igi-global.com • www.igi-global.com

Table of Contents

Preface xii

Chapter 1
A Guide to E-Learning: When the Entire World Was Caught in the Center of a Storm, Technology Played a Critical Role 1
Tahani R. K. Bsharat, Universiti Sains Islam Malaysia, Malaysia
Fariza Behak, Universiti Sains Islam Malaysia, Malaysia
Islam A. Ismail, The English and Foreign Languages University, India

Chapter 2
Aligning Interactive Multimedia Development Practices With Mayer's Split-Attention Effect Principle 11
Yousra Banoor Rajabalee, Mauritius Institute of Education, Mauritius

Chapter 3
Multimodal Assessment in Higher Education: Reflections From Student Perspectives 27
Dorothy Cooshna-Naik, University of Mauritius, Mauritius
Linda Van Laren, University of KwaZulu-Natal, South Africa
Claudia Mitchell, McGill University, Canada

Chapter 4
Rapid Game Development Using LiveCode in SEN and DHH Education 54
Gwendoline Laurissa Chan, University of Mauritius, Mauritius
Jack Whitehead, University of Cumbria, UK

Chapter 5
Use of Scenario-Based Language Learning to Develop English Language Speaking Skills in Online Classrooms 76
Zeynep Çetin Köroğlu, Aksaray University, Turkey
Erkan Yüce, Aksaray University, Turkey

Chapter 6
Designing Goal-Oriented Online Speaking Activities for EFL Learners in a Post-Pandemic World: Insights From CEFR Companion Volume 95
Erkan Yüce, Aksaray University, Turkey
Zeynep Çetin Köroğlu, Aksaray University, Turkey

Chapter 7
A Novel Framework for Developing Digital Platforms for Engineering Students 115
KS Sastry Musti, Namibia University of Science and Technology, Namibia
Harmony Kuitakwashe Musiyarira, Namibia University of Science and Technology, Namibia

Chapter 8
Evaluation and Quality Assurance for Rapid E-Learning and Development of Digital Learning Resources 139
C. V. Suresh Babu, Hindustan Institute of Technolgy and Science, India
B. Rohan, Hindustan Institute of Technology and Science, India

Chapter 9
The Rapid E-Learning Method: A Guide to Developing Interactive Materials Development 171
Mohammad Issack Santally, University of Mauritius, Mauritius
Yousra Rajabalee, Mauritius Institute of Education, Mauritius
Ashvin Beetul, University of Mauritius, Mauritius

Compilation of References 183

Related References 205

About the Contributors 227

Index 231

Detailed Table of Contents

Preface xii

Chapter 1
A Guide to E-Learning: When the Entire World Was Caught in the Center of a Storm, Technology Played a Critical Role 1
Tahani R. K. Bsharat, Universiti Sains Islam Malaysia, Malaysia
Fariza Behak, Universiti Sains Islam Malaysia, Malaysia
Islam A. Ismail, The English and Foreign Languages University, India

The authors pinpoint the fact that e-learning had been successfully implemented in the classroom before the pandemic. This implantation was mainly found in the tutorials. These tutorials were helpful to students through online recorded classes and other learning systems. Together, the present chapter presents a historical development of e-learning from 2000 to the present time. Another promising aim of this chapter is to offer newly employed teachers a proper understanding of types of e-learning; thus, they can employ e-learning effectively in their classes. Planned comparisons were revealed regarding the benefits and drawbacks of e-learning. The chapter concludes that the educational field received a massive change by giving the opportunity for education to carry on during the school shut. E-learning gives both students and teachers a variety of multimedia options to meet the curriculum outcomes without a physical appearance in the classroom.

Chapter 2
Aligning Interactive Multimedia Development Practices With Mayer's Split-Attention Effect Principle 11
Yousra Banoor Rajabalee, Mauritius Institute of Education, Mauritius

Multimedia learning can be defined as the construction of knowledge based on instructions that are delivered through the combined use of visuals such as text, images, animations, etc. It is best described by Richard Mayer, one of the leading researchers in this area who postulated that people learn better from words and pictures than from words alone. Multimedia instructions have for objectives to enhance and promote meaningful learning. The split-attention effect occurs when multimedia instruction is designed in a way that it requires learners to split their attention between, and mentally integrate multiple sources of information that are separate in temporal or physical dimensions/locations. Mayer's principles are guiding constructs, useful for creating effective interactive multimedia materials. This chapter elaborates and sheds light on how to creatively design or develop multimedia learning materials, which can create constructive knowledge by sustaining good engagement in learning and by overcoming and managing the split-attention problems.

Chapter 3
Multimodal Assessment in Higher Education: Reflections From Student Perspectives 27
Dorothy Cooshna-Naik, University of Mauritius, Mauritius
Linda Van Laren, University of KwaZulu-Natal, South Africa
Claudia Mitchell, McGill University, Canada

This chapter explores the implementation of an alternative form of assessment at a higher education institution (HEI) in Mauritius. As part of their module entitled 'Mauritian History,' a group of first year undergraduate students of Faculty of Social Sciences and Humanities were given the opportunity to work on a multimodal assignment which required them to produce a history-related documentary style video. The chapter draws upon students' written reflections collected at different stages of the assignment to share their experiences as creators/producers of knowledge along with their views on this alternative form of assessment at higher education (HE) level. At the end of the assignment, it was found that despite challenges, students felt they gained a lot in terms of content knowledge, personal growth, and emotional development. The implications and recommendations for digitally enhanced multimodal assessment at HE level are presented.

Chapter 4
Rapid Game Development Using LiveCode in SEN and DHH Education 54
Gwendoline Laurissa Chan, University of Mauritius, Mauritius
Jack Whitehead, University of Cumbria, UK

For over 30 years, literacy has been recognized as a key concern in Special Education Needs (SEN) and especially in Deaf and Hard of Hearing (DHH) education. No different in Mauritius, these children struggle to get passing marks in French language at elementary level. Addressing this concern, literature has been reviewed in the context of games for SEN and DHH education. Taking advantage of the potential of gamification, simple letter games have been developed using LiveCode. The games were administered to a sample of 14 SEN and DHH elementary students using the underlying action research theoretical framework. To assess the effectiveness of the games, the students' level of motivation after using the games was measured using the Instructional Materials Motivation Survey (IMMS) based on Keller's (2010) ARCS motivation model. The results demonstrated the potential of using LiveCode to develop timely serious games to support SEN and DHH students' literacy skills.

Chapter 5
Use of Scenario-Based Language Learning to Develop English Language Speaking Skills in Online Classrooms 76
Zeynep Çetin Köroğlu, Aksaray University, Turkey
Erkan Yüce, Aksaray University, Turkey

Developing EFL/ESL learners' speaking skills plays a crucial role to make them capable communicators of target language in a real- life situation. As a recently developing frame or approach, scenario-based language learning may be utilized to foster English language speaking skills of language learners. In this respect the current study contains sections to discuss scenario- based language learning, to present how to use this approach to develop language learners' speaking skills development, to present implementation of scenario-based language learning in online classrooms and propose a sample scenario based speaking task series for EFL learners.

Chapter 6
Designing Goal-Oriented Online Speaking Activities for EFL Learners in a Post-Pandemic World: Insights From CEFR Companion Volume 95
Erkan Yüce, Aksaray University, Turkey
Zeynep Çetin Köroğlu, Aksaray University, Turkey

The Covid-19 pandemic continues to affect every aspect of life. English language education has been shifted from face-to-face education to online education as a result of sudden decisions. English language teachers and learners are expected to adapt to this sudden change and manage the process effectively, without considering their technological competence and knowledge about technology's integration into foreign language pedagogy. In the process of teaching English as a foreign language, speaking skills teaching, which is often neglected compared to other skills, has become more limited in online education due to various reasons. There is not enough study in the existing literature on the design of digital speaking activities. Therefore, the current book section deals with the design of goal-oriented digital speaking skills activities within the framework of the CEFR CV. Additionally, examples of goal-oriented digital speaking activities are presented in the present book chapter. The chapter will guide language teachers to design digital speaking activities appropriate to CEFR CV.

Chapter 7
A Novel Framework for Developing Digital Platforms for Engineering Students.......115
KS Sastry Musti, Namibia University of Science and Technology, Namibia
Harmony Kuitakwashe Musiyarira, Namibia University of Science and Technology, Namibia

This chapter presents a novel framework for the design and development of digital platforms using mature rapid e-learning tools for teaching and learning purposes, specifically in engineering programs. A good number of recent works have been summarized and then the foundation for the chapter is provided. The development process for a simple rapid e-learning tool is outlined, and a 3-tier architecture for a simple digital platform is also presented. Then, the chapter presents a novel framework that uses rapid e-learning tools in the design and development process of digital platforms. Challenges associated with developing digital platforms and important steps in the strategic deployment of the suggested framework are illustrated.

Chapter 8
Evaluation and Quality Assurance for Rapid E-Learning and Development of Digital Learning Resources.......139
C. V. Suresh Babu, Hindustan Institute of Technolgy and Science, India
B. Rohan, Hindustan Institute of Technology and Science, India

E-learning has turned into an undeniably significant instructing and learning mode in instructive organizations and corporate preparation. To guarantee that quality is settled in the use of innovation to accomplish instructive objectives, it is basic to follow the quality checking strategy all through the phases of e-learning asset plan, creation, and conveyance. From a pattern of training of endeavoring to assess numerous e-learning programs, one of the most serious issues has ended up being taking care of the quantity of factors which possibly influence on the viability of the program and concluding what are reliant, free, and unessential factors in a given circumstance. The evaluation of e-learning project has cultivated a more complete construction. This study demonstrates the authoring tool which is used to create the digital learning content and evaluation criteria, and how the quality of e-Learning resources is maintained, and finally the future development of digital learning resources.

Chapter 9
The Rapid E-Learning Method: A Guide to Developing Interactive Materials Development 171
Mohammad Issack Santally, University of Mauritius, Mauritius
Yousra Rajabalee, Mauritius Institute of Education, Mauritius
Ashvin Beetul, University of Mauritius, Mauritius

Rapid e-learning is a method to develop and deploy quality interactive learning materials in a shorter time span, and to address learning needs in different contexts—academic, professional, or commercial. Resources developed via rapid e-learning methods can be used in educational institutions from pre-primary to tertiary levels. They can also be used for professional training, short courses, or more advanced training that leads to alternative qualifications or micro-credentials that are recognised in the workplace. Often, they can be used as agile content to train sales officers on a new product on the market. In such situations, their relevance and lifespan are limited. Rapid e-learning allows for maximum flexibility in terms of re-use of learning materials and modification of content provided it is carefully planned and designed. One has to also design accessibility to ensure inclusiveness in the educational delivery approach. In this chapter, the authors provide an overview of the rapid e-learning method and its application to the development of interactive learning materials.

Compilation of References 183

Related References 205

About the Contributors 227

Index 231

Preface

In recent years, the landscape of education has undergone a significant transformation, fueled by advancements in technology and a growing demand for innovative learning experiences. As a result, the development of interactive digital learning resources has become a crucial endeavor for educators and instructional designers alike. However, the traditional approach to creating such resources was often time-consuming, expensive, and required a multitude of specialized skills.

In this edited reference book, we delve into the world of rapid e-learning, a process model that empowers education practitioners to design and develop interactive multimedia learning resources within shorter time frames and at reduced costs. Gone are the days when content developers, technology experts, and learning designers had to work in separate silos. With the advent of new tools, the fusion of these roles has become seamless, enabling educators to take charge of their own digital resource development without requiring advanced mastery of ICTs.

Our aim with this book is to provide education practitioners, institution heads, and policy-makers with a comprehensive guide to implementing the rapid e-learning method. Drawing on research, case studies, and reports from various contextual applications, we offer a theoretical foundation that underpins the design and development of interactive learning materials. We also delve into the challenges faced and the invaluable learning experiences of students who have engaged with these resources.

Within these pages, readers will find practical examples, techniques, and tools that will enhance their understanding of the rapid e-learning process and facilitate its successful implementation within their own unique contexts. From historical perspectives to the foundations of learning design, from Mayer's Principles of Multimedia Learning to learning design approaches, we cover a wide range of topics that will equip educators with the knowledge and skills needed to create effective interactive digital learning resources.

We also explore the realm of rapid e-learning authoring tools, both open-source and proprietary, offering insights into their functionalities and suitability for different projects. Additionally, we provide guidance on the design and development of interactive digital learning resources, as well as the delivery and tracking of student learning through Learning Management Systems.

Evaluation and quality assurance play vital roles in the rapid e-learning process, and we delve into these areas to help educators ensure the effectiveness and impact of their digital learning resources. Furthermore, we discuss managing large-scale course digitization projects, capacity-building of education practitioners, and the achievements and experiences of students engaging with digital learning resources.

We extend our gratitude to the contributing authors who have shared their expertise and experiences in this book, as well as the reviewers who have provided invaluable feedback. Their collective efforts have made this a comprehensive and insightful resource for all those interested in harnessing the power of rapid e-learning and interactive materials development.

We hope that this book will serve as a valuable guide, informing education practitioners, institutional leaders, and policy-makers about the state-of-the-art practices in interactive digital learning resources. Through the rapid e-learning method, we aspire to decentralize curriculum digitization, empower educators to embrace technology, and foster a culture of sharing and collaboration among peers and practitioners.

CHAPTER OVERVIEW

In the first chapter of our book, titled "A Guide to E-learning," authors Tahani R. K. Bsharat, Fariaz Behak, and Islan A. Ismail shed light on the historical development of e-learning from 2000 to the present time. They emphasize that even before the pandemic, e-learning had already made its mark in classrooms, particularly through the implementation of tutorials. These tutorials, which encompassed online recorded classes and other learning systems, proved to be highly beneficial for students (Kattoua et al., 2016).

The primary objective of this chapter is to provide newly employed teachers with a comprehensive understanding of the different types of e-learning, enabling them to effectively incorporate e-learning strategies into their classes. The authors delve into planned comparisons that reveal both the advantages and disadvantages of e-learning, giving educators a clear perspective on the benefits and challenges associated with this approach.

The chapter concludes by highlighting the significant impact of e-learning on the educational landscape, particularly during times of school closures. E-learning has played a pivotal role in ensuring that education can continue despite physical constraints. By offering students and teachers a wide range of multimedia options, e-learning allows for the fulfillment of curriculum outcomes without the need for a physical presence in the classroom.

Chapter 1 sets the stage for the subsequent chapters in this book, laying a strong foundation by exploring the historical context and benefits of e-learning. It serves as an essential guide for educators, equipping them with the knowledge and insights necessary to navigate the world of e-learning and harness its full potential.

Chapter 2 of our book, titled "Aligning Interactive Multimedia Development Practices with Mayer's Split-Attention Effect Principle," authored by Yousra Banoor Rajabalee, explores the concept of multimedia learning and its impact on knowledge construction. The chapter begins by defining multimedia learning as the process of acquiring knowledge through instructions delivered using a combination of visual elements such as text, images, and animations. Richard Mayer, a prominent researcher in this field, emphasizes that people learn better when information is presented in both visual and verbal formats, rather than relying solely on words.

The chapter focuses on Mayer's split-attention effect principle, which occurs when multimedia instruction requires learners to divide their attention and mentally integrate multiple sources of information that are separate in temporal or physical dimensions. By understanding and applying Mayer's principles, educators can effectively design and develop interactive multimedia learning materials that enhance meaningful learning experiences.

The chapter goes on to explore the creative design and development of multimedia learning materials, emphasizing the importance of sustaining learner engagement and addressing the challenges posed by the split-attention effect. Through practical insights and guidance, educators can overcome these challenges and create interactive multimedia resources that facilitate constructive knowledge construction.

Chapter 2 serves as a valuable resource for educators and instructional designers seeking to align their multimedia development practices with Mayer's principles. By embracing these guiding constructs, they can create engaging and effective multimedia learning materials that optimize the learning experience and promote deep understanding.

Readers will gain a deeper understanding of how to leverage interactive multimedia resources to overcome the split-attention effect and foster meaningful learning outcomes. The chapter provides practical strategies and recommendations for managing the design and development process, ensuring that learners can fully engage with the multimedia content and construct knowledge effectively.

Chapter 3 of our book, titled "Multimodal Assessment at Higher Education: Reflections from Students' Perspective," is authored by Dorothy Cooshna Naik, Linda Van Laren, and Claudia Mitchell. This chapter delves into the implementation of an alternative form of assessment at a Higher Education Institution (HEI) in Mauritius.

The authors focus on a specific module titled "Mauritian History," where first-year undergraduate students from the faculty of Social Sciences and Humanities were given the opportunity to engage in a multimodal assignment. This assignment required students to produce a history-related documentary-style video. Throughout the chapter, the authors draw upon the written reflections of the students, which were collected at different stages of the assignment. By sharing the students' experiences as creators and producers of knowledge, the chapter provides valuable insights into their perspectives on this alternative form of assessment at the Higher Education (HE) level.

The chapter reveals that despite encountering challenges along the way, students felt that they gained significant benefits from engaging in the multimodal assignment. These benefits encompassed not only the acquisition of content knowledge but also personal growth and emotional development. The students' reflections shed light on the transformative nature of this type of assessment and highlight its potential in enhancing the learning experience at the HE level.

By presenting the implications and recommendations for digitally-enhanced multimodal assessment at the HE level, this chapter offers guidance and insights for educators and institutions looking to incorporate innovative assessment methods into their curricula. It underscores the importance of considering students' perspectives and experiences in shaping effective assessment practices that promote meaningful learning outcomes.

Chapter 3 provides a valuable resource for educators, administrators, and researchers interested in exploring multimodal assessment strategies in higher education. By understanding the students' perspectives and their experiences as knowledge creators, readers can gain a deeper understanding of the benefits and challenges associated with this alternative form of assessment.

In Chapter 4, authors Gwendoline Chan and Jack Whitehead explore the application of rapid game development using LiveCode in the context of Special Education Needs (SEN) and Deaf and Hard of Hearing (DHH) education. They highlight the longstanding concern regarding literacy skills among SEN and DHH students, particularly in the French language at the elementary level in Mauritius.

To address this concern, the authors conducted a literature review on the use of games in SEN and DHH education. Recognizing the potential of gamification, they developed simple letter games using LiveCode, a programming language and development environment. These games were then administered to a sample of 14 elementary students with SEN and DHH, following an action research theoretical framework.

To assess the effectiveness of the games, the authors measured the students' level of motivation after using the games using the Instructional Materials Motivation Survey (IMMS), which is based on Keller's ARCS motivation model. The results showcased the potential of LiveCode in developing timely and engaging serious games that support the literacy skills of SEN and DHH students.

This chapter offers insights into the practical application of LiveCode for rapid game development in the field of SEN and DHH education. By leveraging gamification techniques, educators can enhance students' engagement and motivation, thus promoting the development of essential literacy skills. The results of this study serve as evidence for the effectiveness of using LiveCode in developing educational games that cater to the specific needs of SEN and DHH students.

Educators, researchers, and practitioners in the field of special education will find this chapter valuable, as it showcases the potential of game-based learning and highlights the positive impact it can have on literacy skill development. It provides guidance on incorporating rapid game development techniques using LiveCode to create engaging and effective learning experiences for SEN and DHH students.

Chapter 5, authored by Zeynep Çetin Köroğlu and Erkan Yüce, explores the utilization of scenario-based language learning to enhance English language speaking skills in online classrooms. The authors emphasize the significance of developing learners' speaking skills to enable effective communication in real-life situations. They introduce scenario-based language learning as a recently developing approach that can be employed to foster speaking skills among English as a Foreign Language (EFL) learners.

This chapter delves into various sections that discuss the concept of scenario-based language learning, providing insights on how this approach can be used to facilitate the development of speaking skills in language learners. Additionally, the authors present the implementation of scenario-based language learning specifically in online classrooms. They propose a sample scenario-based speaking task series tailored for EFL learners, offering practical guidance for educators in designing effective speaking activities.

Chapter 5 serves as a valuable resource for educators seeking innovative methods to promote English language speaking skills in online environments. By leveraging scenario-based language learning, teachers can create engaging and authentic learning experiences that enable learners to apply their language skills in meaningful contexts. The chapter provides theoretical background, practical examples, and implementation strategies to support educators in incorporating scenario-based language learning into their teaching practices.

In Chapter 6, authors Erkan Yüce and Zeynep Çetin Köroğlu address the challenges faced by English language education in the wake of the Covid-19 pandemic. With the sudden shift from face-to-face education to online learning, teachers and learners are required to adapt to this new reality, often without sufficient technological competence and knowledge of integrating technology into foreign language pedagogy.

The chapter specifically focuses on the teaching of speaking skills, which has become more limited in online education due to various factors. Recognizing the need for effective design of digital speaking activities, the authors explore the concept of goal-oriented online speaking activities within the framework of the CEFR Companion Volume. They offer insights and examples of goal-oriented digital speaking activities, providing language teachers with practical guidance in designing speaking activities aligned with the CEFR Companion Volume.

This chapter addresses the gap in the existing literature regarding the design of digital speaking activities. It equips language teachers with strategies and examples that help facilitate meaningful speaking practice in online settings. By considering the goals outlined in the CEFR Companion Volume, teachers can create engaging and effective digital speaking activities that enhance learners' language proficiency.

Chapter 6 serves as a valuable guide for language teachers navigating the challenges of online education in the post-pandemic world. By incorporating the insights and examples provided, educators can design goal-oriented speaking activities that align with the CEFR Companion Volume and foster the development of learners' speaking skills in online environments.

In Chapter 7, authors K.S Sastry Musti and Harmony Kuitakwashe Musiyarira introduce a novel framework for designing and developing digital platforms tailored for teaching and learning purposes, specifically within the context of engineering programs. The chapter begins by summarizing recent works in the field, providing a foundation for the subsequent discussions.

The authors outline the development process for a simple rapid e-learning tool and present a 3-tier architecture for a basic digital platform. Building upon this, they introduce a novel framework that leverages rapid e-learning tools in the design and development of digital platforms. The chapter sheds light on the challenges associated with developing digital platforms and highlights the important steps involved in the strategic deployment of the proposed framework.

This chapter serves as a comprehensive guide for educators and developers seeking to create effective digital platforms for engineering students. By utilizing rapid e-learning tools and following the outlined framework, educators can enhance the teaching and learning experience, providing engineering students with a dynamic and interactive platform for their studies.

The authors provide valuable insights and practical recommendations for addressing the challenges associated with developing digital platforms. They emphasize the importance of strategic planning and thoughtful deployment to ensure the successful implementation of the framework.

Educators, instructional designers, and developers in the field of engineering education will find this chapter beneficial, as it presents a novel framework that can be applied to create tailored digital platforms. By following the guidelines and leveraging rapid e-learning tools, educators can provide engineering students with engaging and effective learning experiences, fostering their growth and development in the field.

Chapter 8, authored by C. V. Suresh Babu and B. Rohan, addresses the critical aspect of evaluation and quality assurance in the context of rapid e-learning and the development of digital learning resources. As e-learning continues to gain prominence in educational institutions and corporate training, ensuring the integration of quality throughout the process becomes essential.

To achieve educational goals effectively using technology, it is crucial to follow a quality monitoring procedure during the various stages of e-learning resource design, creation, and delivery. One of the challenges in evaluating e-learning programs lies in handling numerous factors that may impact their effectiveness and determining the dependencies, independence, and irrelevance of these factors in a given situation. Evaluating e-learning projects requires a comprehensive framework that considers the complexity of these programs.

This chapter discusses the authoring tools used in creating digital learning content and presents evaluation criteria for assessing the quality of e-learning resources. It explores how the quality assurance process is implemented to ensure the effectiveness and reliability of digital learning resources. Additionally, the chapter examines the future development of digital learning resources, providing insights into potential advancements in the field.

By delving into evaluation and quality assurance in rapid e-learning and digital learning resource development, this chapter serves as a guide for educators and instructional designers. It emphasizes the importance of maintaining high standards of quality throughout the design and implementation process, ultimately enhancing the effectiveness and impact of e-learning initiatives.

Educators, instructional designers, and professionals involved in e-learning development will find this chapter valuable as it provides practical strategies, evaluation criteria, and considerations for maintaining the quality and effectiveness of digital learning resources. It offers insights into the evaluation process, authoring tools, and the future direction of digital learning resource development, enabling readers to make informed decisions and improvements in their e-learning practices.

Chapter 9 of this book, authored by Mohammad Issack Santally, Yousra Rajabalee, and Ashvin Beetul, delves into the realm of rapid e-learning, a method that revolutionizes the development and deployment of interactive learning materials. In today's fast-paced world, where learning needs arise in various contexts such as academia, professional environments, and commercial sectors, the demand for effective and efficient educational resources has reached unprecedented levels. Rapid e-learning emerges as a powerful solution to meet these demands within shorter timeframes.

The potential of resources created through rapid e-learning extends across the entire educational spectrum, from pre-primary to tertiary levels. Additionally, these resources find application in professional training, short courses, and advanced training programs that offer alternative qualifications or micro-credentials recognized in the workplace. They can even be utilized as agile content to train sales officers on new products entering the market, albeit with a limited relevance and lifespan.

A key advantage of rapid e-learning lies in its inherent flexibility, allowing for the maximum reusability and modification of learning materials. However, this flexibility can only be harnessed through careful planning and meticulous design. It is crucial to consider the design principles of accessibility, ensuring inclusiveness in the educational delivery approach. By prioritizing accessibility, we can enable learners from diverse backgrounds and abilities to fully engage with the interactive learning materials.

This chapter serves as an invaluable resource for educators, instructional designers, and e-learning professionals, as it provides a comprehensive overview of the rapid e-learning method and its application in the development of interactive learning materials. By exploring the principles and techniques behind rapid e-learning, readers will gain insights into how to leverage this approach to meet the evolving needs of learners in an ever-changing educational landscape.

IN SUMMARY

As we conclude this preface, we reflect upon the rich and diverse chapters that comprise this edited reference book on implementing rapid e-learning through interactive materials development. The journey through the various chapters has been enlightening, showcasing the evolution and application of innovative approaches in education.

Throughout the book, we have explored the transformative power of rapid e-learning, which has revolutionized the development of interactive digital learning resources. From the historical perspective of e-learning to the practical implementation of scenario-based language learning and multimodal assessment, each chapter has contributed to a comprehensive understanding of how to leverage technology to enhance teaching and learning experiences.

We have seen the emergence of novel frameworks for digital platform development, the alignment of interactive multimedia practices with cognitive principles, and the design of goal-oriented online speaking activities. These contributions have paved the way for educators to embrace technology, adapt to the challenges of online education, and empower learners to thrive in the digital era.

Furthermore, the importance of evaluation and quality assurance in the realm of rapid e-learning has been highlighted, emphasizing the need for continuous improvement and the establishment of effective evaluation criteria. By ensuring the quality of digital learning resources, educators can enhance the learning outcomes and experiences of their students.

As editors, we are grateful to the authors who have shared their expertise, research, and practical insights in this book. Their collective efforts have created a valuable resource for education practitioners, instructional designers, and policy-makers seeking to stay at the forefront of interactive digital learning resources and the rapid e-learning method.

We hope that this book serves as a catalyst for innovation and change, inspiring educators to embrace technology, design engaging learning experiences, and empower learners in their educational journeys. The transformative potential of rapid e-learning is within our grasp, and through its implementation, we can revolutionize education and create a brighter future for learners worldwide.

Mohammad Issack Santally
University of Mauritius, Mauritius

Yousra Rajabalee
University of Mauritius, Mauritius

Ravi Rajputh
University of Mauritius, Mauritius

Chapter 1
A Guide to E-Learning:
When the Entire World Was Caught in the Center of a Storm, Technology Played a Critical Role

Tahani R. K. Bsharat
Universiti Sains Islam Malaysia, Malaysia

Fariza Behak
Universiti Sains Islam Malaysia, Malaysia

Islam A. Ismail
The English and Foreign Languages University, India

ABSTRACT

The authors pinpoint the fact that e-learning had been successfully implemented in the classroom before the pandemic. This implantation was mainly found in the tutorials. These tutorials were helpful to students through online recorded classes and other learning systems. Together, the present chapter presents a historical development of e-learning from 2000 to the present time. Another promising aim of this chapter is to offer newly employed teachers a proper understanding of types of e-learning; thus, they can employ e-learning effectively in their classes. Planned comparisons were revealed regarding the benefits and drawbacks of e-learning. The chapter concludes that the educational field received a massive change by giving the opportunity for education to carry on during the school shut. E-learning gives both students and teachers a variety of multimedia options to meet the curriculum outcomes without a physical appearance in the classroom.

DOI: 10.4018/978-1-6684-4940-0.ch001

DEVELOPMENT OF E-LEARNING FROM 2000 TO THE PRESENT TIME

Research on e-learning has a long tradition. The definition of e-learning received interesting attention among authors worldwide. In the 2000s, an early study completed by Dublin (2003) revealed that the definition of e-learning differs from one author to another based on their interests in the field. The Dublin claim was not clear enough to satisfy the proper understanding of e-learning. The authors brought to the table of discussion a variety of definitions to offer a proper understanding of this concept. To define e-learning effectively, there are a number of questions that should be answered to build a proper understanding. Some of which are these

- Is e-learning meant to be an online material for learners who live far away from the educational institution?
- Is e-learning as same as virtual learning to enhance physical learning?
- Is e-learning similar to blended learning?
- Is e-learning a network method to activate communicational learning?

Later, Oblinger and Hawkins (2005) agreed with Dublin's and Ireland's concerns on the idea that it is perplexing to accept only one definition of e-learning. That is because they are many concepts that should be involved. One year later, Holmes and Gardner (2006) responded to these contradictions. They suggested that e-learning could be defined in many ways. These ways are well documented. Based on these claims, Rossi (2009) suggested a general definition in which e-learning can include a wide option of applications, learning approaches, and techniques.

However, other authors tried to simplify this term by suggesting simple definitions for the public. Oblinger and Hawkins (2005) believed that e-learning is not only teaching through online mode but also goes beyond. This definition was built based on another early article by the European Commission (2001). The European Commission found that e-learning is part of multimedia modern technology that aims at enhancing learning outcomes through offering access to the learning platform. Giving learners the chance to learn from the internet through technological devices is called e-learning. The authors refined this definition wisely to understand the undergoing meaning. They proclaimed that any activity that uses the internet or the web to learn can be called e-learning (LaRose et al., 1998; Keller & Cernerud, 2002). E-learning can be used in many educational situations such as distance and hybrid learning (Maltz et al., 2005). Seminal contributions have been made by OECD (2005). E-learning is used to foster the learning process in schools, colleges, and higher institutions. Previous studies have shown e-learning as the implantation of information from an online platform for students through electronic devices.

This implantation involves using many elements altogether such as a PC, internet connection, and a learning system (Wentling et al., 2000). Other authors insisted on linking e-learning with distance education. They believed that e-learning is more helpful for students who live very far from the educational institution. For instance, other studies conducted on e-learning described it as a revolutionary strategy (Jennex, 2005; Twigg, 2002). They believed that e-learning is a student-centered approach because it requires students to interact, drill, and produce. A number of authors have recognized e-learning as a mode of learning that is based on PCs and the internet to transfer knowledge to students (Welsh et al., 2003). For a successful e-learning experience, many elements should be available such as a web-based atmosphere, platform, proper internet, and a learning system. In addition, e-learning allows many users to connect to the learning system at the same time. In other words, this can save a lot of time for teachers who can give one class to hundreds of students at the same time. This also helps students to access the learning platform at their appropriate time from different parts of the country (Tao et al., 2006).

In 2007, many authors described e-learning as an enjoyable experience for learners. It allows them to interact and build their knowledge in a dynamic way (Liaw et al., 2007). The results of Liaw also indicated that e-learning is a promising mode because it reduces the costs of learning, boosts the quality of education, and makes the learning process goes further faster. Other supporters to e-learning stated that this kind of learning gives the students the chance to learn and continue working on the important things such as work and achieving aims in life without the need to be physically available on the university campus (Borstorff & Lowe, 2007). E-learning received much more interest because it proved itself worthy of providing a high-quality education for learners.

TYPES OF E-LEARNING

Universities and schools start investing in e-learning since it adhered to being effective and flexible for students to learn. As matter of fact, all the students need is a PC and a good internet connection to access knowledge or learning websites. Afterward, the teacher does not need to be available next to the student either in the classroom or at home. E-learning marginalized the role of the teacher in the learning process and gave the chance for students to be centered during the learning process. Moreover, the e-learning allows a student to choose their favorite e-learning style among a variety of options. Some students like to learn by seeing while others are by hearing. These options could be Code Academy, Facebook, Moodle, World Wide Web, blogs, YouTube, Tik-Tok, and so forth. E-learning becomes somehow trustworthy because people usually use many well-known search engines such as

Google, Bing, and Yahoo to look for fundamental information, what to eat, clothes, news, weather, and other industries within their interest. The developer of e-learning believed in the urgent need to offer new versions and a new platform for learning. Therefore, e-learning can be found in many forms and styles. Here are some forms of e-learning:

- Asynchronous: a kind of learning that is simply inserted into a technological device or the internet.
- Synchronous: a style of learning that requires a teacher to monitor it.
- Blended learning: a way of learning that gather two modes together i.e., offline and online learning at the same time.
- Self-study: this learning style requires the learner to log in to learning platforms to learn.
- Self-study with a tutor: a student goes to a private teaching center to study with an expert in the field.
- Teacher-led students: this type of learning fits distance learning the most. Students from different part of the country or the world join a class given by a teacher through a specific platform.
- PC-based learning: learners can access information through a PC's storage device.
- Video-based learning: learners can learn by watching recorded material such as YouTube (Guragain, 2016). Study table (1):

Table 1. Presents the interactivity of different e-learning styles

Type 1	Type 2	Type 3
Low-interactivity: learning that is based on a ridged text.	Medium interactive learning	E-learning systems which is known for high level of interactivity, either between students or between students and teachers, or both.
PowerPoint material Electronic reading books YouTube Recordings	Interactive material on platforms such as moodle. Questions with comprehensive feedback.	Developed blended e-learning platforms. Online learning games Social media groups

Table (1) shows how different types of e-learning are classified based on their interactive capabilities. Although type three systems are more advanced, users may find that type one or two systems are just as necessary, depending on their needs (Guragain,2016).

THE BENEFITS AND DRAWBACKS OF E-LEARNING

There are three major theoretical and conceptual frameworks for the benefits and drawbacks of e-learning. People are going forward in a rapid way in the digital world. For example, the massive change of the digital word van is seen in the future vision of Meta (Previously known as Facebook). Meta platform does many business industries, one of which is education. Investors from all over the world believe that the future is based on the digital world. Therefore, universities and other educational institutions integrated technology into their teaching style to ensure the continuation of the learning process. These styles have been influential because students and teachers were able to cope with this new style. A large number of alternative approaches have been developed over the last few decades in his field. However, one cannot deny that e-learning is a sword with two edges. Although there are thousands of researches on the advantages of e-learning, there still be some drawbacks. Despite the fact that e-learning is useful and students can obtain a huge amount of information, e-learning could be responsible for misleading knowledge and poor training. Although studies have been conducted by many authors, understanding the reality of e-learning is still insufficiently explored. There are key questions and notions that are still not discussed in the literature and this chapter presents now the benefits and drawbacks of e-learning to close this gape,

There are many alternative methods are available for understanding the advantages of e-learning. Here the authors summarize the remarkable advantages of e-learning. These advantages are likely to be found when active learning and a good learning platform is offered based on their level.

- Students will find it convenient if the learning material can be saved or downloaded so students can go back to the material at their convenience or for their own reference.
- An affordable price. E-learning is somehow cheaper than face-to-face learning since both students and teachers do not need to travel and adhere in the classroom. Moreover, the same platform, device, or memory storage can be used for all courses. There is no need to obtain a different device for each course.
- Updated learning material. The e-learning system allows the teacher to update the material from time to time on regular basis. There is no need to print out the updated material. It is simply can be uploaded on the website for a long time.
- A flexible learning style for all students. The e-learning system is a convenient way to learn. The majority of the study materials are kept in a secure location where students can access them whenever they wish. More importantly,

students learn through different learning styles; thus, it allows students who learn best through visual, auditory, reading and writing, and kinesthetic to take their chance and learn comfortably among all of these.

- E-learning technologies contribute to the creation of a global learning society by allowing everyone, regardless of location, to access study resources. Learners can now contribute to study materials using the systems that are now accessible, which helps to keep the contents up to date.
- E-learning allows a tremendous number of students to attend one class.
- Students have a greater degree of autonomy. Learning new concepts might be tough at times. Students can learn the same content again and over as long as they are happy with using e-learning tools.

However, e-learning suffer from some shortcomings and drawbacks, the authors present the most notable disadvantages of e-learning:

- Insufficient motivation because there is no one to supervise them. Learners who suffer from poor communication skills might not fulfill their aims. Learners are in charge of the course's routine and organization, which might lead to lethargy and low motivation at times. Students may drop out of the course early due to a lack of a set schedule and deadlines.
- The complication of technology usage may stand as a hindrance to learning. The authors believe that not all students come from technological backgrounds, especially those who come from ruler areas. Some students may need some time to learn how to use the electronic device before they go ahead on learning from a particular platform.
- Some countries limit the number of websites that may be accessed, therefore access to websites may not be free everywhere.
- Content Reliability The learning material on the web is not necessarily dependable. There are some individuals who intentionally change some information to transfer a wrong idea about a specific matter. Therefore, as learners, they should exercise caution when looking for information and ensure that the content is reliable before studying it.
- Isolation from others for some students.
- Long-term expenditure management. Although e-learning is usually a less expensive choice, it may be prohibitively costly for some institutions for the first time (Guragain,2016).

A FINAL NOTE ON THIS CHAPTER

More generally, these basic notes are consistent with research showing the pros and cons of e-learning. This table summarizes the findings and contributions made to e-learning. Study table (2):

Table 2.

Pros	Cons
It eliminates the possibility to reply n e-learning during emergencies for learning in a distance mode.	It suffers from poor interaction between a student and a student and a student and their teacher.
It is a fixable approach to learn because it can be accessible at any time, from any location, and on demand.	Students and teachers must adhere physically inside the educational institution.
It is a convenient approach to learn because it can be accessible at any time, from anywhere, and on your own schedule.	Students may get demotivated as a result of a lack of stringent standards, leading to early dropouts from educational institution.
An individual-contained personal learning style allows learners to be as flexible as they want.	It might be difficult to assess the dependability of learning systems that have been installed.
It makes use of audiovisual resources, making it simple for students to comprehend.	The learning process might be made more difficult by slow internet connections or server issues.
It is repetitive because the content is kept on storage devices and can be accessed by the student again and again.	Students may need extra time to access, learn, and understand the material from a platform.
Teachers can easily track their students' progress. Some e-learning websites assess student time spent on the platform.	Due to a lack of social engagement, students may feel isolated.
Learning materials have the same content for all users, regardless of where they access them or when they access them.	Students may not be able to engage in real-time interactions when they need them, which can be frustrating.

As seen in the table (2), reliance on e-learning systems has a number of drawbacks in addition to a number of evident benefits. E-learning gives both students and teachers a variety of multimedia options to meet the curriculum outcomes without a physical appearance in the classroom.

However, by attempting to reduce the downsides, a good learning system can be developed. It's also sometimes up to the students to figure out how to get the most out of online learning tools. In addition, teachers should choose the appropriate learning platform for their students to ensure the successfulness of their learning process.

CONFLICT OF INTEREST

The authors submitting this chapter have claimed that they do not have a conflict of interest among themselves.

ACKNOWLEDGMENT

The authors acknowledge all the efforts of those who helped in producing this chapter.

REFERENCES

Abbad, M. M., Morris, D., & de Nahlik, C. (2009). *Looking under the Bonnet: Factors Affecting Student Adoption of E-Learning Systems in Jordan.* The International Review of Research in Open and Distance Learning.

Abo Mokh, A., Shayeb, S., Badah, A., Ismail, I., Ahmed, Y., Dawoud, L., & Ayoub, H. (2021). Levels of Technostress Resulting from Online Learning among Language Teachers in Palestine during Covid-19 Pandemic. *American Journal of Educational Research*, *9*, 243–254. doi:10.12691/education-9-5-1

Ahmed, Y., Ismail, I., Abo Mokh, A., & Hamarsha, M. (2020). *Exploring the effectiveness of technology integration on students' motivation and engagement during Covid-19 from teachers' perspectives: A case study*. İlköğretim Online. . doi:10.17051/ilkonline.2020.04.176

Arkorful, V., & Abaidoo, N. (2015). The role of e-learning, advantages and disadvantages of its adoption in higher education. *International Journal of Instructional Technology and Distance Learning*, *12*(1), 29–42.

Borstorff, P. C., & Lowe, S. L. (2007). Student Perceptions and Opinions toward e-Learning in the College Environment. *Academy of Educational Leadership Journal*, *11*, 13–30.

Bsharat, T. R., & Behak, F. (2020). The impact of microsoft teams' app in enhancing teaching-learning english during the Coronavirus (COVID-19) from the English teachers' perspectives' in Jenin city. *Malaysian Journal of Science Health & Technology, 7.*

Dublin, L. (2003). If You Only Look Under the Street Lamps... Or Nine e-Learning Myths. *The eLearning Developers' Journal.* E-learning Guild. http://www.elearningguild.com/pdf/2/061603MAN.pdf

European Commission. (2001). *The eLearning Action Plan: Designing tomorrow's education.* EC. http://www.elearningeuropa.info

Fry, K. (2001). E-learning markets and providers: Some issues and prospects. *Education + Training*, *43*(4/5), 233–239. doi:10.1108/EUM0000000005484

Guragain, N. (2016). E-*learning benefits and applications.*

Jennex, M. E. (2005). *Case Studies in Knowledge Management. Idea Group Publishing: Hersley.Johnson, L. et al. (2010). 2010 Horizon Report: K-* (12th ed.). The New Media Consortium.

Kattoua, T., Al-Lozi, M., & Alrowwad, A. A. (2016). A review of literature on e-learning systems in higher education. *International Journal of Business Management and Economic Research*, *7*(5), 754–762.

Keller, C., & Cernerud, L. (2002). Students' perception of e-learning in university education. *Learning, Media and Technology*, *27*(1), 55–67.

LaRose, R., Gregg, J., & Eastin, M. (1998). Audio graphic tele-courses for the Web: An experiment. *Journal of Computer-Mediated Communication*, *4*(2), 0. doi:10.1111/j.1083-6101.1998.tb00093.x

Liaw, S.-S., Huang, H.-M., & Chen, G.-D. (2007). Surveying instructor and learner attitudes toward E-learning. *Computers & Education*, *49*(4), 1066–1080. doi:10.1016/j.compedu.2006.01.001

Oblinger, D. G., & Hawkins, B. L. (2005). The Myth about E-Learning. *EDUCAUSE Review*.

OECD. (2005). E-learning in tertiary education [Online]. OECD. http://www.cumex.org.

Rossi, P. G. (2009). Ambiente di apprendimento con elementi di artificial intelligence. JE-LKS. *Journal of E-Learning and Knowledge Society*, *5*(1), 65–75.

Samsuri, N. N., Nadzri, F. A., & Rom, K. B. M. (2014). A Study on the student's perspective on the effectiveness of using elearning. *Procedia: Social and Behavioral Sciences*, *123*, 139–144. doi:10.1016/j.sbspro.2014.01.1407

Tao, Y. H., Yeh, C. R., & Sun, S. I. (2006). Improving training needs assessment processes via theInternet: System design and qualitative study. *Internet Research*, *16*(4), 427–449. doi:10.1108/10662240610690043

Twigg, C. (2002). Quality, cost and access: the case for redesign. In M. S. Pittinsky (Ed.), *The Wired Tower* (pp. 111–143). Prentice-Hall.

Welsh, E. T., Wanberg, C. R., Brown, E. G., & Simmering, M. J. (2003). E-learning: Emerging uses, empiricalresults and future directions. *International Journal of Training and Development*, *2003*(7), 245–258. doi:10.1046/j.1360-3736.2003.00184.x

Wentling, T. L., Waight, C., Gallagher, J., La Fleur, J., Wang, C., & Kanfer, A. (2000). E-learning - a review of literature. *Knowledge and Learning Systems Group NCSA*, *9*, 1–73.

Chapter 2
Aligning Interactive Multimedia Development Practices With Mayer's Split-Attention Effect Principle

Yousra Banoor Rajabalee
https://orcid.org/0000-0003-4885-610X
Mauritius Institute of Education, Mauritius

ABSTRACT

Multimedia learning can be defined as the construction of knowledge based on instructions that are delivered through the combined use of visuals such as text, images, animations, etc. It is best described by Richard Mayer, one of the leading researchers in this area who postulated that people learn better from words and pictures than from words alone. Multimedia instructions have for objectives to enhance and promote meaningful learning. The split-attention effect occurs when multimedia instruction is designed in a way that it requires learners to split their attention between, and mentally integrate multiple sources of information that are separate in temporal or physical dimensions/locations. Mayer's principles are guiding constructs, useful for creating effective interactive multimedia materials. This chapter elaborates and sheds light on how to creatively design or develop multimedia learning materials, which can create constructive knowledge by sustaining good engagement in learning and by overcoming and managing the split-attention problems.

DOI: 10.4018/978-1-6684-4940-0.ch002

INTRODUCTION

The introduction of multimedia learning has become a communication tool in education; it has become a new paradigm in education. It has increasingly alerted and created new impact on education by the evolution of new concepts used in content development and by using innovative methods in teaching and learning. Educators' way of teaching as well as the design of instructional materials have changed and evolved with the use of educational technologies. Consequently, using educational tools and other related technologies have helped educators to shape their course contents for better delivery. Multimedia learning provides a good instructional medium for information delivery, and this has helped learners in a way to have better control on their learning. According to Lindstrom theory (1994), multimedia "provides a means to supplement a presenter's efforts to garner attention, increase retention, improve comprehension, and to bring an audience into agreement", which consequently results in people remembering 20% of what they see, 40% of what they see and hear, but about 75% of what they see and hear and do simultaneously.

With multimedia learning, educators can effectively deliver information that is difficult to explain in textual format. Same could be presented in interactive ways using animation or video or using textual information supported by auditory means. Reliance on educational technology has increased since it offers great potential for multimedia instruction. Instructional materials can be designed in such a way where pedagogical strategies are used to help develop the learning potential of students.

Multimedia learning offers great opportunities and diverse ways to facilitate and entertain learning. You have the possibility of using mixing modes, that is, visual and auditory, in creative ways. However, what is important to know is the fact that learner's brains are able to process information using multiple channels, simultaneously. Multimedia learning helps learners to construct knowledge using multiple modes that include both visual and auditory information. It has been proved by Sweller (2003) that learner's ability to process information is a multi-step process that involves the perception, attention, selection, organization, and integration of information.

Consequently, we should not also forget that the promise of the future does not necessarily lie in technology alone, but in people's ability to use, manage, evaluate and understand it. Therefore, depending on the learning styles and knowledge construction capacity, it might be probable that learners are not able to adapt to the panoply of multimedia tools. Each learner has his or her own individual learning preferences.

In this way, it is important for educators to understand and channel the right teaching repertoire according to the students' style. Arslan (2012) quoted that the flexibility and interactivity elements of multimedia may cause confusion and increase cognitive load in learners' mind. Indeed, one of the limitations that need to be considered has been identified as being the split-attention effect. Hence, the objective of this chapter is to provide a theoretical rationale on multimedia learning design principles aligned with Mayer's (2005) split-attention effect principle.

The aim is to highlight the possible design elements that cause the split-attention effect in learning and how good pedagogical design elements based on multimedia principles can help to improve the effectiveness of multimedia instructional material and address any cognitive load.

BACKGROUND

Multimedia learning provides an informative set of principles to design instructional materials. These materials can include both visual and verbal modes of learning in the form of static pictures and illustrations, animations, on-screen text, etc. It can also involve the use of narration, whereby using audio to highlight essential information all throughout a presentation. The use of sound in multimedia learning helps to enhance learning by providing an extra channel of information to learners. The audio provides additional information that support different learning styles of learners. For instance, a learner might learn and acquire more knowledge while listening to the audio at the same time watching the visual information, than simply reading lines of text on the screen or watching the animated images. Although we say that pictures are worth a thousand words, audio will also add interest to the video. In this way, the instructional message will foster meaningful learning to take place and help learners to build constructive knowledge from the multimedia presentations.

Multimedia learning is best described by Richard Mayer (2005), one of the leading researchers in this area and he postulated that people learn better from words and pictures than from words alone. Multimedia resources which given to learners by adding visuals to verbal, textual and auditory instruction, can result in significant gains in basic or higher-order learning, especially if it is being applied appropriately. The images used in multimedia instructions, enhance the visual aspects of the subject matter discussed and make it have more weight. For example, Figure 1 shows an interface that consists of minimal use of texts, more images, and links, which enable a learner to easily navigate from one screen to another.

Well-designed multimedia instructions help learners to build effective mental models and more accurately. Learners can learn at their own pace with better retention and application of knowledge. Consequently, Mayer (2001) came up with a number of fundamental principles that can be used as guiding constructs for the design and development of interactive multimedia learning materials. But, before we elaborate

Figure 1. Display text and illustration
Source: http://www.articulate.com/community/guru/2009/CPR/

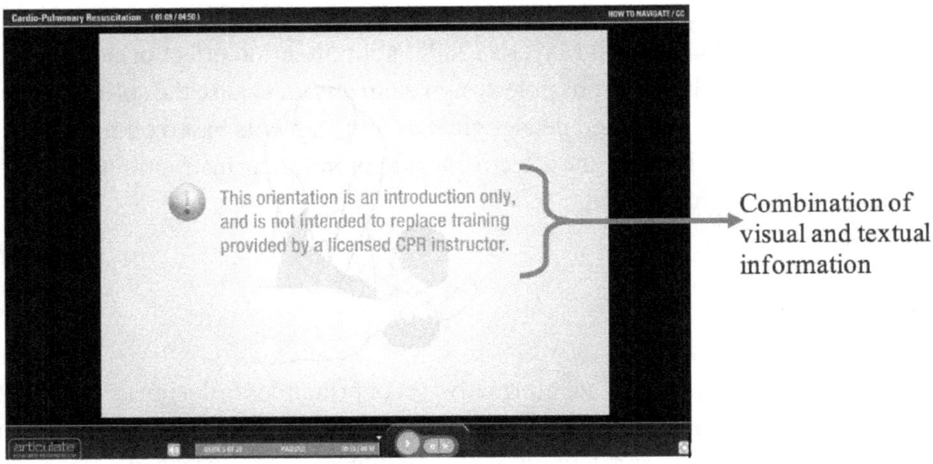

on the principles, let us have a look at the multimedia learning theory which is the theoretical foundation of the said principles.

MULTIMEDIA LEARNING THEORY

The Multimedia Learning Theory was developed by Richard Mayer in 1997 and the objective was to explain how multimedia learning works and how we can best incorporate such instruction for effective learning. The theory refers to the construction of knowledge based on instructions that are delivered through presenting words and pictures. These instructional messages include both visual and verbal modes of learning in the form of pictures and illustrations, animations, on-screen text, etc. The instruction can also involve the use of narration. For instance, a learner might learn and acquire more knowledge while listening to the audio at the same time watching the visual information, than simply reading lines of text on the screen or even by simply watching the animated images. Although we say that pictures are worth a thousand words, audio can also add interest to the video. In this way, the instructional message will foster meaningful learning to take place and help learners to build constructive knowledge from the multimedia presentations.

These multimedia instructions have for objectives to enhance and promote meaningful learning. Multimedia learning helps learners to learn through the use of words and pictures and makes it easier for them to build up mental representations. When words and pictures are presented together as in a narrated animation, students perform well both on retention and transfer tests (Mayer & Anderson, 1991, 1992). Furthermore, the Multimedia Learning Theory also summarizes Mayer's guided principles that are meaningful for the design of materials – which is what we called the multimedia learning design principles.

MULTIMEDIA LEARNING DESIGN PRINCIPLES

The multimedia principles states that under come conditions, learners are better able to construct meaningful learning based on corresponding visual and verbal representations, rather than words alone. The presentation of a simple block of texts or auditory links only is less effective than when the same text or narration is coupled with some visual images. There is a saying that quotes 'A picture is worth a thousand of words', and this is true as a picture or animation will convey a message more easily. An image or picture is a powerful tool that will help a user to better understand the information that is being transmitted. For example, road signs are better illustrated with an image than some lines of text. This is Mayer's *Signaling Principle*. However, we should not ignore the fact that if the image is misinterpreted by any user, then this might be dangerous. So far, the impact of visual presentation is much more positive compared to communication through textual medium.

Empirical research studies have been conducted and support the fact that learning from words and pictures increased when words were presented alone, which makes learners' retention capacity become high. Moreover, learners' retention capacity becomes even higher when instructions were delivered using visual, verbal and auditory mediums. The combination of imagery with text enhances learning experience. This can fall under Mayer's *Personalization Principle.* However, depending on the individual's learning style, some learners may have better performance while using the combination of texts and images modality, while others may simply perform well because they have a prior knowledge of the subject matter.

Multimedia principles focus on the use of visual imagery which is relevant to the subject, and that could enhance instructional materials that would otherwise be presented in textual format only. It also makes use of other mediums such as narration and sound effects to put emphasis on on-screen displays in presentations. Multimedia principles also refer to media-based instructions using media effects to create controlled learning processes. However, using such instructional methods could lead to different learning outcomes as learners are engaged in using different cognitive processes. Mayer (1997) carried out a re-analysis of nine studies, whereby he compared instructional material presented using text and graphics on one hand and computer animation and narration on the other hand. According to his findings, he concludes that it is not the media that matter but rather, how they are used.

Multimedia principles help instruction to be delivered easily by facilitating the acquisition of knowledge through presenting words and pictures. In line with these principles, multimedia learning has made it possible for educators to use authoring tools to develop multimedia content easily and rapidly, with a minimum of technical knowledge. Educators can effectively deliver instruction that is difficult or challenging to explain in textual format. Same could be presented using animation or video or by the use of textual information supported by auditory means. Reliance on educational technology has increased since it offers great potential for multimedia instruction. What is important to know is the fact that learner's brains are able to process information using both channels, simultaneously. Multimedia learning helps learners to construct knowledge using multiple modes that include both visual and auditory information. It has been proved by Sweller (2003) that learner's ability to process information is a multi-step process that involves the perception, attention, selection, organization, and integration of information. Mayer calls this the *Modality Principle.*

However, I also believe that if some people are able to master a particular tool better than others, it's because they feel better adapted to it and those who do not master this same tool might possibly slowdown in learning. Any learner who has a certain prior knowledge of the subject, can significantly impact on the efficacy of the pedagogical strategies used. And, as we know, the effect of embedding multimedia in learning environments is to improve learning experience and performance. It might be possible that the gap diminishes, if multimedia instruction is properly implemented and designed to promote information acquisition, response strengthening and knowledge construction, especially for low achievers who have poor retention ability of knowledge. This is referred to Mayer's *Cognitive Load Principle.*

What is fundamental for learners is that the information that is being presented, encourages their learning, rather than distracts it. The main idea is to help learners to build constructive knowledge based on the information presented, whether it is from computer screen to human's mind or some other way. The goal of the instructional resources is to deliver efficient information to help learners to focus on the meaning of the presented material as well as interpret it in the light of their prior knowledge. Information acquisition occurs when learners can understand the presented materials and interpret them correctly.

However, when it comes to learning, it is important for the human mind to reduce any extraneous cognitive load, especially when there is a need to mentally integrate multiple sources of information – the multimedia learning information. As such, it is fundamental to cater for the split-attention effect, which is directly associated in the design of multimedia learning materials.

THE SPLIT-ATTENTION EFFECT

The split-attention principle states that when designing instruction, including multimedia instruction, it is important to avoid formats that require learners to split their attention between, and mentally integrate multiple sources of information that are separate in temporal or physical dimensions/locations (Mayer 2001).

The split-attention effect occurs when the instructional design of multimedia learning resources is not properly done. More precisely, when learners are required to process two or more sources of information simultaneously, whether it is by using the same modality, that is visual, textual or auditory or even within the same display, this has the tendency to create divided attention in a learner's mind. And, in the query to better manage the cognitive load of what is being presented and heard, very often, the learner finds himself or herself in isolation, without being able to grasp any information. Therefore, this is called the split-attention effect.

The prediction of split-attention effect will arise, when learners are not able to do dual processing of information, which is processing in the working memory, all information presented through the visual and auditory channels simultaneously. Instructional designers, who design multimedia presentations, have the tendency to forget certain important factors that can result in split-attention effects.

We are going to elaborate on some examples and situation where the split-attention effect has arisen.

WORKED EXAMPLES OF SPLIT-ATTENTION EFFECT

The Figure 2 gives an illustration of a multimedia learning resource in which both picture and texts have been used to enhance learning. If a learner reads the text and cross references with the picture, he or she will understand the description and body parts of the butterfly. Basically, the picture shows the different parts of a butterfly and the texts displayed is a brief overview of the body parts of the butterfly. However, if a learner reads the text and then switches his or her attention back and forth to the diagram, this will affect the learner's focus and concentration, as his or her ability to deal simultaneously with different source of visual information is limited. The learner's attention is split between the picture and the texts. Because picture and text cannot be perceived simultaneously, the learner is forced to switch back and forth between the two and integrate them mentally (Tabbers et al, 2000).

Therefore, it is good to note that if the same visual text was summarised and presented in a bulleted format, this would have been easier for a learner to integrate the required information mentally. A summarised verbal information can possibly be more explanatory than lengthy definition paragraphs.

Figure 2. Display of text and picture

Butterfly Body Parts

The butterfly's body can be divided into three segments or parts. The head contains the eyes, the proboscis, and the antenna. The butterfly's proboscis can be called a tongue. The butterfly uncoils or unrolls its proboscis and then uses it to drink nectar from plants or other nutrients. Sometimes they drink out of water puddles. A butterfly uses its antenna as a nose. They sniff the air around them using their antenna.

A butterfly's antenna is shaped like a club while a moth's antenna is feathery. The thorax is the middle section of a butterfly's body. The wings and legs are attached to the thorax. A butterfly has six legs. A butterfly uses three pairs of jointed legs to taste the surface of a petal. They do this by scratching the surface of the petal. The wings are also attached to here. The smallest butterfly's wingspan is 1/8 of an inch long while the largest is over 11 inches. The abdomen mostly contains a butterfly's reproductive organs. Organs that digest food and that get rid of waste products are also located here.

The possibility of catering for such situation could have been having the text as audio. Learner would have listened to the audio and then follow the labels on the diagrams. In this way, this would have prevented learners to switch their focus and attention back and forth the visual information displayed on the screen. And the phenomenon of split-attention effect could have been avoided.

The Figure 3 denotes the use of an animated video on the left of the screen and some textual display on the right of the screen. It is for good purpose to display an informative animated video to learners but when textual information is displayed sometime later, under a timing synchronisation, this has the tendency to impose on a learner's working memory. That is, a learner will try to focus on either one, which is, either the animated video or the synchronised display of the texts. In either case, the learner will try to fill in his mental store but with the risk of missing some parts of either information. The learner might feel frustrated and distracted about whether to support the animated video or to concentrate on the texts that are being synchronised sometimes later. Dealing with such demanding tasks might create cognitive overload efforts on the learner's working memory.

Moreover, there is another split-attention situation whereby a multimedia animation is being displayed from one extremity of the screen and the text is either below completely or on the opposite side of the animation and this makes it difficult for

Figure 3. Display of text and animated video

learners to follow the animation and read the on-screen text at the same time. Even if learners can do both at the same time, they have the tendency to retain only the last part they have viewed, which could be either the text or the animation. Allport (1971) postulates that limits on our ability to see several things at once may reflect both difficulties in dealing with several objects and difficulties in making several similar discriminations.

Mayer and Moreno (1998) states that split-attention occurs when the on-screen text is presented at the bottom on the screen, so while the student is reading, he or she cannot view the animation, and while viewing the animation he or she cannot read the text. This situation creates what Sweller (1999) called a split-attention effect because the learner's visual attention is split between viewing the animation and reading the texts.

The Figure 4 illustrates a multimedia presentation that displays an animation on one side of the screen and some textual display on the opposite side of the animation. If a learner will have to read the textual display as well as visualise the animation on the screen, this will not lead to sustained attention as it will be difficult for the learner to cope and interconnect the displayed information. Mayer *et al* (1995) argued that an important step for meaningful learning to occur was to build connections

Figure 4. Display of text and animation
Source: http://www.articulate.com/community/guru/2009/CPR/

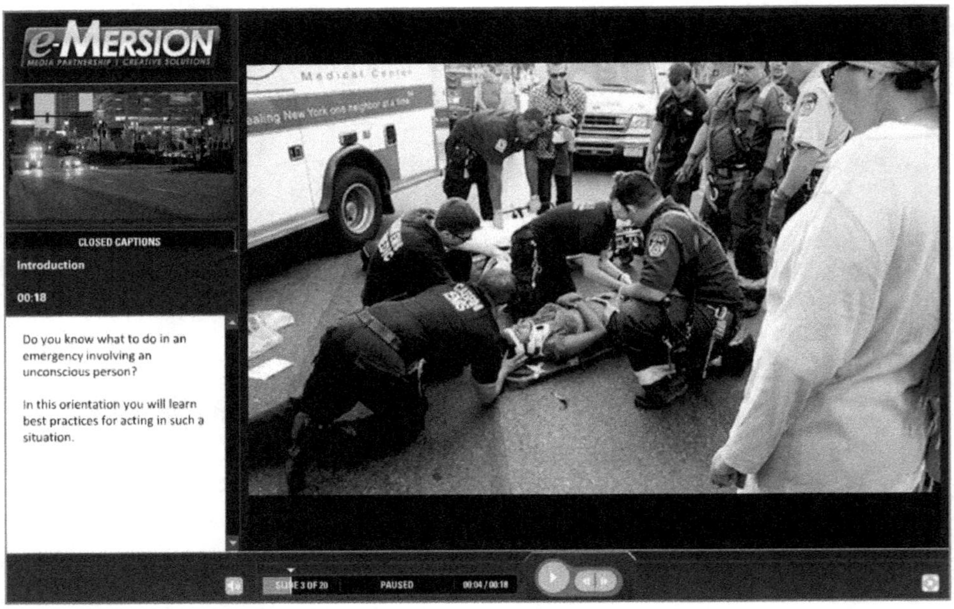

between pictorial and verbal representations and they also argued that this was more likely to occur, when text and illustrations were presented contiguously on the page rather than separately.

According to Moreno and Mayer (1999), they carried out a study which is in a computer-based environment using meteorological tasks. And, they showed that those students who have been working with materials in an integrated format, which means, presenting verbal and visual materials together, have out-performed, those students who have been working with text and diagrams separately, which is on the same screen but opposite to each other. Therefore, it is good practice to avoid splitting the screen with different format of information, which is picture, labels, and texts, etc, as this will divide the attention of learners. Mayer (2001) also formulates that, students learn better when corresponding words and pictures are presented near rather than far from each other on the page or screen (p. 81).

Hence, in contrast with what has been displayed in Figure 3, the verbal texts on the left of the screen, could be represented in auditory format rather than being displayed on the screen.

ALIGNING MULTIMEDIA DEVELOPMENT PRACTICES WITH THE SPLIT-ATTENTION PRINCIPLE

Research found that students have different ways of learning. These modes of learning are learning from on-screen text, learning from printed text and learning from both on-screen text and narration, in multimedia instructions (Mayer et al, 2001). Therefore, learners can still learn in a split-attention environment, whereby they can actively seek to understand the presented material whether it is visual or auditory, by selecting the more relevant and important parts and then mentally organize the information, to finally to create a schema or mental representation in the long-term memory. On the other hand, delivering information to students in multiple ways under more than one modality does not really create a negative impact on their learning.

Learning contents can be presented in different formats to adapt to the different learning styles and preferences of students, but more especially to be able to cater for those learners with disabilities. The importance of accommodating individual differences in learning style has long been recognized in educational psychology (Jonassen & Grabowski, 1993) and has been tested in a Multimedia Learning Environment (Plass *et al.*, 1998). In this context, multiple presentation modes are better than single presentation mode, as it allows learners to choose the modality that best fits their needs and learning styles. Same apply in the case of learners with disabilities. Disabled learners with hearing impairments may opt for information that is presented as printed text or on-screen text rather than auditory format.

Moreover, when presenting instructional materials, very often, instructional designers use video clips to give learners a broader outlook of the subject being taught. A video clip is an appropriate medium to deliver an impactful and highly targeted message based on the subject being taught. This is good idea, especially if it is of topical relevance, as it helps the learners to feel more engaged and interested in learning, without getting bored by following lectures. Adding interesting material to an instructional presentation increases the learner's enjoyment of the presentation, and this causes the reader to pay more attention and work harder to understand the material. In short, emotion grabbing adjuncts improve the learner's affect which in turn improve the learner's cognitive processing. (Garner *et al.* 1992,1989).

But, on the other hand, this has been stated by Garner *et al*, (1992, 1989) that video clips are analogous seductive details in text passages which can be defined as interesting but conceptually irrelevant material that is added to passage to arouse the learner's interest. Consequently, adding interesting video clips or animation that is conceptually irrelevant to the subject matter will divert the attention of the learner from the focus of the subject. Similarly, Harp & Mayer (1997, 1998) reported that adding interesting but conceptually irrelevant illustrations to a text and illustrations explanations results in poorer performance on tests of retention and transfer. This is because learners' attention will be diverted from the explanation if the video clip lacks any structural relevance. Learners can have a negative experience by trying to process on screen text information, and at the same time, trying to focus on the highlighted information in the video clip. Mixing up these two types of information might result in leaving the learner in isolation without understanding anything. Hence, adding interesting but irrelevant video clips to multimedia presentation can hurt learners' understanding of the topic. This has been an extended finding previously done by Harp and Mayer (1997, 1998).

Further research has been conducted by Mayer (2001), where the split-attention hypothesis predicts that adding on-screen text to a narrated animation will result in poorer performance on retention and transfer tests. In his experiment in 2001, he provided evidence that animation and verbal information being displayed concurrently will result in creating cognitive overload in a learner's working memory. This is so, because the verbal information will probably be competing with the animation being played, thus making it difficult for a learner to reconcile both and to build up a mental representation. In this way, when the verbal information is dominating the visual information or vice-versa, the learner's capacity of attending all these information at once becomes limited. Such situation calls for the split-attention effect in which the visual channel gets overloaded with both visual graphic information and verbal information. Similar situation was experimented and confirmed by Mayer and Moreno (1998) using animation and on-screen text.

The split-attention effect will frequently occur when using multimedia as there will always be at least two sources of information involved. Ayres and Sweller (2005), found that split-attention occurs when multiple sources of information are physically separate in a manner that requires the learner to search for the required referents to build an inter-related connection between them. And this act of searching, which is imposed on the learner, creates a split-attention situation and increases the cognitive load.

Chandler and Sweller (1996) talks about the use of different materials where there were interactivity elements. Interactive elements involve users' action that must be simultaneously processed to understand the information. Basically, split-attention effect occurs when interactivity is high in a multimedia instruction. This is because, the interactive elements require more cognitive loads on the working memory. The higher the element of interactivity, the more it is prone to have split-attention situation. For example, Ayres and Sweller (2005) demonstrated that when adding data to a spreadsheet cell using the computer and manual simultaneously, split-attention may have little effect because of low element interactivity. For tasks with high element of interactivity, such as completing a complicated spreadsheet formula, this increases the split-attention effect on learners, because learners will be involved in heavy problem-solving tasks even if the formulae can be computer generated.

Mousavi et al (1995) has suggested that what was previously termed as cognitive load phenomenon, today's research has called it split-attention effect. Learners' attention is divided when they are required to mentally integrate multiple sources of information, especially when using dual modality presentation techniques. There is the need to hold information from one source in the working memory, before attending to the other source. And, this act constitutes of the split-attention effect, as learners have to impose on their working memory to retain information and this creates an overload situation for them. When they have to control their auditory processing capacity to retain incoming auditory information, they have less capacity left to build a schema of the overall information being presented. However, many experiments in various areas have demonstrated that the cognitive load consequences of split-attention can be reduced by integrating multiple sources of information. (Chandler and Sweller, 1991, 1992; Sweller and Chandler, 1994; Sweller, Chandler, Tierney and Cooper, 1990; Tarmizi and Sweller, 1988; Ward and Sweller, 1990). This can be effectively done by eliminating the need for learners to conduct any search to facilitate learning. Thus, reducing load on the working memory.

Based on the research study of Park and Hannafin (1993), who devised a set of instructional guidelines for the design of interactive multimedia, one of its principles states as follows:

Principle 7: Learning improves as the number of complementary stimuli used to represent learning content increases. (p. 72)

Therefore, referring to the above statement, auditory information could rather be considered as an enhancement to learning, rather than be considered as an element that would hinder learning. But auditory material should be restricted to the multimedia material presented to provide relevance to the content of the lesson and should not include any information that will divert learners' attention.

CONCLUSION

The split-attention effect is pervasive, and it is common in any multimedia instruction. Learners have different learning preferences and those whose learning preferences are coherent with multimedia instructional environment are more likely to benefit. Even if all the students master the technology aspect and can navigate through instructional material, there remains the question of assimilating educational content and of "learning" to take place. Multimedia is just a tool, and the onus is on students who need to construct their knowledge irrespective of the tool being used, as long as sound pedagogical approaches are applied to the integration of the tool in the educational process, while also catering for the split-attention effect. Hence, the guidelines discussed in this chapter, can have the potential to considerably improve the design of multimedia instruction.

ACKNOWLEDGMENT

This research received no specific grant from any funding agency in the public, commercial, or not-for-profit sectors.

REFERENCES

Allport, D. (1971). Parallel encoding within and between elementary stimulus dimensions. *Perception & Psychophysics*, *10*(2), 104–108. doi:10.3758/BF03214327

Arslan, P. Y. (2012). A Review of Multimedia Learning Principles: Split-Attention, Modality, and Redundancy Effects. *Mersin Üniversitesi Eğitim Fakültesi Dergisi*, *8*(1), 114–122.

Ayres, P., & Sweller, J. (2005). The split-attention principle in multimedia learning. The Cambridge handbook of multimedia learning, 2, 135-146.

Chandler, P., & Sweller, J. (1991). Cognitive load theory and the format of instruction. *Cognition and Instruction*, *8*(4), 293–332. doi:10.12071532690xci0804_2

Chandler, P., & Sweller, J. (1992). The split-attention effect as a factor in the design of instruction. *The British Journal of Educational Psychology*, *62*(2), 233–246. doi:10.1111/j.2044-8279.1992.tb01017.x

Chandler, P., & Sweller, J. (1996). Cognitive load while learning to use a computer program. *Applied Cognitive Psychology*, *10*(2), 151–170. doi:10.1002/(SICI)1099-0720(199604)10:2<151::AID-ACP380>3.0.CO;2-U

Garner, R., Brown, R., Sanders, S., & Menke, D. J. (1992). Seductive details" and learning from text. *The role of interest in learning and development*, 239-254.

Garner, R., Gillingham, M. G., & White, C. S. (1989). Effects of'seductive details' on macroprocessing and microprocessing in adults and children. *Cognition and Instruction*, *6*(1), 41–57. doi:10.12071532690xci0601_2

Harp, S. F., & Mayer, R. E. (1997). The role of interest in learning from scientific text and illustrations: On the distinction between emotional interest and cognitive interest. *Journal of Educational Psychology, 89*(1), 92–102. doi:10.1037/0022-0663.89.1.92

Harp, S. F., & Mayer, R. E. (1998). How seductive details do their damage: A theory of cognitive interest in science learning. *Journal of Educational Psychology, 90*(3), 414–434. doi:10.1037/0022-0663.90.3.414

Jonassen, D., & Grabowski, B. (1993). *Handbook of individual differences, learning and instruction.* LEA.

Lindstrom, R. L. (1994). *Business Week guide to multimedia presentations.* New York: Osborne McGraw-Hill.

Mayer, R., & Mayer, R. E. (Eds.). (2005). *The Cambridge handbook of multimedia learning* (pp. 1–16). Cambridge university press. doi:10.1017/CBO9780511816819

Mayer, R. E. (1997). Multimedia learning: Are we asking the right questions? *Educational Psychologist, 32*(1), 1–19. doi:10.120715326985ep3201_1

Mayer, R. E. (2001). *Multimedia learning*. Cambridge University Press. doi:10.1017/CBO9781139164603

Mayer, R. E., & Anderson, R. B. (1991). Animations need narrations: An experimental test of a dual-coding hypothesis. *Journal of Educational Psychology, 83*(4), 484–490. doi:10.1037/0022-0663.83.4.484

Mayer, R. E., & Anderson, R. B. (1992). The instructive animation: Helping students build connections between words and pictures in multimedia learning. *Journal of Educational Psychology, 84*(4), 444–452. doi:10.1037/0022-0663.84.4.444

Mayer, R. E., Heiser, J., & Lonn, S. (2001). Cognitive constraints on multimedia learning: When presenting more material results in less understanding. *Journal of Educational Psychology, 93*(1), 187–198. doi:10.1037/0022-0663.93.1.187

Mayer, R. E., & Moreno, R. (1998). A split-attention effect in multimedia learning: Evidence for dual processing systems in working memory. *Journal of Educational Psychology, 90*(2), 312–320. doi:10.1037/0022-0663.90.2.312

Mayer, R. E., Steinhoff, K., Bower, G., & Mars, R. (1995). A generative theory of textbook design: Using annotated illustrations to foster meaningful learning of science text. *Educational Technology Research and Development, 43*(1), 31–41. doi:10.1007/BF02300480

Moreno, R., & Mayer, R. E. (1999). Cognitive principles of multimedia learning: The role of modality and contiguity. *Journal of Educational Psychology*, *91*(2), 358–368. doi:10.1037/0022-0663.91.2.358

Mousavi, S. Y., Low, R., & Sweller, J. (1995). Reducing cognitive load by mixing auditory and visual presentation modes. *Journal of Educational Psychology*, *87*(2), 319–334. doi:10.1037/0022-0663.87.2.319

Park, I., & Hannafin, M. J. (1993). Empirically-based guidelines for the design of interactive multimedia. *Educational Technology Research and Development*, *41*(3), 63–85. doi:10.1007/BF02297358

Plass, J. L., Chun, D. M., Mayer, R. E., & Leutner, D. (1998). Supporting visual and verbal learning preferences in a second-language multimedia learning environment. *Journal of Educational Psychology*, *90*(1), 25–36. doi:10.1037/0022-0663.90.1.25

Sweller, J. (1999). Instructional Design in Technical Areas. Australian Education Review, 43. PCS Data Processing. Inc. USA.

Sweller, J. (2003). Evolution of human cognitive architecture. *Psychology of Learning and Motivation*, *43*, 216–266. doi:10.1016/S0079-7421(03)01015-6

Sweller, J., & Chandler, P. (1994). Why some material is difficult to learn. *Cognition and Instruction*, *12*(3), 185–233. doi:10.12071532690xci1203_1

Sweller, J., Chandler, P., Tierney, P., & Cooper, M. (1990). Cognitive load as a factor in the structuring of technical material. *Journal of Experimental Psychology. General*, *119*(2), 176–192. doi:10.1037/0096-3445.119.2.176

Tabbers, H. K., Martens, R. L., & van Merriënboer, J. J. (2000). *Multimedia instructions and cognitive load theory: Split-attention and modality effects*. In *National Convention of the Association for Educational Communications and Technology*, Long Beach, CA.

Tarmizi, R. A., & Sweller, J. (1988). Guidance during mathematical problem solving. *Journal of Educational Psychology*, *80*(4), 424–436. doi:10.1037/0022-0663.80.4.424

Ward, M., & Sweller, J. (1990). Structuring effective worked examples. *Cognition and Instruction*, *7*(1), 1–39. doi:10.12071532690xci0701_1

Chapter 3
Multimodal Assessment in Higher Education:
Reflections From Student Perspectives

Dorothy Cooshna-Naik
University of Mauritius, Mauritius

Linda Van Laren
University of KwaZulu-Natal, South Africa

Claudia Mitchell
McGill University, Canada

ABSTRACT

This chapter explores the implementation of an alternative form of assessment at a higher education institution (HEI) in Mauritius. As part of their module entitled 'Mauritian History,' a group of first year undergraduate students of Faculty of Social Sciences and Humanities were given the opportunity to work on a multimodal assignment which required them to produce a history-related documentary style video. The chapter draws upon students' written reflections collected at different stages of the assignment to share their experiences as creators/producers of knowledge along with their views on this alternative form of assessment at higher education (HE) level. At the end of the assignment, it was found that despite challenges, students felt they gained a lot in terms of content knowledge, personal growth, and emotional development. The implications and recommendations for digitally enhanced multimodal assessment at HE level are presented.

DOI: 10.4018/978-1-6684-4940-0.ch003

INTRODUCTION

Assessment forms an integral part of students' academic journey as well as that of educators. Through assessment, educators can work on the improvement of their teaching strategies and also improve students' learning. The teaching and learning process includes students' evaluation at different key stages to fulfil specific purposes. Within HE settings, most programmes of study are assessed using coursework (formative assessment) and written and/or practical exams (summative assessment). While summative assessment acts as a mechanism to certify the level of achievement/ performance of students at the end of a course, formative assessment enables students to engage in tests and assignments of different types and receive constructive feedback from the educator. Through such feedback, students can judge and reflect on their own achievements and what they should do to improve their learning. Across the literature, there have been ongoing discussions about aspects related to assessment practices and their effectiveness in supporting student learning (Areekkuzhiyil, 2019; Fook & Sidhu, 2014; Rawlusyk, 2018). Researchers such as Boud (2000) addressed the notion of sustainable assessment as one "that meets the needs of the present and prepares students to meet their own future learning needs" (p. 1). This resonates with the Education for Sustainable Development (ESD), an integral part of the United Nations Educational, Scientific and Cultural Organization (UNESCO) Sustainable Development Goal (SDG 4) on quality education which contends that learning should go beyond educational needs and provide opportunities for students to develop "the knowledge, skills, and values they need to thrive as global citizens in the twenty-first century" (UNESCO, 2015). According to Boud and Falchikov (2006), assessment should not only serve the purpose of certification and to facilitate learning, but also consider "assessment to foster learning throughout life" (p. 400).

Despite the increasing call for a reform in assessment practices to promote the development of broader life skills and attributes as highlighted by scholars in the literature (Baleni, 2015, Gilles et al., 2011, Postareff et al., 2012; Masters,2013), some Higher Education Institutions (HEIs) still appear to prioritise the traditional or conventional forms of assessment such as paper-based formal tests or exams over other alternative assessment methods which take into consideration not just students' cognitive abilities, but also the demonstration of students' skills and competencies. Hence, it is important for educators to shift their focus on assessment *of* learning to assessment *for* learning to optimise the potential of assessment.

This chapter puts forward the idea of assessment *for* learning and in particular multimodal assessment within a higher education context. It draws on findings from a pedagogical intervention implemented in a first year undergraduate History course entitled '*Mauritian History*', included in the first year of three programmes of study from the Faculty of Social Science and Humanities of a Higher Education

Institution in Mauritius, namely BA(Hons)Joint Humanities, BA(Hons) History and Political Science and BA (Hons) History and Sociology. The common approach to assessment in this module is continuous assignments, tests and written exams. The assignments normally take the form of written work such as essays and presentations. However, following discussion with the course instructor who shared concerns about students' difficulties in connecting the past and present, in visualising and demonstrating imaginative reconstruction of text-intensive lecture notes and also the challenge to arouse an interest and a sense of belonging to the subject, it was decided to integrate a multimodal assignment as part of the formative assessment of the module. For this assignment, students were expected to create a digital multimodal text in the form of a history-related documentary style video. It was hoped that this multimodal assessment would provide opportunities for students to demonstrate their knowledge, give them a voice, and help them develop transferable and cross-curricular skills and competencies. The chapter intends to encourage HEI academics to explore the potential of digitally enhanced multimodal assessment so as to provide students the opportunities to develop not only content knowledge but also equip them with skills and competencies, important for them to thrive in the 21st century workforce (Cooshna-Naik, 2018).

This chapter draws upon students' reflective written summaries about their experiences as knowledge producers to explore and better understand the challenges, value and pedagogical implications of this multimodal form of assignment at HE level. It attempts to answer the following research questions:

(i) What were the students' thoughts and reactions before and after the video assignment?
(ii) How did the students experience the whole process of creating a video as an assessment task?
(iii) Does video creation as an assessment task have a place at Higher Education level?

The chapter begins with a review of assessment at HE level and puts forth the notion of students as knowledge producers. Next, the methodology section provides a description of the video assignment and its implementation within the context of the study, presents the study participants and explains how their reflective written summaries, used as data source, were analysed to address mainly the first two research questions. The findings section elaborates on the themes derived from the analysis and use illustrative excerpts from the participants' written reflections in order to justify the analysis. The chapter ends with a discussion section which reviews and interprets the findings in relation to pedagogical considerations and in response to the third research question present implications and recommendations for multimodal assessment at HE level. Some suggestions for future research are also offered.

BACKGROUND

Allen (2009) and McLaren (2007) argued that traditional approaches to assessment may appear to be unauthentic and not appropriate for 21st century teaching and learning. Essay writing and other types of written work do not necessary provide opportunities for students to develop the full range of digital literacies, necessary for graduates to face the challenges of an increasingly digitalised world. Assessment *for* learning is the way forward and can be supported by alternative assessment (Alderson & Banerjee, 2001; Nasab, 2015) which is based on a constructivist view of learning whereby students are constructors of knowledge and assessment activities are authentic (Janisch et al., 2007). When discussing alternative assessment, researchers often refer to performance-based and authentic assessments (Alkhateeb, 2018; Letina, 2015) which are regarded as important elements of assessment *for* learning. Such types of assessments include, but not limited to portfolios, presentations, journals, self-assessment, video and audio recordings (Letina, 2015; Phongsirikul, 2018; Pop, 2020).

The use of digital technologies is often discussed with reference to generations or age groupings. Generations have been categorized according to the birth year range. However, there is no standard explanation for when a generation begins and ends across the literature. Although researchers working on the concept of generations do not often agree on the birth date limits of respective generations, there seems to be a general view that a generation lasts for a period of approximately 15-20 years (Carter, 2018). As noted by the theorists, Neil Strauss and William Howe (1991, 1997), specialists in the study of generations, the modern population consists of four broad generations namely the Baby Boomers (1943-1960), the Generation X (born 1961-1981), the Generation Y most commonly referred to as the Millennials or the NetGen (born in 1982 to roughly 2004) and the Generation Z to those born between 2005-2018. The students involved in the case study discussed in this chapter, belong to a generation, who based on their birth year fall under the 'millennials' (Strause & Howe, 1991). They are the first generation growing up in an internet age and live in a society already filled with new forms of communication, a society with increased connectivity and new technological devices. Millennials are said to be supposedly different from their predecessors (Calk & Patrick, 2017; Prensky, 2001a, 2001b) and as learners they are believed to have interests and expectations which are sometimes ignored by educators (Prensky, 2001a). They are assumed to be digital natives and therefore digitally proficient as compared to previous generations

(MacKenzie Jr & Scherer, 2019; Prensky, 2001a, 2001b; Shah & Abraham, 2009; Tapscott, 1998; Zur & Zur, 2011). Some scholars have shown concerns about these assumptions on the millennials which according to them are broad generalisations, are too deterministic and not substantiated by empirical research (Bennet et al., 2008; Margaryan et al.,2011; Sorrentino,2018). The digital skills of this generation are often restricted to entertainment, communication and socialising (Kirschner & De Bruyckere, 2017) and their use of technology for learning are quite limited. According to Sorrentino (2018), the millennials use technology in the context of learning as passive consumers of information rather than as creators of content. Some studies have shown that it is too simplistic to determine Information and Communications Technology skills of the so called digital natives only on the basis of age. Factors such as experience, breadth of use, gender, preference and familiarity with the digital medium, and social status are also important (Brown & Czerniewicz, 2010; Helsper & Enyon, 2010).

Involving students as producers of digital content is an innovative and emerging form of assessment across many HEIs across the globe (Hawley & Allen, 2018; Schofield et al., 2017) where the accent is put on students becoming producers of knowledge instead of being simply consumers of knowledge (Doyle et al., 2021; Snowball & McKenna, 2017). The use of cellphilming which involves using cellphones to produce short videos (Burkholder & Frawley, 2019; MacEntee et al.,2016) has been explored in the social science discipline to address community issues such as sexual and gender-based violence (Sadati & Mitchell, 2021), or with pre-service social studies teachers (Burkholder & Chase, 2021; Burkholder, 2020; Lemieux et al., 2019).

A literature review by Hawley and Allen (2018) on the use of student generated video creation from around the world across institutions and educational levels and subjects noted that student-generated videos as assessment task has several benefits. Video creation as a learning task promotes active learning which helps in transforming students from being passive recipients of knowledge to knowledge constructors (Greene & Crespi, 2012; Ryan, 2013). A high level of motivation and engagement (Alpay & Gulati,2010; Greene & Crispi, 2012; Pereira et al., 2014), satisfaction (Elsom, 2009; Orús, et al., 2016), and enjoyment are other positive outcomes noted when students engaged in video creation (Hawley & Allen, 2018). Many studies revealed that through their involvement in producing videos as part of assessment, students not only enhanced their competency and ability in using technology (Alpay & Gulati, 2010; Pereira et al., 2014) but also developed other skills such as digital skills and communication skills while working in authentic learning situations. Furthermore, video creation as an assessment has been found to be relevant and helpful in reinforcing concepts taught in class (Greene & Crespi, 2012). Along with reported benefits of video creation as assessment task, some studies also pointed to some challenges which mainly relate to technical issues, access to proper equipment and software, technological skills (Beetham & Sharpe, 2013; Pereira et al., 2014).

Some researchers have argued that it is important not to overlook students' usage of technologies outside the classroom. Jorm et al., (2019) note that students are not mere consumers of videos but are often regular producers of content that they share on Facebook and YouTube, yet it is reported that some HEIs and programmes are slow in implementing learning which considers students as producers of digital content (Lipps, 2018). This situation is also relevant to HEIs in Mauritius where assessment methods are still very much traditional.

METHODOLOGY

The Multimodal Assessment

This section describes the approach used for the multimodal assessment in the module '*Mauritian History*'. which was implemented in the first semester of academic year 2015-2016 (Cooshna-Naik, 2018). Students were given the choice of two topics on producing a documentary-style video: (i) *What's in a name: Family name or family History* (ii) *What's in a name: Your street name*. Previously, at the start of the semester, these topics were given to the students for research and for practicing writing short essays. The video assignment was intended to act as an extension of the essay task requiring students to communicate their perspectives on the chosen topic in a multimodal format that integrates moving and still images, text and audio (Yearta & Kelly, 2021). To help students with the creation of their video, four short workshops of two hours were organised focusing on tools and techniques of video editing. Students had the opportunity to become familiar with the process of video creation which included pre-production, production and post-production phases.

Students were given some specifications for the video: duration (3-5 minutes), style (e.g. using a mix of still and moving images and sound (including audio in the form of narration and/or music. As for the language of expression for the video, irrespective of whether it was written or verbal, they were allowed to use English, French, Creole or even a mix of these languages. They could use their mobile phones and/or digital camera to record video footage and were free to use any video editing software. They were taught how to manipulate specific software such as Audacity, Windows Movie Maker and PowerPoint during the workshop. Students had to complete and submit a storyboard and the final published video after eight weeks.

The act of reflection where one thinks over and thinks through what one is experiencing is said to be crucial for transformative learning (Mezirow, 1981).

Table 1. Guiding questions for each reflective account

Reflection phases	Guiding questions
Before creation of the video	How did you react when you learnt that you had to create a video? What did you think about having a video assignment as part of the assessment of this module? Choose the emoji(s) that best define(s) your feelings/emotions prior to the creation of the video. *(a sheet with a list of different emojis was provided to the students)*
During creation of the video	What are your thoughts, feelings and emotions you experienced during the creation of the video? Note also the moments that you are enjoying and moments you are not enjoying, the difficulties (if any) that you are encountering. The actions you are taking to solve the issues you are having. Choose the emoji(s) that best define(s) your feelings/emotion during the creation of the video. *(a sheet with a list of different emojis was provided to the students)*
After creation of the video	What do you think about your creation? What did you find particularly satisfying about either the process of creation or the finished product? Describe any difficult /frustrating moments (if any) you encountered during the process of this video assignment. If you had the chance to do this assignment again, what changes would you consider? How do you feel after having created the video? *(a sheet with a list of different emojis was provided to the students)*

Therefore, as part of the video production, students were given the chance to write reflective accounts where they could share their reactions, attitudes, feelings and emotions at different phases of the assignment- (i) before the making of the video, (ii) during the making of the video and (iii) after completing the video. For each of the reflective accounts, some guiding questions (see Table 1) were given to students to help them write their reflections. Furthermore, a list of emojis was given to them, so that they could highlight the ones that best define their feeling/emotions at each phase in the creation of the multimodal task.

Study Participants, Data Collection, and Data Analysis

Although all students (n=109) were involved in the video assessment, only a purposeful sample of 19 students across the three programmes of study was considered as research participants. The selection of participants was done so as to ensure that there was maximum diversity in the data collected through participants' written reflective accounts. Inclusion criteria was based on (i) completion of rich reflective summaries about their experience of the video assignment, (ii) completion of the documentary-style video as per requirements and (iii) those who showed an interest in participating in the study. Aged between 18-22 years old, the participants included three males and 16 females as displayed in Table 2. The low number of male participants is due to the fact that most of the students across the three different programmes were females.

Table 2. Composition of participants as per the programme of studies

BA (Hons) Joint Humanities	BA(Hons) History and Sociology	BA(Hons) History and Political Science
• 5 females • 1 male	• 6 females • No male	• 5 females • 2 males

DATA ANALYSIS

The chapter draws on the written data gathered through the reflective accounts of the above-mentioned participants that were collected at three different stages of the video assignment. A qualitative content analysis was chosen to analyse these reflective accounts, as this approach helps in getting deeper insights and understanding of "a particular phenomenon by providing structure in a large amount of textual data through a systematic process of interpretation" (Kleinheksel et al., 2020, p.127). The approach was to analyse either the manifest or the latent content of the data (Graneheim & Lundman, 2004).

First, each participant's written reflective accounts were read and re-read so as to get familiar with the whole context. This was then followed by an inductive content analysis. Meaning units were identified, condensed and assigned to open codes by focusing on the manifest content of the data. The codes were then consolidated into categories based on similarities and differences. The next step consisted of finding and interpreting the underlying meaning in the data, and this was done by organising the categories into themes. The coding process considered a combination of *a priori*

Table 3. Extract of analysis process from meaning unit to theme

Meaning Unit *(Verbatim quotations from participant)*	**Condensed Meaning Unit**	**Code**	**Category**	**Theme**
The creation of the video is filled with lots of ups and downs, and also excitement. Since I am not using windows movie maker, but another software, I am exploring another programme with loads of editing styles. I am getting to use several different features. At first while creating the video, I felt confident at times and sometimes confused and also I had mixed feelings.	Creation of the video is filled with lots of ups and downs Excitement I am exploring another programme I am getting to use several different features I had mixed feelings.	Ups and downs Exploration of software and features Mixed feelings	Video creation is a process filled with ups and downs Getting familiar to technology Mixed feelings	Emotional journey filled with ups and downs.

codes and emergent codes. The *a priori* codes were derived from the research questions and the literature on concepts related to student learning experience, development of skills and competences. Table 3 provides an extract of how the analysis of meaning units led to developing the themes.

FINDINGS

The main themes that emerged from the analysis of the written reflective accounts (pre-production, during-production and post-production) revealed that the video assignment was a transformative learning experience for the participants in a number of ways. Video creation as an assessment was experienced: as a new and creative way of learning; as an emotional journey filled with ups and down, as an opportunity to extend one's horizon and as personal growth and development (Cooshna-Naik, 2018). In this section, each theme is elaborated using illustrative quotes from the participants' written reflections to justify the analysis.

A New and Creative Way of Learning

The first set of reflections written prior to starting the digital video creation revealed that participants were quite shocked and amazed to have a video assignment in their subject discipline. There was an assumption that assignments involving the need to manipulate software and digital devices are generally targeted towards students having an Information Technology background. For some of the participants, it represented a change from the '*classic*' or '*typical*' assessment in Social Sciences and Humanities discipline which they are familiar with. Generally, students from the History discipline are often required to demonstrate their analytical skills through research and writing tasks and therefore a digital multimodal assignment was something *'outside of the circle'* as commented by one of the participants. It was something unexpected as illustrated by the comment of one participant who wrote *'we are going to learn something new that we never even thought about doing.'* Seen as a new way of learning for many, the video assignment was assigned a higher level of importance as compared with other types of student assignments. Comments such as '*it is on a higher level compared to the assignments I have been doing earlier*' or '*having to do a video assignment was quite surprising and innovative as it is on a higher level compared to the assignments I have been doing earlier'* are illustrative of the importance attached to the video assignment.

Furthermore, the video assignment was considered to be an interesting and creative task. Some participants acknowledged that such an assignment offers them wider choices to present their research creatively. They did not have to only rely on textual

Figure 1. Sample screenshots from a participants' video showing the use of visual effects and typography

form of communication. When they compared this assignment to writing text-based long essays, they felt that this assignment was less restrictive, less monotonous and more creative, as they were free to use various semiotic modes such as still and moving images, as well as narration and music. It was a way of making knowledge visible through new forms of expression.

Extracts from students' reflections prior to creating the video such as *'Having a video assignment is really creative and, much more attractive to students* 'or ' *In my point of view, I think it is kind of attractive, charismatic, thought provoking, and insightful to display history through a video, to unveil the past and whatever it holds.*' or ' *A video is much more appealing and brings a kind of enthusiasm, as it will have the music, the images as slides and the animations'* clearly illustrate that participants saw the video assignment as something more creative than conventional types of assignments due to its audio-visual format.

It was interesting to see how some participants "demonstrated modal preferences and relied on the communicative and associative aspects of specific modes to convey meanings in their video" (Cooshna-Naik, 2018, p. 201). For instance, one participant highlighted the importance of choosing an appropriate music for her video: "*I am still looking for the songs as I must look for one that is pleasant to the ears. I want to make my video attracting and not boring*". Similarly, another participant who was working on the street name topic, felt it was appropriate to choose the French national anthem as soundtrack for a section of her video which displayed content related to the French revolution. Some of the videos also displayed the use of visual effects, animations and typographic enhancements which some participants felt gave them the opportunity to make their work more creative and appealing as shown in Figure 1.

An Emotional Journey Filled With Ups and Downs

This theme considers the different emotions and feelings that were reported by the participants from the video assignment commencement to its completion. The video making process was far from being *'a bed of roses'* or was *'filled with lots of ups and downs'* as reported by most of the participants. This assignment yielded a mix of emotions at different stages and emotional shifts were noted as the work progressed. The analysis of the reflections written in the pre-production phase showed that both positive and negative feelings and emotions were present amongst the participants, upon hearing that they would need to produce a video as an assignment. For instance, some of the participants admitted to feeling *'enthusiastic'*, *'excited and eager'* but at the same time there was a sense of apprehension. There were some who were *'anxious and puzzled'* yet were *'determined'* to embark on the video task which they found *'challenging'*.

The reflections on the process of creating the video (during-production) also showed evidence of various emotional states depending on various situations the participants were experiencing. Various emotional shifts were noted. For instance, one of the participants who admitted to being *'pessimist and frightened at the mere thought of creating a video'* yet showed a more positive emotional stance during the process of producing the video by stating the following:

As I am doing the video, I am realising how much I am actually loving it! And this is something very interesting and unbelievable. As far as I know myself, I would never choose to create a video or anything related with graphics, effects, animations, IT stuffs… As such, it is like a new experience. I am enjoying it, to be honest.

Furthermore, there were participants who at the beginning showed determination but when things did not go as planned, they became anxious, stressed, felt discouraged or disappointed which led to frustration. Some participants were stressed throughout the process of video production for various reasons which were related to the lack of resources, technical issues, unexpected situations. The fear of not being able to complete the work or to submit a good quality work was expressed in the following reflective writings:

During the video I encountered a lot of stress because I know it will not be my best video. This is because I lack many resources.

I have completed half of the work, but I am very anxious to not be able to finish my video. I have the impression that it is not becoming the way I wanted it to be... Finally, I am still much stressed.

Truthfully, it is the most stressing moment since I have started the assignment. I am having some difficulties with transferring my interview and there are parts that are missing from my introduction.

For most of the participants, completing a video assignment seemed very much like going through a roller coaster experience with good moments that led to positive feelings and emotions, and bad moments that led to negative feelings and emotions.

An Opportunity to Extend One's Horizon

Regardless of whether the participants had previous exposure to video making, the multimodal assignment was viewed as an opportunity to learn new things about the history of Mauritius through their research and also acquire skills in using digital tools and technologies. Although they were guided through the different steps in producing a digital video during the workshops, the participants were responsible for working on the assignment individually. In so doing, they learnt new things which helped them either enhance or gain new skills that are considered to be critical to thrive in today's world. Some were pleased to have had the chance to learn to use specific tools and technologies despite the challenges they faced. The following quotes from the written reflections of three participants show the importance attached to their skill development:

First of all I have gained knowledge of how to use a video editing software.

I've been able to know how to use other type of software and I must say it was really interesting, I really appreciated it.

Using the different software can bring students to a level of exploring the technological world that would definitely help each and everyone as we are now living in a technological era.

For this assignment, the participants had to move out of their comfort zone and carry out tasks that they were not familiar with such as storyboarding, filming, video and audio editing. This contributed to the development of their self-confidence, problem-solving skills, critical thinking and creativity. Many encountered unexpected issues such as background noise when they were filming, something going wrong with their laptop, and weather related conditions. However, they admitted that they tried to solve the problems by finding alternatives so that they could complete and submit the assignment. This is illustrated by the quote '*I have the camera but I will not able to record voices with it so I will have to put all the information in subtitles*'

Additionally, the video assignment provided opportunities to view historical knowledge through another perspective. Their fieldwork research involved going beyond sources of information such as books, documents and archives. Their physical presence and interaction with the community was required so that they could collect historical evidence such as video recordings of interviews with people or recording video footage and taking pictures of the places they were investigating. This helped them feel more connected to their work and allowed them to take a critical stance towards historical knowledge. Some learnt to value aspects of Mauritius' history that were before uninteresting to them prior to the video assignment as illustrated by this comment: '*It was a reflective work so it made me think about things that I did not give any importance like everyday I pass in front of that school, but I never take it into consideration.*' Another participant described how she was motivated to extend her research and how meaningful and valuable this was as follows:

I was not too interested in-knowing the independence of Mauritius, I know as a whole but since the time I came to know about this person's story, I became very sad, emotional. I went to look for every detail that there was on independence of Mauritius.

Some participants also expressed their satisfaction about having had the chance to connect with their own family history by engaging in this video assignment. For instance, one participant who was working on the topic '*What's in a Name-Family Name*' expressed the importance she attached to going back into past memories.

One of my most favourite parts was to look for old pictures. Some of them brought back very good memories. There were also some of my grandmother's photos that I had never seen and I was happy to have such an opportunity.

This theme emphasised the opportunities that the video assignment offered the participants in terms of content knowledge as well as digital skills.

Personal Growth and Development

Overall the video assignment was seen as a transformational journey for most of the participants as it contributed to their personal growth and development. Their sense of achievement, self-esteem and pride were evident in their reflections written after completing the assignment. A handful of the participants was of the opinion that their work was not of good quality or could have been better but at the same time they were aware of their personal growth as a result of facing and overcoming apprehensions, challenges, and of social interaction and support. Irrespective of whether the final video was good or bad, the fact that they were able to carry out the task on their own and overcoming the difficulties was regarded as an important aspect of their learning experience. In their written reflections post the production of the video, they highlighted their hard work, dedication and how they felt proud of themselves. For many, having been able to create a video for the first time in their life was an achievement and this helped in boosting their self-esteem. For example, the following comments show how they valued their creation:

After having lost sleep, after having concentrated hard on a particular assignment, you kind of get a good feeling. A feeling of relief. And why not proud of yourself? That's how I felt.

It is quite time consuming but seeing the end result makes it worth all the efforts invested in it and we are filled with a sense of satisfaction while watching the end product.

Furthermore, the video assignment empowered the participants to take ownership of their learning and promoted active and autonomous learning. Some participants acknowledged the fact that through their involvement in the video assignment, they became more '*independent*'. The assignment required personal investment as reflected by one participant comment '*Since we have to do interviews and we have to move to those places and film by ourselves, so it's fruitful since we have to move at that place and go by ourselves'*.

Through their reflections, it is noted that although some participants were struggling or were frustrated at times, they were determined and motivated in completing their work. They became resourceful and relied on the help and suggestions from friends, family and tutorials from the internet. This showed their determination and interest in completing the work assigned to them.

The video assignment allowed some of the participants, especially those who were shy by nature to overcome their inhibitions. It was an opportunity for them to develop their intrapersonal and interpersonal skills. One participant admitted that what she found most satisfying was being able to express herself in front of the camera. Another mentioned '*I felt a bit awkward as well because people from the street were staring at me like thinking of what I'm doing. But I did not pay attention to them because I was so dedicated to my work'*.

DISCUSSION

Within the majority of Humanities or Social Sciences courses, reliance on language or textual-based assessment such as essays and written exams (Pace, 2011; Ross et al.,2020) is common. The increased use of digital resources by the young generation today is something that cannot be overlooked. Students enrolling at HE have diverse backgrounds and thus diverse experiences and despite their increased use of digital resources, their access to literacy, texts and digital resources vary (Jewitt, 2012; New London Group [NLG], 1996). Rethinking educational assessment while simultaneously taking into consideration the students' backgrounds and diverse digital experiences was at the core of the study reported in this chapter.

The first research question explored the students' thoughts and reactions before and after the video assignment. The video assignment required the creation of a type of digital text that went beyond the printed form. The generation of students who participated in this study frequently labelled as '*millennials*', based on their birth year are said to stand out for their use of technology (Jiang, 2018; MacKenzie Jr & Scherer, 2019). It is suggested that their communication habits are different from previous generations as they are familiar with social networks and mobile devices and consume a variety of digital texts. Despite the claims made about the '*millennials*' use of technology and digital access, the study reported in this chapter revealed that the experience of the participants as producers of digital texts were limited to non-existent. A handful of the participants had at some point used for instance YouTube tools to create small video clips but they never created a digital video using specific software as an assessment requirement. Their past experience of assessment was rather conventional as in secondary schools they would generally be assessed through class tests, exams and essays. The video assignment came as a big surprise and was seen as a novelty in their field of study, both in terms of process and product. Some of the participants questioned the relevance of the video assignment at the start of the project but as they progressed through the work, they recognised its contribution to their academic and personal development. Compared to the essay as an assignment, they realised that the video assignment offered them new avenues for expression, flexibility in knowledge construction and presentation along with opportunities to demonstrate their creativity. This is in line with the findings of Ross et al. (2020) who state that the creation of multimodal texts "offer authentic opportunities for students to engage with disciplinary knowledge in ways that are innovative, creative and imaginative" (p. 292). Although the participants found this digital learning approach to the History of Mauritius a novelty, Koch et al. (2018) consider this novelty when it comes to new media as "an increase in the perceived usability of something, on account of its newness. When novelty eventually fades, usage patterns and/or perceived usability changes" (p.3). But at the same time, technologies will keep on evolving and represent opportunities for teaching and learning. Educators should not overlook the fact that some young people, as part of their Do-It Yourself practices outside educational contexts, are often found to be intrinsically motivated to create media such as videos, podcasts and disseminate these on online spaces (Mitchell, 2014; Yi, 2008) and technology therefore represents opportunities for young people to become proactive, curious and creative.

The second research question looked into how whole process of creating a video as an assessment task was experienced by the students. The findings suggest that in general, the video as an assessment task was experienced as challenging yet relevant and valuable for their academic and personal development. All three domains of learning were successfully addressed through the video assignment as participants not only enhanced their subject knowledge but experienced various feelings and emotions that contributed either positively or negatively to their learning. Emotional experiences have been found to have a direct influence on learning and academic performance (Artino et al., 2010; Febrilia et al.,2011; Pekrun et al.,2011). Positive emotions such as happiness and enjoyment normally tend to boost learning while negative emotions such as frustration lead to disengagement in the task. In this study, participants evoked a variety of feelings and emotions from the start of the learning task to its completion. As in the study by Ryan (2013), there were different emotions at different stages during the video production. For instance, at the beginning there were feelings of stress, confusion and anxiety but also curiosity and enthusiasm. Once participants started the process of the video creation, some started to feel less anxious especially those who felt that they were coping with the work they had planned. Stress and frustration appeared for those who encountered difficulties for instance during the recording or during the editing phase. But there were also some who, despite facing some difficult situations, enjoyed what they were doing. It was interesting to note that those participants who faced difficult or unexpected situations, such as change in the weather or noisy background during recording, did not give up and were willing to complete the work. Similar to the study findings by Herrington and Parker (2013), there was a sense of pride and relief after completing the video. Their emotive words in their reflections post the completion of the video suggested that they were relieved and felt happy and proud to have been able to overcome the challenges and submit the completed assignment. Some participants also showed some disappointment for not being able to achieve what they had planned but generally they were satisfied because they managed to submit the assignment. So the video assignment can be said to have yielded a mix of positive and negative experiences filled with affective shifts (Mitchell, 2021) depending on their experiences during different stages of the video production.

Furthermore, the findings showed that participants were motivated in different ways to complete the video assignment. There are various reasons and motives that determine the extent to which students devote time to a certain task. The motivational factors may be intrinsic and/or extrinsic. Student agency which assumes that learners are "generally self-motivated, agentic and inspired-striving to learn, to extend themselves, to master new skills, and to apply their talents" (Ryan & Deci, 2000, p.68) was manifested during the video assignment which was different from what they were usually required to do in assessment tasks. They were mainly motivated when they felt that they were coping with the assigned task. Their personal interest and enjoyment contributed to the "intrinsic motivation by sustaining the willingness to continue and persist in the activity" (Reeve, 1989, p. 83). In some cases, participants were encouraged when being helped by others and felt determined to continue their learning journey despite the ups and downs. The fact that the video was a graded assignment also acted as an extrinsic source of motivation for some participants who were interested in completing the work not only for the sake of submitting an assignment, but to score good marks. Some were aiming to do their best in obtaining good quality audio recordings, pictures, to search for appropriate music so as to produce an interesting, meaningful and valuable video that others would enjoy watching.

The Bloom's Digital Taxonomy proposed by Churches (2008) considers the ability to create as an important cognitive process that contributes to the development of "higher-order thinking skills and 'provides students with an authentic learning experience"(Lightie, 2011, p. 9). This domain of learning was addressed through the video assignment which was based on a learning by doing approach. This type of assignment fostered active and self-directed learning and made students feel empowered which in turn promoted a greater sense of ownership of their learning. As part of the video making process, students had to devise their own planning strategies, make certain decisions, learn beyond the four walls of the classroom and engage with their community. As noted by Veletsianos (2011), the participants were being empowered to take control of their learning. As they progress through their work, they became more autonomous. While they acknowledged that the workshop was helpful, they also said that they sought help from other sources such as family members, elders, experts and other people they felt could provide them with information. The students also sought documentary evidence from archives, books and also the internet. From being passive recipients of information, the participants became active knowledge constructors. The alternative assessment in the form of the digital video creation showed that participants were able to achieve a complex task by relying not only on the lecturer's guidance but also on their own resourcefulness. The video assignment further helped participants develop a deeper understanding of the topic they were investigating by being actively involved in the process. In this study participants were involved in active learning as they were involved "in doing things and thinking about the things they are doing" (Bonwell & Eison, 1991, p.2).

Through the act of multimodal composing, students engaged with a range of modes such as text, images, sound, music, gestures and other social symbols to communicate and create meaning. This mediated a range of skills and competencies other than digital skills such as time management, problem-solving, communication, empathy, research and analytical skills, creativity skills (Alpay & Gulati, 2010; Orús et al., 2016; Pirhonen & Rasi, 2017; Pereira et al., 2014). This alternative multimodal assessment made it possible to promote new literacy practices and is regarded as a positive approach to learning in the digital age, by many proponents of multimodality and multiliteracies (Cope & Kalantzis, 2015; Jewitt, 2003). The video assignment pushed the participants out of their comfort zone. Their role as knowledge producers was more complex as they had to create meaning by using new semiotic resources other than text which was something that was new to most of them. These semiotic modes of communication and meaning making were encountered as consumers but very rarely as creators. Going through this change in mode of assessment was no doubt a deep learning curve for the participants as they were required to explore and engage in new learning processes to produce a learning artifact that went beyond the conventional text-based work. The participants recognised that the learning by doing approach of the video assignment was indeed very enriching on both personal and academic level.

IMPLICATIONS AND RECOMMENDATIONS

As compared to more conventional types of assignments, a video assignment requires more time, especially when students need to acquire new skills to successfully master the process of video creation. Participants in this study acknowledged the usefulness of the pre-assignment digital video workshop. As such, it is indeed essential to devise strategies to scaffold students' learning particularly when new modes of assessment are incorporated in the curriculum. The shift from conventional modes of assessment to cater for alternative and authentic assessment is the way forward for HEIs if they want to achieve one of their key roles which is to prepare graduates to be creative thinkers, problem-solvers and leaders of tomorrow. It is the responsibility of HEIs to provide the opportunities for students to become active and independent learners while they engage in new forms of assessments relevant to the digital age. The importance of emerging technologies as cognitive tools for authentic learning should not be overlooked as the video assignment confirmed that despite initial fear, apprehension and anxiety about the use of technology, students in general learnt about the affordances offered by technologies. To encourage academics to consider alternative assessments and the affordances of emerging technologies to support teaching and learning, it is crucial to have staff professional development that focus on building academics confidence in digital technologies and in assessments methods suited for the digital age. These can help them feel more prepared to explore innovative forms of assessment that tap into the potential of technologies. For the participants, although the video creation assignment felt like a rollercoaster ride, the take away was overall positive. It left most of them with a feeling of accomplishment and pride while being aware of having gained quite a lot in terms of academic and personal development. Thus this study demonstrates that multimodal assessments such as the video creation do have its "*raison d'être*" at HE level.

CONCLUSION AND FUTURE RESEARCH DIRECTIONS

The findings from this fieldwork conducted several years ago (and pre-Pandemic) are even more relevant to the academic community now. The educational landscape has changed since the outbreak of the COVID-19 pandemic, forcing teachers and students to shift to various types of digital technologies to allow the continuity of teaching and learning. Students have been following online classes and have been accessing different forms of digital media to support their learning in the form of video lessons, webinars and other digital applications. The burgeoning work on mobile technologies and in particular research with and about cellphilms (MacEntee et al., 2016; Mitchell et al., 2019; Sadati & Mitchell, 2021; Starr & Mitchell, 2020) has been key. This shift has brought forward the importance for educational institutions to explore the affordances that emerging technologies may offer to support assessment and more transformative approaches. Focusing future research on students' digital learning practices and the impact on their academic performance would be helpful in guiding assessment *for* learning in light of the changing educational landscape and technological developments.

ACKNOWLEDGMENT

A special thanks to all students who participated in this research and to their lecturer, Dr Vijaya Teelock for her support and collaboration in implementing the pedagogical intervention reported in this chapter.

REFERENCES

Alderson, J. C., & Banerjee, J. (2001). Language testing and assessment (Part 1): State-of-the-art review. *Language Teaching*, *34*(4), 213–236. doi:10.1017/S0261444800014464

Alkhateeb, M. A. (2018). The effect of using performance-based assessment strategies to tenth-grade students' achievement and self-efficacy in Jordan. *Cypriot Journal of Educational Sciences*, *13*(4), 489–500. doi:10.18844/cjes.v13i4.2815

Allen, M. (2009). Authentic assessment and the internet:Contributions within knowledge networks. In *Proceedings of World Conference on E-Learning in Corporate, Government, Healthcare, and Higher Education* (pp. 1505-1510). Chesapeake, VA: AACE.

Alpay, E., & Gulati, S. (2010). Student-led podcasting for engineering education. *European Journal of Engineering Education*, *35*(4), 415–427. doi:10.1080/03043797.2010.487557

Areekkuzhiyil, S. (2019). Assessment practices in higher education. *University News*, *57*(11), 18–20.

Artino, A. R., La Rochelle, J. S., & Durning, S. J. (2010). Second-year medical students' motivational beliefs, emotions, and achievement. *Medical Education, 44*(12), 1203–1212. doi:10.1111/j.1365-2923.2010.03712.x PMID:21091760

Baleni, Z. (2015). Online formative assessment in higher education: Its pros and cons. *Electronic Journal of e-Learning, 13*(4), 228–236.

Beetham, H., & Sharpe, R. (Eds.). (2013). *Rethinking Pedagogy for a Digital Age: Designing for 21st Century Learning*. Routledge. doi:10.4324/9780203078952

Bennett, S., Maton, K., & Kervin, L. (2008). The 'digital natives' debate: A critical review of the evidence. *British Journal of Educational Technology, 39*(5), 775–786. doi:10.1111/j.1467-8535.2007.00793.x

Bonwell, C. C., & Eison, J. A. (1991). Active Learning: Creating Excitement in the Classroom. ASHE-ERIC Higher Education Report, School of Education and Human Development, George Washington University, Washington DC.

Boud, D. (2000). Sustainable assessment: Rethinking assessment for the learning society. *Studies in Continuing Education, 22*(2), 151–167. doi:10.1080/713695728

Boud, D., & Falchikov, N. (2006). Aligning assessment with long-term learning. *Assessment & Evaluation in Higher Education, 31*(4), 399–413. doi:10.1080/02602930600679050

Brown, C., & Czerniewicz, L. (2010). Debunking the 'digital native': Beyond digital apartheid, towards digital democracy. *Journal of Computer Assisted Learning, 26*(5), 357–369. doi:10.1111/j.1365-2729.2010.00369.x

Burkholder, C. (2020). Looking within and looking around: On cellphilming with pre-service Social Studies teachers in Prince Edward Island. In K. C. Schmitz, M. Cotnam-Kappel, & N. Grant (Eds.), *Infiltrating, interrupting, investigating: Radical youth pedagogy in education* (pp. 167–178). DIO Press.

Burkholder, C., & Chase, A. (2021). Exploring the creative geographies of work with pre- service social studies teachers: Exposing intersections of time and labour in New Brunswick, Canada. *McGill Journal of Education, 55*(3), 1–20. https://mje.mcgill.ca/issue/view/573. doi:10.7202/1083423ar

Burkholder, C., & Frawley, A. (2019). Revisiting and disrupting uncritical diversity narratives through autoethnography and cellphilming. *LEARNing Landscapes, 12*(1), 63–76. doi:10.36510/learnland.v12i1.979

Calk, R., & Patrick, A. (2017). Millennials through the looking glass: Workplace motivating factors. *Journal of Business Inquiry, 16*(2), 131–139. http:www.uvu.edu/woodbury/jbi/volume16

Carter, T. (2018). Preparing Generation Z for the Teaching Profession. *SRATE Journal, 27*(1), 1–8.

Churches, A. (2008). Bloom's digital taxonomy. *Bloom's Revised Digital Taxonomy Map*, 6-8. Bloom.

Cooshna-Naik, D. (2018). *Undergraduate students' experiences of learning with digital multimodal texts*. [Unpublished doctoral dissertation], University of KwaZulu-Natal, Durban, South Africa

Cope, B., & Kalantzis, M. (2015). *The things you do to know: An Introduction to the pedagogy of multiliteracies*. doi:10.1057/9781137539724_1

Doyle, E., Buckley, P., & McCarthy, B. (2021). The impact of content co-creation on academic achievement. *Assessment & Evaluation in Higher Education, 46*(3), 494–507. doi:10.1080/02602938.2020.1782832

Elsom, J. (2009). A creative assessment strategy to improve student motivation and engagement in biochemistry. In J. Barlow, G. Louw, & M. Price (Eds.), *Social Purpose and Creativity: Integrating Learning in the Real World*. University of Brighton Press.

Febrilia, I., Warokka, A., & Abdullah, H. H. (2011). University students' emotional state and academic performance: New insights of managing complex cognitive. *The Journal of Learning in Higher Education*, 1–15. doi:10.5171/2011.879553

Fook, C. Y., & Sidhu, G. K. (2014). Assessment practices in higher education in United States. *Procedia: Social and Behavioral Sciences, 123*, 299–306. doi:10.1016/j.sbspro.2014.01.1427

Gilles, J., Detroz, P., & Blais, J. (2011). An international online survey of the practices and perceptions of higher education professors with respect to the assessment of learning in the classroom. *Assessment & Evaluation in Higher Education, 36*(6), 719–733. doi:10.1080/02602938.2010.484880

Graneheim, U. H., & Lundman, B. (2004). Qualitative content analysis in nursing research: Concepts, procedures, and measures to achieve trustworthiness. *Nurse Education Today, 24*(2), 105–112. doi:10.1016/j.nedt.2003.10.001 PMID:14769454

Greene, H., & Crespi, C. (2012). The value of student created videos in the college classroom-an exploratory study in marketing and accounting. *The International Journal of the Arts in Society*, *5*(1), 213–283.

Hawley, R., & Allen, C. (2018). Student-generated video creation for assessment: Can it transform assessment within Higher Education? *International Journal for Transformative Research*, *5*(1), 1–11. doi:10.2478/ijtr-2018-0001

Helsper, E. J., & Enyon, R. (2010). Digital natives: Where is the evidence? *British Educational Research Journal*, *36*(3), 503–520. doi:10.1080/01411920902989227

Herrington, J., & Parker, J. (2013). Emerging technologies as cognitive tools for authentic learning. *British Journal of Educational Technology*, *4*(4), 607–615. doi:10.1111/bjet.12048

Janisch, C., Liu, X., & Akrof, A. (2007). Implementing alternative assessment: Opportunities and obstacles. *The Educational Forum*, *71*(3), 221–230. doi:10.1080/00131720709335007

Jewitt, C. (2003). Re-thinking assessment: Multimodality, literacy and computer-mediated learning. *Assessment in Education: Principles, Policy & Practice*, *10*(1), 83–102. doi:10.1080/09695940301698

Jewitt, C. (2012). Multimodal methods for researching digital technologies. In S. Price, C. Jewitt, & B. Brown (Eds.), *The Sage handbook of digital technology research* (pp. 250–265). Sage.

Jiang, J. (2018). *Millennials stand out for their technology use, but older generations.* Pew Research Center. https://www.pewresearch.org/fact-tank/2019/09/09/us-generations-technology-use/

Jorm, C., Roberts, C., Gordon, C., Nisbet, G., & Roper, L. (2019). Time for university educators to embrace student videography. *Cambridge Journal of Education*, *49*(6), 673–693. doi:10.1080/0305764X.2019.1590528

Kirschner, P. A., & De Bruyckere, P. (2017). The myths of the digital native and the multitasker. *Teaching and Teacher Education*, *67*, 135–142. doi:10.1016/j.tate.2017.06.001

Kleinheksel, A. J., Rockich-Winston, N., Tawfik, H., & Wyatt, T. R. (2020). Demystifying content analysis. *American Journal of Pharmaceutical Education*, *84*(1), 127–137. doi:10.5688/ajpe7113 PMID:32292185

Koch, M., Luck, K. V., Schwarzer, J., & Draheim, S. (2018). The novelty effect in large display deployments - Experiences and lessons-learned for evaluating prototypes. *16th European Conference on Computer-Supported Cooperative Work*, (pp. 1-19). Nancy, France. 10.18420/ecscw2018_3

Lemieux, A., Burkholder, C., & Ribiero, J. (2019). Pedagogies of empathy-building: Canadian and Azorean perspectives of film-viewing in higher education. In G. Barton & S. Garvis (Eds.), *Compassion and empathy in educational contexts* (pp. 271–288). Palgrave MacMillan. doi:10.1007/978-3-030-18925-9_14

Letina, A. (2015). Application of traditional and alternative assessment in science and social studies teaching. *Croatian Journal of Education, 17*(1), 137–152. doi:10.15516/cje.v17i0.1496

Lightle, K. (2011). More than just the technology. *Science Scope, 34*(9), 6–9. PMID:21980630

Lipps, R. (2018). *Beyond the Bitrate: Ensuring Campus Video Success* [Paper presentation]. Media and Learning Conference Leuven.

MacEntee, K., Burkholder, C., & Schwab-Cartas, J. (2016). *What's a cellpilms? Integrating mobile technology into participatory visual activism and activims*. Sense.

MacKenzie, W. I. Jr, & Scherer, F. R. (2019). Millennial research on fleek: Suggestions for improving generational research design. *The Journal of Social Psychology, 159*(2), 119–124. doi:10.1080/00224545.2019.1572967 PMID:31002294

Margaryan, A., Littlejohn, A., & Vojt, G. (2011). Are digital natives a myth or reality? University students' use of digital technologies. *Computers & Education, 56*(2), 429–440. doi:10.1016/j.compedu.2010.09.004

Masters, G. N. (2013). Reforming educational assessment: Imperatives, principles and challenges. Camberwel: Australian Council for Educational Research.

McLaren, S. V. (2007). An international overview of assessment issues in technology education: Disentangling the influences, confusion and complexities. *Design and Technology Education: An International Journal, 12*(2), 10–24.

Merizow, J. (1981). A critical theory of adult learning and education. *Adult Education, 32*(1), 3–24. doi:10.1177/074171368103200101

Mitchell, C. (2014). Digital Media and the knowledge-producing practices of young people in the age of AIDS. In K. Sandford, T. Rogers, & M. Kendrick, Cultural Studies and Transdisciplinarity in Education (Vol. 1, pp. 81-93). Springer. doi:10.1007/978-981-4451-03-1_6

Mitchell, C., Burkholder, C., Magubane, S., & Saioojee, S. (2019). Ethically significant moments in stirring up memories. In K. Pithouse-Morgan, D. Pillay, & C. Mitchell (Eds.), *Memory mosaics: Researching teacher professional learning through artful memory-work* (pp. 175–192). Springer. doi:10.1007/978-3-319-97106-3_10

Mitchell, J. (2021). Affective shifts: Mood, emotion and well-being. *Synthese, 199*(5-6), 11793–11820. doi:10.100711229-021-03312-3

Nasab, G. F. (2015). Alternative versus traditional assessment. *Journal of Applied Linguistics and Language Research, 2*(6), 165–178.

New London Group. (1996). A pedagogy of multiliteracies: Designing social futures. *Harvard Educational Review, 66*(1), 60–92. doi:10.17763/haer.66.1.17370n67v22j160u

Orús, C., Barlés, M. J., Belanche, D., Casaló, L., Fraj, E., & Gurrea, R. (2016). The effects of learner-generated videos for YouTube on learning outcomes and satisfaction. *Computers & Education, 95*, 254–269. doi:10.1016/j.compedu.2016.01.007

Pace, D. (2011). Assessment in History: The case for"decoding" the discipline. *The Journal of Scholarship of Teaching and Learning, 11*(3), 107–119.

Pekrun, R., Goetz, T., Frenzel, A. C., Barchfeld, P., & Perry, R. P. (2011). Measuring emotions in students' learning and performance: The Achievement Emotions Questionnaire (AEQ). *Contemporary Educational Psychology, 36*(1), 36–48. doi:10.1016/j.cedpsych.2010.10.002

Pereira, J., Echeazarra, L., Sanz-Santamaría, S., & Gutiérrez, J. (2014). Student-generated online videos to develop cross-curricular and curricular competencies in nursing studies. *Computers in Human Behavior, 31*, 580–590. doi:10.1016/j.chb.2013.06.011

Phongsirikul, M. (2018). Traditional and alternative assessments in ELT: Students' and teachers' perceptions. *Reflections: The SoL Journal, 25*(1), 61–84. https://so05.tci-thaijo.org/index.php/reflections/article/view/136267

Pirhonen, J., & Rasi, P. (2017). Student-generated instructional videos facilitate learning through positive emotions. *Journal of Biological Education, 51*(3), 215–227. doi:10.1080/00219266.2016.1200647

Pop, A. (2020). Alternatives in assessment: Student-generated videos and online written case presentations in medical English. *The 15th International Conference on Virtual Learning ICVL 2020*. Bucharest. https://www.researchgate.net/publication/352090551_Alternatives_in_Assessment_Student-generated_Videos_and_Online_Written_Case_presentations_in_Medical_English

Postareff, L., Virtanen, V., Katajavuori, N., & Lindblom-Ylänne, S. (2012). Academics' conceptions of assessment and their assessment practices. *Studies in Educational Evaluation*, *38*(3-4), 84–92. doi:10.1016/j.stueduc.2012.06.003

Prensky, M. (2001a). Digital natives, digital immigrants, part 1. *On the Horizon*, *9*(5), 1–6. doi:10.1108/10748120110424816

Prensky, M. (2001b). Digital natives, digital immigrants Part 2: Do they really think differently? *On the Horizon*, *9*(6), 1–6. doi:10.1108/10748120110424843

Rawlusyk, P. E. (2018). Assessment in higher education and student learning. *Journal of Instructional Pedagogies*, *21*, 1–34.

Reeve, J. (1989). The interest-enjoyment distinction in intrinsic motivation. *Motivation and Emotion*, *13*(2), 83–103. doi:10.1007/BF00992956

Ross, J., Curwood, J. S., & Bell, A. (2020). A multimodal assessment framework for higher education. *E-Learning and Digital Media*, *17*(4), 290–306. doi:10.1177/2042753020927201

Ryan, B. (2013). A walk down the red carpet: Students as producers digital video-based knowledge. *International Journal of Technology Enhanced Learning*, *5*(1), 24–41. doi:10.1504/IJTEL.2013.055950

Ryan, R. M., & Deci, E. L. (2000). Self-determination theory and the facilitation of intrinsic motivation, social development, and well-being. *The American Psychologist*, *55*(1), 68–78. doi:10.1037/0003-066X.55.1.68 PMID:11392867

Sadati, S. M. H., & Mitchell, C. (2021). Narrative imagination and social change: Instructors in agricultural colleges in Ethiopia address sexual and gender-based violence. *Educational Research for Social Change*, *10*(2), 124–141. doi:10.17159/2221-4070/2021/v10i2a8

Schofield, L., Baker, K., Vo, D., Pham, T., Lindsay, L., & Han, B. (2017). How does the option of video assessment impact on student choice and grades? In S. Nash, & L. M. Patston (eds.), Spaces and Pedagogies: New Zealand Tertiary Learning and Teaching Conference 2017 Proceedings (pp. 67-78). Auckland, New Zealand: ePress, Unitec Institute of Technology.

Shah, N., & Abraham, S. (2009). Digital natives with a cause?A knowledge survey and framework. The Centre for Internet and Society, San Francisco:Hivos Knowledge Program

Snowball, J. D., & McKenna, S. (2017). Student-generated content: An approach to harnessing the power of diversity in higher education. *Teaching in Higher Education, 22*(5), 604–618. doi:10.1080/13562517.2016.1273205

Sorrentino, P. (2018). The mystery of the digital natives' existence: Questioning the validity of the Prenskian metaphor. *First Monday, 23*(10). doi:10.5210/fm.v23i10.9434

Starr, L. J., & Mitchell, C. (2020). Cellphilming as a feminist tool. In D. Clover, S. Dzulkifli, H. Gelderman, & K. Sanford (Eds.), *Feminist adult educator's guide to aesthetic, creative and disruptive strategies in museums and communities* (pp. 119–128). University of Victoria Gender Justice, Creative Pedagogies and Arts-Based Research Group., https://onlineacademiccommunity.uvic.ca/comarts/

Strauss, W., & Howe, N. (1991). *Generations*. Harper Perennial.

Strauss, W., & Howe, N. (1997). *The fourth turning: An American prophecy—What the cycles of history tell us about America's next rendezvous with destiny*. Broadway Books.

Tapscott, D. (1998). *Growing up digital: the rise of the net generation*. McGraw-Hill.

UNESCO. (2015). *Global citizenship education: Preparing learners for the challenges of the twenty-first century*. UNESCO. https://en.unesco.org/news/global-citizenship-education-preparing-learners-challenges-twenty-first-century-0

Veletsianos, G. (2011). Designing opportunities for transformation with emerging technologies. *Educational Technology, 51*(2), 41–46.

Yearta, L., & Kelly, K. (2021). Digital storytelling to enhance social studies content knowledge, explore multiple perspectives, and advocate for social justice. In L. Hass & J. Tussey (Eds.), *Connecting disciplinary literacy and digital storytelling in K-12 education* (pp. 235–256). IGI Global. doi:10.4018/978-1-7998-5770-9.ch012

Yi, Y. (2008). Relay writing in an adolescent online community. *Journal of Adolescent & Adult Literacy, 51*(8), 670–680. https://www.jstor.org/stable/40012404. doi:10.1598/JAAL.51.8.6

Zur, O., & Zur, A. (2011). *On digital immigrants and digital natives: How the digital divide affects families, educational institutions, and the workplace?* Zur Institute - Online Publication. http://www.zurinstitute.com/digital_divide.html

Chapter 4
Rapid Game Development Using LiveCode in SEN and DHH Education

Gwendoline Laurissa Chan
University of Mauritius, Mauritius

Jack Whitehead
University of Cumbria, UK

ABSTRACT

For over 30 years, literacy has been recognized as a key concern in Special Education Needs (SEN) and especially in Deaf and Hard of Hearing (DHH) education. No different in Mauritius, these children struggle to get passing marks in French language at elementary level. Addressing this concern, literature has been reviewed in the context of games for SEN and DHH education. Taking advantage of the potential of gamification, simple letter games have been developed using LiveCode. The games were administered to a sample of 14 SEN and DHH elementary students using the underlying action research theoretical framework. To assess the effectiveness of the games, the students' level of motivation after using the games was measured using the Instructional Materials Motivation Survey (IMMS) based on Keller's (2010) ARCS motivation model. The results demonstrated the potential of using LiveCode to develop timely serious games to support SEN and DHH students' literacy skills.

DOI: 10.4018/978-1-6684-4940-0.ch004

INTRODUCTION

For over 30 years, literacy has been recognized as a key concern in Special Education Needs (SEN) and especially in Deaf and Hard of Hearing (DHH) education. No different in Mauritius, around 25% of children with disability are categorized as severe to profound, and these children struggle to get passing marks in French language at elementary level. The latter subject being a prerequisite to passing the Primary School Achievement Certificate (PSAC) assessment classified as the first level on the National Qualification Framework. Addressing this concern, literature has been reviewed in the context of games for SEN and specially DHH education. Serious games have proved to benefit children with special needs, increasing their motivation level and supporting their literacy skills at the same time. Taking advantage of the potential of gamification in SEN and DHH education, simple letter games have been developed using LiveCode, a cross-platform development tool. This authoring tool allowed for the rapid design and development of the games' prototype for evaluation and testing purposes before the final deployment of the software. The games were administered to a sample of 14 SEN and DHH elementary students using the underlying action research theoretical framework. While the rapid game development stages meet those of the outlining phases of action research, the latter framework served as basis for the methodologies and evaluation protocols employed in this project. To assess the effectiveness of the games, the students' level of motivation after using the games was measured using the Instructional Materials Motivation Survey (IMMS) based on Keller's (2010) ARCS motivation model.

The following sections give an overview of literature, a brief description of the methodology employed and describe each stage of the game development; from gathering users' requirements to prototyping, testing and deployment of the games.

BACKGROUND

Special Educational Needs (SEN) refer to learners with learning, developmental, and physical disabilities; communication, emotional, and behavioral disorders; and learning deficiencies (Bryant et al., 2019). In Mauritius, around 25% of children with disability are categorized as severe to profound, and those children normally attend SEN schools because they need resource assistance or require direct attention from Special Needs teachers (Ministry of Education Tertiary Education Science and Technology, 2017). A sub-category of SEN includes Deaf and Hard of Hearing (DHH) children. The delayed exposure to a first language in DHH children affects language acquisition and the development of a second one (Humphries et al., 2014; Mayberry, 2007).

Over the past decades, research has shown that performance on short-term memory (STM) and working memory (WM) tasks highly predicted academic achievement in reading and language comprehension (Cain & Oakhill, 2006). Research suggests that learning fails or is hampered when the task demand exceeds memory capacity (Ayres & Van Gog, 2009). Further, deficits in memory processes have been found for children with disabilities (Pickering, 2006); such as reading disabilities (Swanson et al., 2009), speech and language impairments (Archibald & Gathercole, 2006), attention deficit or hyperactivity disorder (Rapport et al., 2008), and intellectual disabilities (Henry & Winfield, 2010).

Research has also shown that gamification has had the most success with struggling learners or students with SEN (El Mawas et al., 2019; Jong, 2015; Lan et al., 2018; Wajiuhullah et al., 2018). The studies (Cano et al., 2018; El Mawas et al., 2019; Jong, 2015; Wajiuhullah et al., 2018) indicated a higher level of motivation and learning participation when games were used with children having SEN. These students often receive this type of specialized instruction because of the lack of success with the sole use of a traditional approach (de Freitas, 2018; Jong, 2015). Nowadays, teaching strategies not only include frameworks from past approaches, but support their incorporation with new findings and technologies for the growth of the education system (de Freitas, 2018; Florian, 2021).

Differentiating games according to cognitive characteristics such as visual attention, text comprehension skills and memory abilities turn out to be crucial for the suitability and accessibility of students with SEN, and more specifically those with sensory deficiencies such as hearing impairment (Mascio et al., 2013). According to deaf studies (Marschark & Hauser, 2008), the reading skills of DHH people are lagging behind compared to those who hear, while both groups are considered to have similar visuoperceptual skills. Such differences call for specific guidelines when designing educational games that are both accessible and usable for DHH and SEN students.

Di Mascio and colleagues (2013) suggest developing digital learning systems that follow the Evidence Based Design and the User-Centered Design. To produce pedagogically effective systems, the Evidence Based Design framework ensures that the system design is based on empirical evidence gathered from domain experts, whereas User-centered Design places the users at the center of the design process using iterative prototype evaluation to produce usable systems. Di Mascio and colleagues (2013) provide guidelines clustered into five main areas for the design of digital pedagogical games for DHH children: words, other characteristics and position of textual elements, choices and interaction, feedback, game genres and devices. Unambiguous, familiar and short words should be favoured, and the surrounding context should easily infer meaning. Relevant textual information should be simple and short, and visual cues should direct a student's attention to key textual information. Including only necessary choices while avoiding distracting stimuli should aid the attention and recall of DHH children. Using single communication and interaction channel at a time is encouraged because DHH children cannot answer and listen simultaneously as hearing ones do. Immediate feedback can compensate the usually short attention span of DHH children. Illustrations provided in games should be highly coherent and pertain to displayed texts. In most cases, DHH children prefer single-player games, and male children prefer adventure and sport elements, progressive challenges and extrinsic rewards.

Users' experiences in operating a system are an important goal of test and evaluation. Specific forms of social interactions such as surveys are suitable for measuring such user experience. People's opinions, thoughts and feelings are systematically measured through surveys. Users go through several mental processes to respond using response options provided by researchers. For this reason, survey design should formulate questions which facilitate a user's ability to recall relevant information, understand the question and respond honestly. (Gideon, 2012; Wojton et al., 2016) Another important aspect is the question of validity when surveying students with SEN. Nusser and colleagues report on this issue when using a survey questionnaire for SEN students with learning difficulties in Grade 5 and Grade 9. Congruency between students' and parents' reports and completion rate were the main issues they encountered. Validity was reduced and response rates lower when items without mental representations were presented to the students, while simple items yielded valid and accurate responses. The mode of administering the questionnaire is yet another aspect to be considered when working with students with SEN (Nusser et al., 2016). Interviewers are especially helpful when the survey includes more than one person in the household, when the survey is long and that additional data has to be collected, and when participants need an interpreter, as in the case of SEN and DHH children. As such training and instructions should be provided to interviewers to minimize variation in the administration of the survey. (Gideon, 2012)

Keller's (2010) ARCS motivation model has been extensively used to provide guidance in motivational aspects of instructional design and teaching. The model is represented by four categories which when applied to instructional materials, can condition students to be fully motivated (Li et al., 2018). Over the years, the ARCS model has been used to understand learners' language learning efficiency, and researchers found that students' achievement in English as Foreign Language was enhanced (Li et al., 2018); positively increasing their confidence, autonomy and learning motivation (Li et al., 2018; Refat et al., 2020). The Likert scale is an important aspect of the ARCS model survey. Pictorial scales are commonly used to survey children to replace text response options (Hall et al., 2016). In smiley face scales, respondents match their emotions or attitude on a scale showing faces with varying curvature of the mouth line, systematically varying from a grimace to a large smile (Toepoel et al., 2019). Stange and colleagues (2018) found that the smiley faces could speed up processing of questions, especially for lower literacy respondents, and made the question-answering process more enjoyable (Toepoel et al., 2019).

METHODOLOGY

This chapter describes part of a bigger project in the development of serious games for SEN and DHH elementary students to support French literacy. For a comprehensive understanding of the purpose of developing serious games, this section gives a brief overview of the methodology employed.

Advocating for both qualitative and quantitative methods to complement limitations and strengths of the different approaches, the project was based on the pragmatic paradigm while the theoretical framework was based on action research. Pragmatism as a research paradigm finds its philosophical foundation in the historical contributions of the philosophy of pragmatism and as a result embraces plurality of methods. The paradigm is based on the proposition that the methodological approach which works best for particular research problems being investigated should be employed. Action Research is a process whereby a researcher tries to both acquire knowledge of and improve the real-world situation he found himself in. Rather than dealing with the theoretical, participants examine their own educational techniques and engage in research; assuming that participants: work best on problems they identified for themselves, assess their own work and come up with personalised solutions, and work collaboratively to help generate new ideas and grow professionally (Watts, 1985). The process is so practical that in any case the practitioners often say that this is what they do; there is no difference in practice (McNiff & Whitehead, 2005). Based on the four-phase which are: Plan, Act, Observe and Reflect, the research completed 2 cycles of Action Research. The first cycle served to refine the methods employed and to inform subsequent research decisions in the second cycle. The Plan phase consisted of gathering data about the difficulties faced by the children in French language and their gaming preferences, which then informed the Act phase on the collaborative design and administration of the pedagogical games. The Observe phase ensured that students' educational data were gathered to be interpreted in the Reflect phase, where each participant reflected on his own action.

Through the purposeful sampling strategy, a SEN school which includes DHH students was chosen. Data was gathered using techniques which included surveys, interviews, observations and focus group discussions through the lenses of narrative inquiry.

Initially, surveys were used to gather information about research subjects to inform research methods, tests and required resources. They were then paired with interviews to interpret the different point of views of students, teachers, and parents. This also allowed for the requirements elicitation for game development. Interviews were carried out in a face-to-face style or through telephone calls depending on the availability of participants. Observation was used in both participant and non-participant styles to balance closeness and better understanding of participants and to avoid biased interpretations through objectivity and neutrality. The focus group discussion technique was mainly employed to understand teaching and assessment methods that the teachers used at school, and to also inform research decisions.

Analysis of data gathered allowed for the construction of different models which helped in designing an adaptive solution. The latter solution was then used to address some of the difficulties faced by the students. In implementing those models, several vocabulary tests were designed and administered within specific timeframes to the students to capture academical progress in French language, although not discussed here. Afterwards, a survey was also designed and administered to the students to measure motivation levels and understand learning preferences.

RAPID GAME DEVELOPMENT

Pre-Production

The pedagogical games which were co-developed with the teachers were aimed at being used as learning aid for the children. The games requirements were gathered from interviews with the children, the SEN teachers together with observations of their French classes. Implementation of the games was driven by several factors: being able to play and all the while learn from home and adapt to the new sanitary measures imposed by the pandemic Covid-19 when schools remained closed.

Although not all of the students owned a mobile phone, all played and liked console or mobile games. A frequent response was that of time constrained games among the students: "I like racing in the games". The boys were especially responsive to points and challenges: "I like competitions" or "I like to win". Most of the students struggled with both reading and writing of common nouns. The latter being the building block of French literacy in the context of the primary school curriculum, the teachers thought that simple letter games would be appropriate tools in assisting learning as well as teaching. Through observation of activities carried out in French classes and brainstorming sessions, the teachers and the researcher drew drafts of the games' design and mechanics. Important features included recording students' scores, the games they played, and the time taken to complete each game.

The choice of technology used for game development was influenced by two main criteria: rapid development and cross-platform deployment. The games have therefore been developed in LiveCode, a cross-platform rapid application development runtime system inspired by HyperCard and imported as both mobile and desktop applications. The database technology chosen was MySQL, an open-source relational database management system. This was primarily used to store students' gaming data and the different sets of words that would be used for the purpose of research. This allowed for the dynamic loading of different set of words for each teaching and learning session. Before the final administration of the game, several prototypes have been deployed to ensure a good usability of the games' interface and that the intents of implementing pedagogical games were met.

Production

Design

The games were based on the adaptive model described by Chan and colleagues (2019); and complemented the teachers' teaching methods while addressing the children's vocabulary learning needs by enabling the "learning for fun" concept. Also based on Keller's (2010) ARCS model to include motivational aspects, the different game elements used were classified into each of the four categories of Attention, Relevance, Confidence and Satisfaction, as described in Table 1.

Table 1. ARCS model applied to game elements

Attention	Relevance	Confidence	Satisfaction
• Graphics • Animated mouse-overs • Colors • Dynamic content • Variety of games	• Personalized • Game choice • Consequences • Rewards • Score board	• Objectives • Game prompts • Score board • Feedback • Dynamic content	• Feedback • Score points • Objectives • Reward system

In Attention, game elements such as graphics, animated mouse-overs and dynamic content are used to achieve the goals of perceptual and inquiry arousal through a variety of games; while in relevance, game elements such as personalized graphics, rewards and score boards are aimed at achieving familiarity and matching motive and goals. To meet learning requirements and success opportunities, game elements such as game prompts and feedback messages are used to achieve confidence; while the score boards, individual game scores and feedback messages are used to reinforce intrinsic motivation through extrinsic rewards and equity which results in satisfaction.

Following guidelines from Di Mascio and colleagues (2013) on the designing of games for DHH children, short-worded and familiar instructions are given on the main screen and are accompanied by their respective signs (i.e.: ‘Choose a game’) as illustrated in Figure 1.

Figure 1. The main menu

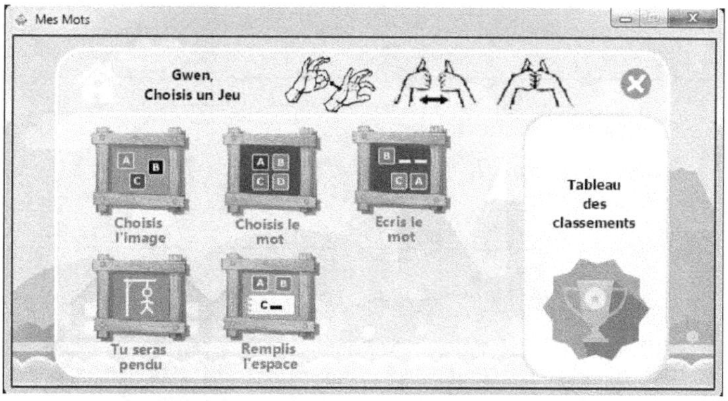

Moreover, icons used to indicate home or exit buttons were consistently used across the screens to aid the recall of DHH children. Each game was designed to require single interaction tasks from the children. Although initially designed to be single-player games, as generally preferred by DHH children (Mascio et al., 2013), the desktop version installed on the school laptop allowed for collaborative play in class, with each child taking turns as directed by their teachers. Since the games focused on vocabulary learning, the pictorial representations of each word were carefully selected and validated by the teachers to ensure that they easily inferred meaning.

As a result, five distinct games have been used as teaching and learning aids. The first (‘Tu seras pendu’) is a classical hangman game allowing for only 5 mistakes; while the second (‘Choisis l’image’) is a multiple-choice game with 3 options to choose from; and the third (‘Ecris le mot’) is a re-ordering letters game with the aim of forcing the player to complete the whole word correctly before proceeding to the next round. The fourth (‘Choisis le mot’) is another multiple-choice game with 4 word options to choose from, and the fifth (‘Remplis l’espace’) is a fill in the blank activity with no pictorial representations. Each game is made up of ten rounds (10 words) allowing for a maximum of ten points. The time taken to complete a game is also recorded for each student. The score board was designed in three

Figure 2. The score board

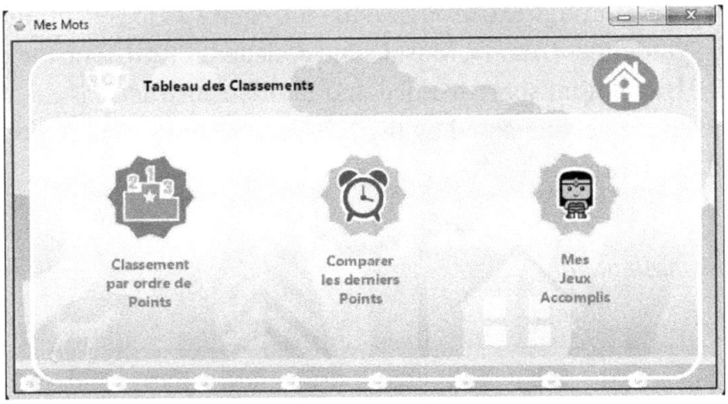

Figure 3. The third score board

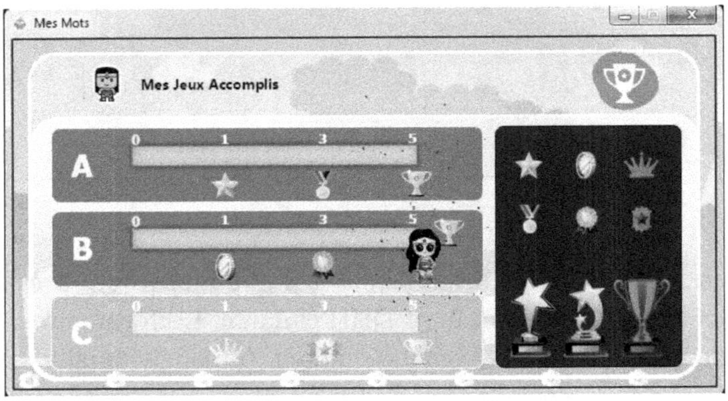

parts as illustrated in Figure 2. A first to compare the highest score obtained in the minimum possible time, a second to compare the last score obtained, and the last, as illustrated in Figure 3, to evaluate the player's overall performance; giving a statistic of the number of times distinct games were played, and badges and trophies for each milestone. For research purposes, three sessions (A, B, C) have been considered in the third score board to represent the three teaching strategy sessions which included the games as learning aid.

Implementation

The possibility to develop games in a timely manner was an important factor which was considered when choosing the technology for research-based game development. The visual development environment provided by LiveCode made it both easy and quick to implement fully featured controls through drag and drop. The ability to live edit the application also allowed for an uninterrupted workflow while developing the games. Because LiveCode is cross-platform, coding was done once and deployed to both desktop and mobile platforms. This effectively reduced development time, otherwise each platform would have required rewriting each application anew. The following paragraphs describe how some of the game mechanics were rapidly developed.

The first step was that of creating the login page. This will determine which content to display based on the student's grade, gender and the set of words linked to the student's learning path. As described below, global variables storing the student's data were initialized so they would be accessible across the application.

```
global myName
global myGender
global myGrade
global myGroup
```

To address the short attention span of DHH, an interactive loading screen was designed to keep the students entertained and engaged while waiting for the games to load. As seen in Figure 4, the illustration depicting hands with wiggling fingers was purposefully added to mean "wait" in ASL. The interaction included a spaceship which would fly and move forward in a loop as the lower button is pushed. A progress bar was also included to indicate the remaining loading time. The following codes show how the short loading animation is called when the *openCard* event is triggered.

```
on openCard
          -- start load animation
          show group "Load_game"
          show btn "Boost"
          put true into sRun
          mainEventLoop // Execute the main run loop.
...
on openCard
```

Word and image pairs were randomly presented for each game to draw on the strengths of DHH students in free recall of unordered lists, and to maintain the appearance of unpredictability. The following snippet shows how random numbers were generated using a local function. To call the function, three parameters are defined: the range of possible numbers, and the amount of numbers to return.

Figure 4. The loading screen

```
function randList pMin, pMax, pAmount
   local mycount
   put 1 into mycount
   repeat with n = pMin to pMax
      put n & comma after tList
   end repeat
   delete char -1 of tList
   sort items of tList by random(2^31)
   return item 1 to pAmount of tList
end randList
```

The hangman game ("Tu seras pendu"), as seen in Figure 5, was particularly tricky to implement. For each round, placeholders or underlines amounting to the number of letters in the random word had to be displayed. Moreover, letters included in the random word had to be specifically positioned to replace appropriate placeholders. The below codes show how loops were implemented with the *repeat* keyword, while arrays were easily read using the *of* keyword. LiveCode's high level language effectively reduced blocks of codes to fewer or single English programming language sentences.

```
repeat with x = 1 to the number of words of tAnswer
      add the number of chars of word x of tAnswer to
sAnswerCharacters
      repeat with y = 1 to the number of characters of word x
of tAnswer
         put "letter" & x & y into tButtonName
```

```
        put "underline" & x & y into tUnderlineName
        put character y of word x of tAnswer into tCharacter
        put tCharacter & ".png" into tImageName

        set the cLetter of button tButtonName of group
"Answer" to tCharacter
        set the icon of button tButtonName to the id of image
tImageName of card "Image Store"
        set the visible of graphic tUnderlineName of group
"Answer" to true
     end repeat
end repeat
```

Figure 5. "Tu seras pendu" game

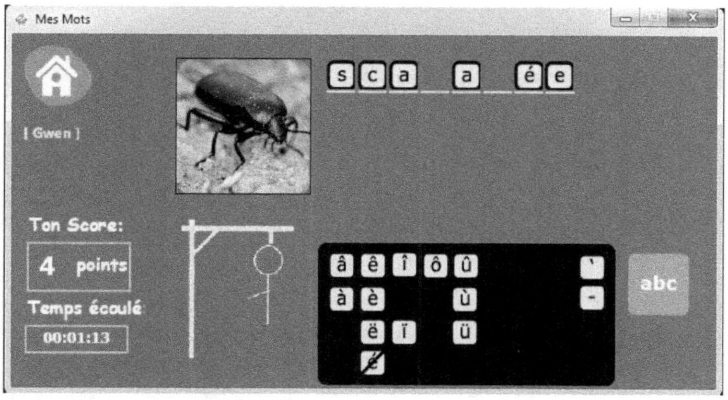

Both multiple choice games, and the fill in the blank activity ('Choisis l'image', 'Choisis le mot', 'Remplis l'espace'), as seen in Figures 6, 7, and 8, required scripts to be dynamically attached to the correct and wrong option buttons. The game mechanic included determining the next random answer, setting the correct answer button, generating different random wrong answers and setting their scripts respectively. Although the latter option buttons could be directly added to the user interface as objects, their properties had to be altered for each of the 10 rounds. As described below, the script and icon properties could be altered using the simple command of *set the script of button* or *set the icon of button.*

```
repeat with i = 1 to 3
     if myRandAns=i then
```

```
    -- correct answer
            put "hint" & tID into myImg
            put "btn_" & myRandAns into myBtn
            set the icon of button myBtn to the id of image myImg
            set the script of button myBtn to "on mouseUp" & cr &
"showCorrect" & cr & "end mouseUp"
        else
    -- random wrong answer
            put myRandAns into myRandAnsOther
            repeat until myRandAnsOther is not in myRandAnsList
               put randList(1, 10, 1) into myRandAnsOther
            end repeat
            put myRandAnsList, myRandAnsOther into myRandAnsList
            put "hint" & myRandAnsOther into myImg
            put "btn_" & i into myBtn
            set the icon of button myBtn to the id of image myImg
            set the script of button myBtn to "on mouseUp" & cr &
"showWrong" & cr & "end mouseUp"
        end if;
        put (myAnsCount + 1) into myAnsCount
end repeat
```

Figure 6. "Choisis l'image" game

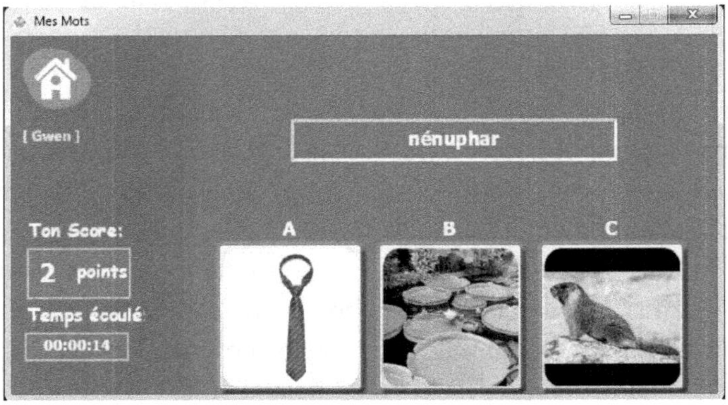

Figure 7. "Remplis l'espace" game

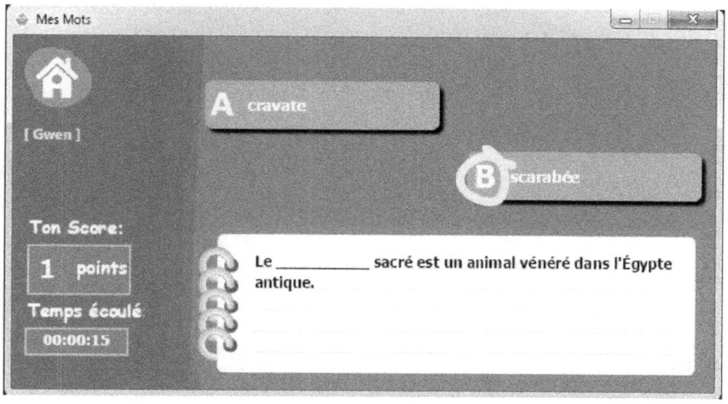

Figure 8. "Choisis le mot" game

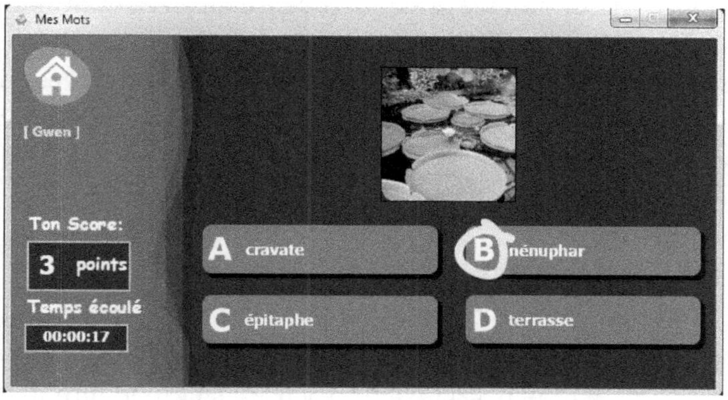

For the reorder letters game ('Ecris le mot'), as seen in Figure 9, a *setUpAlphabets* function was created for code reusability. The below snippet demonstrates how this function takes the answer as parameter and processes each letter to attach scripts which would determine the correct letter position in the word, as the letters are dragged to a placeholder during play.

```
on setUpAlphabets lAnswer
   put lAnswer into myAnswer
   replace space with "" in lAnswer
   replace space with cr in mAnswer
   add the number of chars of lAnswer to lCharacters
   put randList(1, lCharacters, lCharacters) into myRandLetters
   split myRandLetters by comma
```

```
   ...

   repeat for (the number of characters of lAnswer) times

      set the script of button myCount2 of group "Alphabet" to
"global cX, cY, oX, oY, uletterCount" & CR & \

         ...

   end repeat

end setUpAlphabets
```

This section described how the games were conceptualized from the requirements gathering phase and effectively developed in around five months, considering the ongoing testing, realignment of requirements and several prototypes deployed. In software engineering, this evolutionary prototyping method was especially useful and suitable for research purposes.

Post-Production

At the end of the development phase and after testing several prototypes of the games with the teachers, the games were introduced to the children. After a first demonstration of how to play each game, each student took turn to give a try at playing the vocabulary games. From the impressions shared by the teachers and

Figure 9. "Ecris le mot" game

observed by the researcher, adjustments were made to ready the game for the upcoming experiment and survey.

During the experiment period, the games were used as a class activity where each child would take turn to play the games; or sometimes as a collaborative one where the whole class would participate using their mini whiteboards to write their answers. The teachers and students often played the games in a sort of friendly competition to score the most points in the least amount of time. The games were also used as refresher training for students who missed class lessons.

Survey and IMMS Questionnaire

This subsection briefly describes contents of the survey questionnaire and gives details of the results obtained. Although not the focus of this chapter, it is important to shed light on the purpose of developing the games so the reader can grasp a better understanding of the whole research and how choosing the right development environment was crucial in implementing pedagogy for SEN and DHH students. For a more comprehensive description on the research process, please refer to "Gamification as Technology Enabler in SEN and DHH Education" by Chan and colleagues (2022).

Derived from the ARCS model, as previously discussed, the survey questionnaire was also based on Keller's (2010) four motivation categories: Attention, Relevance, Confidence and Satisfaction. Consisting of a total of 16 questions, each category of ARCS was addressed by 4 questions. For example, the first four questions pertained to Attention with questions such as "I liked using the games to learn new words", or "I wanted to know what the games were about". The fifth to eighth questions pertained to Relevance and included questions such as "Learning words through the games will help in my communication skills", "Learning words through games is easier for me". The ninth to twelfth questions were to evaluate Confidence with questions such as "Using the games can increase my knowledge and vocabulary" and "If I score more points in the games, I will also perform better in vocabulary tests". The last four questions were for evaluating Satisfaction and consisted of items such as "I feel that I am learning to read using the games" and "I feel satisfied/ happy when I score points in the game".

Because of the relatively small sample size of 14 SEN and DHH students, it was irrelevant to calculate Cronbach's Alpha for internal reliability of items (Taber, 2018), and that an overall Cronbach Alpha of 0.73 for the whole instrument was acceptable. This describes the general link between the different items in the survey; meaning that the instrument is reliable and captures motivation level. The following table describes the students' overall motivation level after having played the games.

Table 2. ARCS overall motivation level

ARCS subcategories	Agree + SA (N=56)	N%	Mean *	Mode **
Attention	52	93%	4.36	4
Relevance	45	80%	4.04	4
Confidence	42	75%	4.05	5
Satisfaction	49	88%	4.29	5
* mean on a total of 56 responses for each category with median 2.5, and overall mean of 4.18 ** on a Likert scale where – 1: strongly disagree, 2: agree, 3: neutral, 4: agree, 5: strongly agree				

As can be observed, most of the 56 responses reported for each subcategory measuring motivation were positive: ranging from 75% to 93%. The average response calculated for each subcategory was well over the median value of 2.5; and the most frequent response for all subcategories was relatively positive; meaning that most children thought that the pedagogical games met their motivational requirements.

SOLUTIONS AND RECOMMENDATIONS

LiveCode's open-source version and MySQL database are highly suitable for the purpose of research. The technology employed allowed for the rapid development of multiple games within acceptable timeframes. The implementation process was easy and smooth once the software engineer became accustomed to the high-level programming language of LiveCode. Although no proficient programming skills are required to develop simple applications in LiveCode, it was definitely an advantage having programming backgrounds and assuming both roles of researcher and programmer. This effectively reduced overall development and deployment time, and the need to translate requirements from the two roles. The ability to import to different platforms was also a contributing factor to reducing implementation time. No additional programming environment was necessary to deploy the games as both mobile and desktop applications.

FUTURE RESEARCH DIRECTIONS

For research purposes, this study took into consideration the requirements that pertained to PSAC and the French curriculum which, as at now, do not assess sign languages. Integrating MSL and ASL into the games may further develop and assert the communication skills of elementary DHH students. Implementing difficulty levels within each game should also be considered to maintain students' engagement in the games, although a thorough study is required to balance existing literacy skills and challenge levels. It is to be noted that the target audience deals with SEN and DHH students and that unsolvable additional challenge may deter low performing students and adversely impact their short attention span, as previously reviewed (Ayres & Van Gog, 2009). From a practical perspective, developing an interface to enable teachers to upload their own set of words with the respective images is to be taken into consideration. Empowering both teachers and students with the right technological tools while assessing the appropriate pedagogy and addressing the urgency of pragmatic methodologies, will most likely foster favourable learning environments and help students realize their full potential (de Freitas, 2018; Florian, 2021).

CONCLUSION

This chapter describes the rapid development of interactive pedagogical games in French literacy. The technology employed was crucial for the swift deployment of the games for research purposes. LiveCode was deemed a suitable programming environment because of its high-level language and the ability to import the interactive games to different platforms to accommodate each student's need. A survey was later administered to evaluate the efficacy of the games in terms of Keller's (2010) ARCS model. The results demonstrated the potential of using LiveCode to develop timely serious games to support SEN and DHH students' literacy skills.

ACKNOWLEDGMENT

This research received no specific grant from any funding agency in the public, commercial, or not-for-profit sectors.

REFERENCES

Archibald, L. M. D., & Gathercole, S. E. (2006). Short-term and working memory in specific language impairment. *International Journal of Language & Communication Disorders*, *41*(6), 675–693. doi:10.1080/13682820500442602 PMID:17079222

Ayres, P., & Van Gog, T. (2009). State of the art research into Cognitive Load Theory. *Computers in Human Behavior*, *25*(2), 253–257. doi:10.1016/j.chb.2008.12.007

Bryant, B. R., Bryant, D. P., & Smith, D. D. (2019). Teaching Students with Special Needs in Inclusive Classrooms. Sage Publications.

Cain, K., & Oakhill, J. (2006). Profiles of children with specific reading comprehension difficulties. *The British Journal of Educational Psychology*, *76*(4), 683–696. doi:10.1348/000709905X67610 PMID:17094880

Cano, S., Collazos, C. A., Aristizabal, L. F., Moreira, F., Peñeñory, V. M., & Agredo, V. (2018). Designing Collaborative Strategies Supporting Literacy Skills in Children with Cochlear Implants Using Serious Games. *Advances in Intelligent Systems and Computing*, *746*, 1317–1326. doi:10.1007/978-3-319-77712-2_126

Chan, G. L., Santally, M. I., & Whitehead, J. (2019). Portrait of a Deaf Mauritian Student: How I propose to use educational games to ease up struggles faced in French elementary classes. *Pan-Commonwealth Forum 9 (PCF9), 2019*. http://hdl.handle.net/11599/3254

Chan, G. L., Santally, M. I., & Whitehead, J. (2022). Gamification as technology enabler in SEN and DHH education. *Education and Information Technologies*, *27*(7), 9031–9064. doi:10.100710639-022-10984-y PMID:35345601

de Freitas, S. (2018). Are Games Effective Learning Tools? A Review of Educational Games. *Journal of Educational Technology & Society*, *21*(2), 74–84. https://www.jstor.org/stable/26388380

Di Mascio, T., Gennari, R., Melonio, A., & Vittorini, P. (2013). Designing games for deaf children: First guidelines. *International Journal of Technology Enhanced Learning*, *5*(3/4), 223. doi:10.1504/IJTEL.2013.059493

El Mawas, N., Bratu, M., Caraman, D., & Muntean, C. (2019). Investigating the Learning Impact of Game-based Learning when Teaching Science to Children with Special Learning Needs. *30th Annual Conference of the Society for Information Technology and Teacher Education SITE*. HAL. https://hal.archives-ouvertes.fr/hal-02251329

Florian, L. (2021). The Universal Value of Teacher Education for Inclusive Education. In A. Köpfer, J. J. W. Powell, & R. Zahnd (Eds.), *Handbuch Inklusion international / International Handbook of Inclusive Education* (1st ed., pp. 89–106). Verlag Barbara Budrich. doi:10.2307/j.ctv1f70kvj.8

Gideon, L. (2012). Handbook of Survey Methodology for the Social Sciences. In L. Gideon (Ed.), *Handbook of Survey Methodology for the Social Sciences*. Springer New York. doi:10.1007/978-1-4614-3876-2

Hall, L., Hume, C., & Tazzyman, S. (2016). Five Degrees of happiness: Effective Smiley Face Likert scales for evaluating with children. *Proceedings of IDC 2016 - The 15th International Conference on Interaction Design and Children*, (pp. 311–321). ACM. 10.1145/2930674.2930719

Henry, L., & Winfield, J. (2010). Working memory and educational achievement in children with intellectual disabilities. *Journal of Intellectual Disability Research*, *54*(4), 354–365. doi:10.1111/j.1365-2788.2010.01264.x PMID:20236191

Humphries, T., Kushalnagar, P., Mathur, G., Napoli, D. J., Padden, C., & Rathmann, C. (2014). Ensuring language acquisition for deaf children: What linguists can do. *Language*, *90*(2), e31–e52. doi:10.1353/lan.2014.0036

Jong, M. S. Y. (2015). Does online game-based learning work in formal education at school? A case study of VISOLE. *Curriculum Journal*, *26*(2), 249–267. doi:10.1080/09585176.2015.1018915

Keller, J. M. (2010). The Arcs Model of Motivational Design. In *Motivational Design for Learning and Performance* (pp. 43–74). Springer US. doi:10.1007/978-1-4419-1250-3_3

Lan, Y.-J., Hsiao, I. Y. T., & Shih, M.-F. (2018). Effective Learning Design of Game-Based 3D Virtual Language Learning Environments for Special Education Students. *Journal of Educational Technology & Society*, *21*(3), 213–227. https://www.jstor.org/stable/26458519?seq=1#metadata_info_tab_contents

Li, C.-L., Chen, Y.-H., & Li, H.-Y. (2018). Technical College Students' ARCS Learning Motivation on Hospitality English Vocabulary. *International Journal of Human Resource Studies*, *8*(1), 189. doi:10.5296/ijhrs.v8i1.12370

Marschark, M., & Hauser, P. C. (2008). Cognitive underpinnings of learning by deaf and hard-of-hearing students: Differences, diversity, and directions. In *Deaf cognition: Foundations and outcomes* (pp. 3–23). Oxford University Press. doi:10.1093/acprof:oso/9780195368673.003.0001

Mayberry, R. I. (2007). When timing is everything: Age of first-language acquisition effects on second-language learning. *Applied Psycholinguistics*, *28*(3), 537–549. doi:10.1017/S0142716407070294

McNiff, J., & Whitehead, J. (2005). *Action research for teachers: a practical guide* (1st ed.). David Fulton Publishers. https://www.routledge.com/Action-Research-for-Teachers-A-Practical-Guide/McNiff/p/book/9781843123217

Ministry of Education Tertiary Education Science and Technology. (2017). *Salient Features Inclusive Education for Children and Youth with Special Needs in Mauritius Concept to Reality Policy Framework and Strategy Document*. METEST. https://education.govmu.org/Documents/educationsector/Documents/Special Education Needs/Salient Features Startegy Doc (1).pdf

Nusser, L., Heydrich, J., Carstensen, C. H., Artelt, C., & Weinert, S. (2016). Validity of Survey Data of Students with Special Educational Needs— Results From the National Educational Panel Study. In H. Blossfeld, J. Von Maurice, r M. Baye, & J. Skopek (Eds.), Methodological Issues of Longitudinal Surveys (pp. 251–266). Springer Fachmedien Wiesbaden. doi:10.1007/978-3-658-11994-2_15

Pickering, S. J. (2006). Working Memory and Education. In *Working Memory and Education*. Elsevier. doi:10.1016/B978-012554465-8/50011-9

Rapport, M. D., Alderson, R. M., Kofler, M. J., Sarver, D. E., Bolden, J., & Sims, V. (2008). Working Memory Deficits in Boys with Attention-deficit/Hyperactivity Disorder (ADHD): The Contribution of Central Executive and Subsystem Processes. *Journal of Abnormal Child Psychology*, *36*(6), 825–837. doi:10.100710802-008-9215-y PMID:18317920

Refat, N., Kassim, H., Rahman, M. A., & Razali, R. (2020). Measuring student motivation on the use of a mobile assisted grammar learning tool. *PLoS One*, *15*(8), e0236862. doi:10.1371/journal.pone.0236862 PMID:32857762

Stange, M., Barry, A., Smyth, J., & Olson, K. (2018). Effects of Smiley Face Scales on Visual Processing of Satisfaction Questions in Web Surveys. *Social Science Computer Review*, *36*(6), 756–766. doi:10.1177/0894439316674166

Swanson, H. L., Zheng, X., & Jerman, O. (2009). Working Memory, Short-Term Memory, and Reading Disabilities. *Journal of Learning Disabilities*, *42*(3), 260–287. doi:10.1177/0022219409331958 PMID:19255286

Taber, K. S. (2018). The Use of Cronbach's Alpha When Developing and Reporting Research Instruments in Science Education. *Research in Science Education*, *48*(6), 1273–1296. doi:10.100711165-016-9602-2

Toepoel, V., Vermeeren, B., & Metin, B. (2019). Smileys, Stars, Hearts, Buttons, Tiles or Grids: Influence of Response Format on Substantive Response, Questionnaire Experience and Response Time: *Sage, 142*(1), 57–74. doi:10.1177/0759106319834665

Wajiuhullah, A., Ashraf, S., & Majad, S. (2018). Development of Number Concepts in Students with Intellectual Disability by using Digital Game based Learning. *The Journal of Educational Research, 21*(1), 122–129. https://www.bbc.co.uk/bitesiz/ks1/maths

Watts, H. S. (1985). When Teachers Are Researchers, Teaching Improves. *Journal of Staff Development*, 6.

Wojton, H., Snavely, J., & Mary, J. (2016). *Introduction to Survey Design*. Institute for Defense Analyses. https://www.jstor.org/stable/resrep22713

KEY TERMS AND DEFINITIONS

Acoustic Awareness: This refers to the perception of sound or the sense of hearing.

Deaf: This refers to people with a hearing loss so severe that there is very little to no functional hearing.

Hard of Hearing: This is when there may be enough residual hearing that auditory devices, such as hearing aids, provide adequate assistance to process speech.

Phonological Awareness: The ability to understand and recognize the sound structure of the spoken language.

Phonological Coding: This refers to the mapping between 'seen' speech and its cognitive representations in the development of phonological awareness in Deaf learners and does not necessarily include acoustic awareness.

SEN Schools: These are those that provide educational services to children with special education needs due to disabilities such as motor, physical, visual, auditory, intellectual or due to other specific educational needs.

SEN Teachers or Educators: This refers to teachers who have been trained in special education and are qualified in the SEN sector.

Special Education Needs: A learner with Special Education Needs is one having learning, developmental, and physical disabilities; communication, emotional, and behavioral disorders; and learning deficiencies.

Chapter 5
Use of Scenario-Based Language Learning to Develop English Language Speaking Skills in Online Classrooms

Zeynep Çetin Köroğlu
https://orcid.org/0000-0002-9456-8910
Aksaray University, Turkey

Erkan Yüce
https://orcid.org/0000-0003-2716-5668
Aksaray University, Turkey

ABSTRACT

Developing EFL/ESL learners' speaking skills plays a crucial role to make them capable communicators of target language in a real- life situation. As a recently developing frame or approach, scenario-based language learning may be utilized to foster English language speaking skills of language learners. In this respect the current study contains sections to discuss scenario- based language learning, to present how to use this approach to develop language learners' speaking skills development, to present implementation of scenario-based language learning in online classrooms and propose a sample scenario based speaking task series for EFL learners.

DOI: 10.4018/978-1-6684-4940-0.ch005

INTRODUCTION

We live in a constantly changing and evolving world with the help of developing technologies which expose unlimited information. In such a world, utilizing the new technologies to achieve educational aims especially in the field of foreign language learning is inescapable (Şeker, 2016). Scenario based education is a recently developed approach to use situations with educational purposes by creating scenarios through various digital tools (Misfeldt, 2015). Scenario- based interactive videos promote self-regulated learning, collaboration among language learners and can solve common problems in foreign language education such as lack of motivation, anxiety, affective filters, and negative attitudes towards language learning (Taşlıbeyaz, 2020). Scenario based learning can foster language learners' sense of responsibility by working on a problem in the scenario (Zhuang, 2014). Another positive contribution of scenario-based learning is that it may increase language learners' motivation by enabling them to actively participate in scenarios. Thus, motivation is one the key factors to promote language learning (Choi, 2014; Eitan & Harel, 2011). Similarly, Pernice (2003) states that engaging learners in authentic situations simulating real life can lead them to empathize with others in the scenarios, support their thinking skills by providing different perspectives and increase their motivation towards learning. Within this frame, scenario-based language learning has numerous positive effects on both language learners and learning environments. However, some points must be considered in preparation of a well-prepared scenario. The scenario should be appropriate for the subject and objectives of the course. The scenario should assign a key role to the students to solve the problem or conflict presented in the scenario which reflects the real-life situations so that students participate in the scenario actively and eagerly (Naidu et al., 2007). Additionally, scenarios should present useful information, pose problems that can be solvable, and present tips or clues to support learners (Naidu et al., 2007). Scenario based learning is also applicable in digital learning environments (Avci & Bayrak, 2013). Digital scenarios generally "use complex simulations and other interactive performance tasks that replicate important features of real environments" (p. 372). Language learners are engaged in goal- oriented activities through which the learners should link their previous knowledge with the new information, and they should produce a product to complete the given task (Benarjee, 2019). Scenario based tasks enable language learners to interact with simulated peers, using background information and digital literacy in a real-life alike setting (Benarjee, 2019). Thus, "people are natural scenario planners; it is how we make sense of the world and how we decide upon which source of action to take in everyday life" (Van der Heijden, 2002, p. 117). In this perspective scenario- based tasks should contain some necessary features such as a) individual goal orientation with purposeful multi-stage activities, (b) integration and synthesis of language skills (Sabatini et al., 2011) and (c) motivating and engaging tasks not directly focused on language skills, and (d) language use for problem solving.

Scholars and researchers pointed out that the core construct of second or foreign language proficiency is multi-componential, and the basic goal of language learning process is to communicate with others in a meaningful way (Bachman, 2007; Purpura, 2004). Benarjee (2019) stated that language learners' suitable knowledge and language level are key elements in L2 learners' successful representation of their communicative skills in situations. As the goal of the language learning process is communication, language learners' communicative skills development through developing and enhancing approaches and tools should be fostered in learning environments. Scenario based language learning may serve this mission by providing purposeful, interactive, and strategic features in it. In this perspective, few studies have shown that scenario-based language learning provides a positive impact on language learners' skills development (Taşlıbeyaz, 2020; Almazova, et. al. 2021). In this perspective the present study contains sections to discuss scenario- based language learning, to present how to use this approach to develop language learners' speaking skills development, to present implementation of scenario-based language learning in online classrooms and propose a sample scenario based speaking task series for EFL learners.

THEORETICAL FRAMEWORK

Communicative Competence

Broadly speaking, communication stands for a process of sharing and exchanging of ideas, feelings, and emotions by using various means to satisfy needs, come to a conclusion, and understand contextual issues in various contexts. To be successful in communication on an ordinary day, individuals need to develop their competences from different perspectives in communication. Furthermore, the crucial role of communication takes further attention when it comes to communicating in a language having interlocutors from different language backgrounds. In this regard, within the scope of the current study, this section will focus on communicative competence, communicative strategies training in online classrooms, scenario-based language learning, and related research studies in literature to shed light on how to use scenario-based language learning to enhance EFL speaking skills in online classrooms.

The term "communicative competence" after proposed by Chomsky in 1965, has become the main interest of innumerable research studies regarding foreign/ second language teaching and learning contexts. Communicative competence can be explained as the awareness of individuals on how to benefit from their linguistic systems in a correct way with regard to the differing needs and features of particular situations (Tarone, 1981). To extend the term comprehensively, Canale and Swain (1980) reconsidered communicative competence related with four dimensions of grammar, discourse, sociolinguistics, and strategy. Grammatical competence addressed the ability of creating grammatically correct utterances and sentences. Discourse competence highlights the ability of creating coherent and cohesive utterances and sentences. Sociolinguistics draws attention to the ability of creating sociolinguistically relevant utterances and sentences. Strategic competence puts emphasis on the ability of solving communication problems when they emerge. Strategic competence requires using verbal and non-verbal communicative strategies concurrently to exclude or compensate for possible restrictions between or among individuals to reach a clear communication. Dörnyei and Thurrel (1991) advocated communicative strategies as an indispensable part of communicative competence. Recently, education contexts witnessed innumerable changes due to various developments across the globe. One, probably the most important, of them was the Covid-19 pandemic affecting all aspects of life including education. Most of the education processes conducted in conventional classrooms were transferred to online environments. This shift forced most educators to reconsider educational processes to reach predetermined outcomes of courses. Related to our study, communicative strategy training in online classrooms one of them and we will take attention to this aspect of foreign/second language learning in the following part

Communicative Strategies Training in Online Classrooms

Tarone (1980) described communication strategies as "mutual attempts of two interlocutors to agree on a meaning in a situation where the requisite meaning structures do not seem to be shared" (p. 420). Faerch and Kasper (1983) interpreted communication strategies as conscious plans followed by individuals to reach a particular communicative aim in communicative exchanges. Literature presents several taxonomies regarding communication strategies. For example, Tarone's (1977) taxonomy classifies communication strategies as avoidance, paraphrase, and borrowing/conscious transfer. Avoidance strategy involves message abandonment, and topic avoidance; paraphrase involves approximation, and word coinage; and borrowing/conscious transfer involves literal translation, language switch, appeal for assistance, and mime. Nakatani (2006) proposed a taxonomy of communication strategies dealing with speech problems involving eight dimensions, and they are social affective strategies, fluency-oriented strategies, negotiation for meaning while speaking strategies, accuracy-oriented strategies, message reduction and alteration strategies, nonverbal strategies while speaking, message abandonment strategies, and attempt to think in English strategies. The list of taxonomies from various authors can be added to the list. Regarding online education contexts, effective communication in online courses also requires strategies to follow to achieve a smooth exchange of information. Venable (2011) proposed seven communication strategies for effective communication in online courses to carry out a successful communication. They are clarity, completeness, conciseness, concreteness, correctness, courtesy, and consideration. First, clarity stands for ensuring your messages are clear to the target audience without any ambiguity or confusion. To ensure clarity, we can cross-check our written documents and have them proofread by a colleague. Second, completeness means completing all of the necessary parts of a task or an assignment without any deficiencies. To achieve completeness, we can design a checklist involving critical points so that we can avoid any missing parts. Third, conciseness refers to expressing your ideas shortly by focusing on key points. To be concise, we can eliminate details and unnecessary parts in our documents. Fourth, concreteness means making your important ideas concrete by sharing visuals, photos, etc. for the listeners. Using visual material from reliable sources can help our ideas be concrete. Fifth, correctness refers to conveying correct information from reliable sources to your audience. Data from appropriate references can ensure the correctness of information we negotiate. Sixth, courtesy stands for showing respect to others during communication in online courses. Waiting others to communicate their messages and giving enough time to avoid any connection problems can prevent overlapping of mutual utterances that causes misunderstanding problems. Last, consideration means keeping in mind the features of your target audience and preparing your messages accordingly in online courses. Considering the specific features of the audience may increase the efficiency of communication in online environments. However, one important point that comes to fore to mention here is related with their teachability in foreign/second language education contexts. Research explored that they could be taught in foreign/second language education contexts. Additionally, explicit instruction was proposed as the most useful way of teaching communicative strategies (Faucette, 2001).

Scenario-Based Language Learning

Scenario-based language instruction in foreign/second language teaching in online courses can be benefited as an effective interactive approach as it presents challenges requiring communication strategies similar to real world ones (Almazova et al., 2021). Scenario-based language instruction can be accepted as an essential approach fostering active learning (Sorin et al., 2012). In education contexts, scenario-based language learning refers to educational approaches that encourage implementation of scenarios to achieve learning outcomes (Errington, 2010). A wide variety of issues reflecting real life can be designed as scenarios in foreign/second language education. They can help language learners to apply the theory in real life practices since they present authentic language learning experiences through enabling simulations of activities, reconsidering experiences, taking decisions and evaluating their suitability, practicing cooperation with other language learners and teachers (Errington, 2010). Different types of scenarios that can be used in foreign/second language education context are presented in the literature. For example, Errington (2005) proposed five types of scenarios that can be benefited in education contexts. They are skill-based scenarios, problem-based scenarios, issues-based scenarios, speculative-based scenarios, and gaming-based scenarios. Skill-based scenarios allow learners to perform their available skills through exact and clear procedures. Problem-based scenarios present a problem to overcome for learners. Issues-based scenarios provide different perspectives to reach the appropriate solution. Speculative-based scenarios require learners to think about the future based on the available information. Gaming-based scenarios benefit from the gaming approach to learning with the intention of including fun to the learning process (Errington (2005). Additionally, Di Pietro (1987) describes scenario types with regard to the role types performed. Basic scenario involves two groups in which two interlocutors interact with each other on behalf of the other group members. Multiple role scenarios comprise various roles assigned to different participants with distinct purposes. Group scenarios require reacting to all participants to a situation individually in a way that affects each member of the group. Open-ended scenarios enhance long-term interrelated roles and episodes take several class sessions. Depending on the features of foreign/second language courses and learners, appropriate scenario types can be chosen and integrated into education context to foster communicative competences of language learners. Well designed and chosen scenarios may increase the efficiency of education contexts and encourage language learners to participate in tasks and activities by providing engaging language learning environments for the learners.

Proposed for general education contexts, these scenarios can also easily be applied in foreign/second language education contexts by taking several factors into account. Educators need to choose scenarios appropriate to language learning objectives and processes. The scenarios should be based on real life as much as possible by involving problems for learners. Also, learners should undertake some responsibilities, roles to manage communicative aims. Furthermore, scenarios should involve curiosity and learning opportunities for learners to encourage active involvement in processes (Avci & Bayrak, 2013; Naidu et al., 2007; Taslibeyaz, 2020).

Related Research

Literature presents many research studies regarding the use of scenario-based instruction in foreign/second language education contexts from various perspectives.

Several studies in the literature indicated the positive impacts of scenario-based instruction on EFL learners' language skills. For example, Miccoli (2003) provided findings regarding using drama in a higher education context in Brazilia. The study used a case study approach to the application of drama in a speaking skill class, giving details about course outline and classroom implementations. The study reported learners' reflections, evaluated results, and presented drawbacks and possible solutions. The study suggested the use of drama to develop oral skills in language learning. Similarly, Hsu (2006) searched for the impact of drama activities on eleventh grade learners' EFL reading comprehension in Taiwan. For this purpose, drama activities and a drama contest were designed in the EFL classroom. A quasi-experimental design was used in the study, and the students were assigned in two experimental groups (Group A and Group B) and two control groups (Group C and Group D). The results from reading comprehension examination and questionnaire reported that drama-based activities improved the learners' language skills, grammatical knowledge, and motivated them towards language learning. Furthermore, Al-Attar (2019) probed the effectiveness of implementing scenario-based learning instruction in enhancing eleventh grade EFL students' speaking and prospective thinking skills. The study benefited from a quasi-experimental design and 72 students were allotted to experimental group and control group appropriately. A checklist was designed to measure the students' posttest results. The findings showed that scenario-based instruction affected students' speaking and prospective thinking skills in the experimental group.

Additionally, the literature also revealed the contribution of scenario-based instruction to EFL learners' interests, motivations, achievements, and self-regulated learning behaviors. For instance, Liu (2012) conducted scenario-based training in both face-to-face instruction and virtual classes in EFL learning in a college in China. Each scenario was designed in terms of several criteria such as vocation relatedness, setting, characters, authenticity, etc. The study collected data from a survey and observations. The results showed that scenario-based instruction improved learners' interests and motivations in EFL courses. Moreover, Taşlıbeyaz (2020) investigated the influence of scenario-based interactive videos regarding learners' achievements and self-regulated learning behaviors in an English grammar course. The research followed an experimental design with a sample of 84 participants from an elementary school. Scenario-based interactive videos were used in the experimental group, while non-scenario-based interactive videos were used in the control group. The posttest scores of the participants in the experimental group were higher than the scores in the control group in terms of achievement and self-regulated learning behaviors.

The related literature supported the implementation of scenario-based instruction in foreign/second language education contexts from various perspectives. In this regard, the current study will present several scenarios for EFL education contexts to develop speaking skills in online courses.

HOW TO DESIGN A SCENARIO FOR ONLINE LANGUAGE CLASSROOMS

Scenario based e-language learning combines virtual language learning and real-life alike situations with hands-on activities in a digital environment. In this respect, language learners gain learning experiences in a relatively shorter period rather than actual learning opportunities. One of the significant features of scenario-based e language learning is that language learners learn new language items by trial and error. While language learners need to face the consequences of wrong decisions in real life situations, they have other trial chances in scenario-based e-language learning environments. Moreover, they do not have to face the negative effects of wrong decisions in such environments as well. Scenario-based e-language learning can be used to foster both productive and receptive skills Sabatini et al., 2011). In this perspective, a well-prepared scenario can combine different language skills and make language learners involved in scenarios in virtual environments.

Some points should be taken into consideration while preparing a scenario for language teaching. A scenario is a representation of a real-life-like story which has a plot, characters, setting and a problem. Depending on the scenario type the story may vary in its context. According to Errington (2019) there are four types of scenarios that are;

- Skill-based scenarios
- Problem based scenarios
- Subject based scenarios
- Fiction-based scenarios

Skill-based scenarios are used to make learners show their skills and competencies about the topic. The skill-based scenario type is more useful in terms of students when they understand the issue well and when the scenario includes steps and procedures in it. The second scenario type is problem-based scenarios. The problem-based scenarios pose a problem which is open-ended. Students need to think about the problem based on their existing information, they need to find a reasonable solution by utilizing their problem solving and critical thinking skills. The third type is subject based scenarios which provides different perspectives to the learners. The learners need to think about an issue from various perspectives through these scenarios. The fourth type is fiction-based scenario which provides fictitious learning environments. Students can use their imagination to predict the future of fictitious cases which were presented in the scenario (Errington, 2019).

Language teachers should follow a few steps to create meaningful and effective scenarios for language learners. At first, the teacher should identify the target language learners and their needs. By doing so, the teacher can create more engaging and fruitful scenarios related to their learning needs. The second step is defining learning outcomes of the scenarios. Each scenario should have an aim to be reached by the learners. At this step, the teacher should consider difficult, important, and frequent situations in which language learners should think critically and face the same situation in real life frequently. The third step is choosing a situation, plot, and characters for the scenario. Designing the story for the scenario has a significant role because language learners should resolve the conflict, or the problem presented in it. Another important aspect is providing interaction opportunities to language learners through the scenario. Thus, language is the means of communication between individuals.

A SAMPLE SCENARIO-BASED SPEAKING TASK FOR ONLINE CLASSROOMS

Scenario based speaking task was designed for an online classroom which is presumed to contain EFL learners at B2 levels English proficiency. The task was designated as an interactive scenario because interactive scenarios enable language learners' real-life simulations in which they can practice their language skills. In this scenario, language learners need to participate in interaction to proceed in the scenes.

In designing process, settings, characters and plot we selected appropriate for the presumed online language classrooms. In the present scenario, a web 2.0 tool called 'vyond', which is accessible at https://www.vyond.com/, was used to create video. The scenario and tasks were explained in detail below.

My Pen-Pal's 3 Days Visit to Aksaray

Level: B2

Graders: 12 graders of High School

Topic & Skills: Giving recommendations & suggestions, expressing ideas & thoughts, Speaking skills

Materials: Computer, headphones, zoom.

Targeted Vocabulary: itinerary, commencement, recreation, podcast, excursion, garment bag, souvenir.

Figure 1. Presentation of setting

Approaches & techniques: student-centered learning, scenario- based instruction, Role-play

Procedure: In this speaking activity, the teacher creates groups which consist of two students. Each group utilizes one computer to watch the full scenario through vyond web 2.0 tool. In this interactive scenario, there are totally 3 different scenes in which different speaking tasks were integrated in them. The first scene presents the main characters of the story who are 'Ahmet' and 'Carol'. Ahmet is a university student who studies at Aksaray university in the English language teaching department. He has a pen-pal who is 'Carol'. Carol lives in England and she studies at London Metropolitan University. In her summer holiday, Carol decided to visit Aksaray for three days. In their first encounter Ahmet mentions his plan for three days and asks Carol's plan. The video extract is presented below.

First, they met at Aksaray University's campus because on their first day Ahmet wanted to show around to Carol. Then, he planned a city tour in which they visited Ulu Mosque at the city center. Since Carol is Christian, she has some hesitations about visiting a mosque. She explained his hesitations about the case. In the first speaking task students are supposed to use phrases such as "(If I was/were) in that (that kind of) situation, I'd ...Have you thought about ...? If it was/were me, I'd ...Make sure you (don't) ...The sooner you ... the better. Whatever you do, ...Your only option is to ...You have no choice but to"

The first speaking task for the students is that;

- If you were Ahmet, what would you suggest to Carol?
- If you were Ahmet how do you react in such a case?
- If you were Ahmet, what kind of plan would you prepare for three days?

Students can complete the task by using zoom chat rooms or they can record their responses to a tape or voice recorder. They can send it to the teacher. In traditional classrooms, students may have a role-play to complete the first task.

Figure 2. Task 1- First encounter at the campus

Due to the scenario, Ahmet and Carol visited the mosque and they sat at a cafe in the second scene. In this scene Ahmet asks Carol's ideas about the Ulu Mosque and wants her to describe her experience and Ulu Mosque as if she was telling someone else. In the second task students can search information about the Ulu Mosque from the internet. Then they could describe the mosque with their own sentences as if one of them was Carol and another student was Ahmet or someone else. In the second speaking task students are supposed to use phrases such as "I think.... I believe.... I feel.... I suppose.... I guess.... According to me.... In my view.... In my opinion.... In my eyes.... It seems to me that.... From my perspective.... From my point of view.... From my viewpoint.... As far as I'm concerned.... Personally, I think.... I'd like to point out that.... What I mean is.... Generally, it is thought that.... Some people say that.... Well, it is considered that.... It is generally accepted that.... My impression is that.... It goes without saying that.... I hold the view that.... I'm of the opinion that" The video extract is presented below.

Language items were provided as language hints within the scenario before each task as follows.

The third task aims to make students learn by making suggestions in each context. In this scene, Ahmet and Carol went to a store and Carol wanted to buy some gifts

Figure 3. Task 2- Describing the mosque

Figure 4. Language hints extract from the scenario

and souvenirs for her family and friends. Ahmet leads Carol to buy more traditional gifts instead of regular ones. In this speaking task students search for information about traditional objects of Aksaray. The third speaking task for the students is that.

- If you were Ahmet what would you recommend Carol to buy?
- If you were Ahmet, how do you explain your reasons for buying traditional objects or gifts?

The fourth scene takes place in the airport where Carol is headed to England after she completed her three days visit in Aksaray. Ahmet wants from Carol to prepare a podcast about her three days visit in which she needs to tell her short vacation. Then she needs to upload it to Edmodo (learning management tool). In the last speaking task, students need to create the podcast by using different web 2.0 tools such as powtoon, vyond or videoscribe. The video extract is presented below. The task details are.

- Please prepare a podcast about Carol's three days visit and upload it to Edmodo.

Figure 5.

Figure 6. Task 4-Creating a podcast

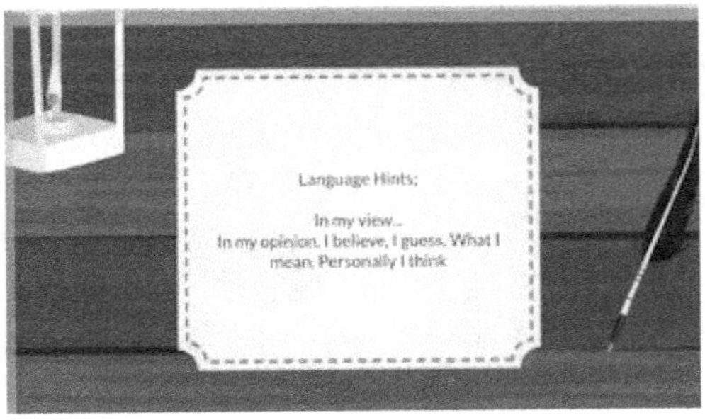

Assessment: Teacher evaluates language learner's speaking performance by using a pre-prepared rubric in terms of accuracy, fluency, pronunciation, grammar structure and vocabulary use.

DISCUSSION

The use of information and communication technology (ICT) increased dramatically in education contexts after the worldwide spread of the Covid-19 pandemic, and this led to change in the understanding of teaching and learning. Traditional face-to-face education contexts transformed to online ones in which teachers and learners conduct educational activities in a distant way. Interaction in online education became a one of the problematic issues in these contexts for educators, and several studies revealed that learners favor traditional face-to-face classes in terms of interaction with their teachers (Megat-Abdul-Rahim et al., 2021). It becomes even harder when it comes to foreign/second language education, especially with regard to speaking skills, in these contexts. Heng and Linda (2003) reported that students with low level of speaking skills preferred online education since they think that this mode of education does not require them to take part in activities actively. Furthermore, Sze (2006) informed that less confident students opt for online education as it decreases anxiety levels of these learners during communications compared to real time communications. To this end, professionals are in need of innovative teaching tools and ways to raise the attention and desire of language learners for interaction in online contexts.

A number of studies reported that online learning platforms can foster learning effectively compared to face-to-face learning since online materials can be more flexible, engaging, and exciting (Li, 2016; Megat-Abdul-Rahim et al., 2021; Wang et al., 2015). Moreover, there are studies proving that integrating technology has a crucial part in education as it eases learning and presents opportunities for learners to interest in the learning process (Kuama & Intharaksa, 2016; Li, 2016). In this regard, scenario-based language learning presented through diverse online platforms and technological tools can benefit in enhancing foreign/second language learners' English language speaking skills in online classrooms. Various scenario-based tasks and activities addressing different oral communication purposes can be designed and integrated to online foreign/second language lessons in an innovative way which may result in active participation and increased interests of learners.

LIMITATIONS

This study involved several limitations. First, the study was designed as a theoretical one which presents ideas and discusses the implementation of scenario-based language learning in enhancing foreign/second language learners' English language speaking skills in online classrooms. Data-driven studies, experimental or quasi-experimental studies, can be designed in the future to evaluate the effectiveness of scenario-based language learning regarding speaking skills in online classrooms. Next, the current study focused only on speaking skills. New studies focusing on the influence of scenario-based language learning on listening, writing, and reading skills can be designed. Last, scenario-based language learning can be searched both in face-to-face lessons and online lessons in a comparative way by considering various psychological constructs in educational contexts.

PRACTICAL IMPLICATIONS

Within this scope, some practical implications can be suggested for educational contexts. First, designing engaging scenario-based tasks and activities involving various aspects of real life needs of foreign/second language learners may help teachers to promote the desires of learners to participate in online lessons. Second, choosing appropriate Web tools and platforms for presenting scenarios may help language teachers grasp the attention of learners in online lessons. Last, considering foreign/second language learners' language levels and needs in designing scenarios may promote interests of learners in online lessons.

CONCLUSION

Enhancing communicative competences of EFL/ESL learners' speaking skills holds an essential part in bringing up effective communicators in the target language.

Many new approaches and tools are suggested to make language learning engaging and meaningful for educational contexts each day with emerging technology and developments. In this regard, scenario-based language instruction has gained attention recently to promote especially speaking skills of language learners by presenting real-life, authentic, and challenging situations.

The Covid-19 pandemic changed the nature of conventional language classes in which language teachers conduct lessons on a face-to-face basis with their learners. The emergent online learning situation forced language educators to be innovative in their courses to reach their students' attention and interest. Accordingly, scenario-based language instruction can be benefited in online foreign/second language education as an effective way to enhance learners' speaking skills. After providing a theoretical background, the current chapter provided a sample scenario-based speaking task for online classrooms. This chapter may present insights for those desiring to improve their learners' foreign/speaking skills in online language education.

REFERENCES

Al-Attar, R. H. (2019). *The effectiveness of using scenario-based learning strategy in developing EFL eleventh graders' speaking and prospective thinking skills* [Unpublished master's thesis, The Islamic University of Gaza].

Almazova, N., Rubtsova, A., Kats, N., Eremin, Y., & Smolskaia, N. (2021). Scenario-based instruction: The case of foreign language training at Multidisciplinary University. *Education Sciences, 11*(5), 1–18. doi:10.3390/educsci11050227

Avci, D. E., & Bayrak, E. B. (2013). Investigating teacher Candidates' Opinions related to scenario-based learning: An action research. *Elementary Education Online*, *12*(2), 528–549.

Bachman, L. F. (2007). What is the construct? The dialectic of abilities and contexts in defining constructs in language assessment. In J. Fox, M. Wesche, D. Bayliss, L. Cheng, C. E. Turner, & C. Doe (Eds.), *Language testing reconsidered* (pp. 41–71). University of Ottawa Press. doi:10.2307/j.ctt1ckpccf.9

Banerjee, H. L. (2019). Investigating the Construct of Topical Knowledge in Second Language Assessment: A Scenario-Based Assessment Approach. *Language Assessment Quarterly*, *16*(2), 133–160. doi:10.1080/15434303.2019.1628237

Bennett, R. E. (2015). The changing nature of educational assessment. *Review of Research in Education*, *39*(1), 370–407. doi:10.3102/0091732X14554179

Canale, M. (1983). From communicative competence to communicative language pedagogy. In J. C. Richard & R. W. Schmidt (Eds.), *Language and Communication* (pp. 2–14). Longman.

Canale, M., & Swain, M. (1980). Theoretical bases of communicative approaches to second language teaching and testing. *Applied Linguistics*, *1*(1), 1–47. doi:10.1093/applin/1.1.1

Choi, E. (2014). Second language learning through drama: Practical Techniques and Applications. Joe Winston (Ed.). New York, NY: Routledge. 2012. TESOL Journal, 5(4), 792–795.

Di Pietro, R. J. (1987). The scenario principle in the teaching of Italian literature. *Italica*, *64*(3), 365–376. doi:10.2307/478496

Dörnyei, Z., & Thurrell, S. (1991). Strategic competence and how to teach it. *ELT Journal*, *45*(1), 16–23. doi:10.1093/elt/45.1.16

Eitan, N., & Harel, D. (2011). Adaptive behavioral programming. Paper presented at *the tools with Artificial Intelligence (ICTAI), 2011 23rd IEEE International Conference*. IEEE. 10.1109/ICTAI.2011.109

Errington, E. (2005). *Creating learning scenarios: A planning guide for adult educators*. Cool Books New Zealand.

Errington, E. (2019). *As close as it gets: Developing professional identity through the potential of scenario based learning*. Life Wide Education. http://www.lifewideeducation.uk/uploads/1/3/5/4/13542890/c3._edward_errington.pdf

Errington, E. P. (2010). Preparing graduates for the professions: Achieving employability through the exploration of near-world scenarios. *The International Journal of Interdisciplinary Social Sciences: Annual Review*, *5*(5), 1–10. doi:10.18848/1833-1882/CGP/v05i05/51723

Faucette, P. (2001). A pedagogical perspective on communication strategies: Benefits of training and an analysis of English language teaching materials. *Second Lang. Stud.*, *19*, 1–40.

Hsu, M. H. (2006). *The effects of dramatic activities on reading comprehension of senior high school EFL students in Taiwan* [Unpublished doctoral dissertation, College of Graduate Studies Texas A & M University-Kingsville].

Kuama, S., & Intharaksa, U. (2016). Is online learning suitable for all English language students? *PASAA*, *52*, 53–82.

Li, E. (2016). The study on higher vocational English O2O teaching experiment from the perspective of MOOC. *Journal of HUBEI Correspondence University, 29*, 136–137.

Liu, Z. (2012). Construction and application of scenarios in college EFL learning. *International Forum of Teaching and Studies, 8*(2), 32-40.

Megat-Abdul-Rahim, P. T., Idris, S. L., Rahman, Z. I. A., Ya Shaq, M. S., & Nasir, N. F. (2021). Approaching listening and speaking skills using online to facilitate interactive learning from students' perspectives. [AJUE]. *Asian Journal of University Education, 17*(2), 203–214. doi:10.24191/ajue.v17i2.13400

Miccoli, L. (2003). English through drama for oral skills development. *ELT Journal, 57*(2), 122–129. doi:10.1093/elt/57.2.122

Misfeldt, M. (2015). Scenario Based Education as a Framework for Understanding Students Engagement and Learning in a Project Management Simulation Game. *Electronic Journal of e-Learning, 13*(3), 181–191. www.ejel.org

Naidu, S. (2010). Using scenario-based learning to promote situated learning and develop professional knowledge. In E. P. Errington (Ed.), *Preparing graduates for the professions using scenario- based learning* (pp. 39–49). Post Pressed.

Naidu, S., Menon, M., Gunawardena, C., Lekamge, D., & Karunanayaka, S. (2007). *How scenario-based learning can engender reflective practice in distance education.* Lawrence Erlbaum Associates, Publishers New Jersey.

Nakatani, Y. (2006). Developing an oral communication strategy inventory. *Modern Language Journal, 90*(1), 151–168. doi:10.1111/j.1540-4781.2006.00390.x

Pernice, R. (2003). Writing-in-role: Helping students explore emotional dimensions. In E. Errington (Ed.), *Developing scenario based learning: Practical insights for tertiary educators* (pp. 145–153). Dunmore Press.

Purpura, J. E. (2004). *Assessing grammar.* Cambridge University Press. doi:10.1017/CBO9780511733086

Sabatini, J., Bennett, R. E., & Deane, P. (2011). *Four years of cognitively based assessment of, for, and as learning (CBAL): Learning about through course assessment (TCA)* [Symposium presentation]. Invitational research symposium on through-course summative assessments, Atlanta, GA, United States.https://www.ets.org/Media/Research/pdf/TCSA_Symposium_Final_Paper_Sabatini.pd

Sorin, R., Errington, E., Ireland, L., Nickson, A., & Caltabiano, M. (2012). Embedding graduate attributes through scenario-based learning. *J. NUS Teach. Acad., 2*, 192–205.

Şeker, M. (2016). Scenario-Based Instruction Design as a Tool to Promote Self-Regulated Language Learning Strategies. *SAGE Open*, *6*(4), 1–11. doi:10.1177/2158244016684175

Sze, P. M. (2006). Developing students' listening and speaking skills through ELT podcasts. *Education Journal*, *34*(2), 115–134.

Tarone, E. (1977). Conscious communication strategies in interlanguage: A progress report. In H. D. Brown, C. A. Yorio, & R. C. Crymes (Eds.), *On TESOL 77* (pp. 194–203). TESOL.

Tarone, E. (1980). Communication strategies, foreigner talk, and repair in interlanguage. *Language Learning*, *30*(4), 417–431. doi:10.1111/j.1467-1770.1980.tb00326.x

Taslibeyaz, E. (2020). The effect of scenario-based interactive videos on English learning. *Interactive Learning Environments*, *28*(7), 808–820. doi:10.1080/10494820.2018.1552870

Venable, M. (2011). *The 7 Cs of effective communication in your online course.* Online College.org.

Wang, S., Liu, J., & Fu, W. (2015). A study on the content-based college ESP instruction under the background of MOOC era. *China Educational Technology*, 98-120.

Zhuang, Y. L. (2014). *A Research of the Application of Visual Simulation Technology in College English Teaching*. Paper presented at the Advanced Materials Research. Scientific Net. 10.4028/www.scientific.net/AMR.1044-1045.1565

ADDITIONAL READING

Şeker, M. (2016). Scenario-based instruction design as a tool to promote self-regulated language learning strategies. *SAGE Open*, *6*(4), 1–11. doi:10.1177/2158244016684175

Taslibeyaz, E. (2020). The effect of scenario-based interactive videos on English learning. *Interactive Learning Environments*, *28*(7), 808–820. doi:10.1080/10494820.2018.1552870

KEY TERMS AND DEFINITIONS

Scenario Based Learning: A curricular design approach that assigns students a specific role and problem situation, usually drawn from real-world contexts. It involves using resources to support learning while producing an authentic product.

Chapter 6
Designing Goal-Oriented Online Speaking Activities for EFL Learners in a Post-Pandemic World:
Insights From CEFR Companion Volume

Erkan Yüce
Aksaray University, Turkey

Zeynep Çetin Köroğlu
Aksaray University, Turkey

ABSTRACT

The Covid-19 pandemic continues to affect every aspect of life. English language education has been shifted from face-to-face education to online education as a result of sudden decisions. English language teachers and learners are expected to adapt to this sudden change and manage the process effectively, without considering their technological competence and knowledge about technology's integration into foreign language pedagogy. In the process of teaching English as a foreign language, speaking skills teaching, which is often neglected compared to other skills, has become more limited in online education due to various reasons. There is not enough study in the existing literature on the design of digital speaking activities. Therefore, the current book section deals with the design of goal-oriented digital speaking skills activities within the framework of the CEFR CV. Additionally, examples of goal-oriented digital speaking activities are presented in the present book chapter. The chapter will guide language teachers to design digital speaking activities appropriate to CEFR CV.

DOI: 10.4018/978-1-6684-4940-0.ch006

INTRODUCTION

The current chapter addresses goal-oriented online speaking activities designed for English as a Foreign Language (EFL) learners in online interactions after experiencing the Covid-19 pandemic effects in foreign/second language education contexts globally. First, after giving brief information about the current situation regarding the pandemic, this chapter focuses on distance online language education during the pandemic. Next, it informs the readers about the Common European Framework of Reference for Languages (CEFR), the CEFR Companion Volume (CEFR-CV), and online transactions and collaboration. Then, it discusses the features of EFL speaking skills in digital environments and presents goal-oriented speaking activity samples. Last, it concludes with some insights into foreign/second language education contexts.

Covid-19, short for "coronavirus disease 2019", emerged in and spread from Wuhan City, Hubei Province of China, on December 31, 2019, and became a severe pandemic in a short time all across the world (World Health Organization [WHO], 2020a, 2020b). The Covid-19 pandemic has affected all walks of life severely. As of October 16, 2021, there are 4.879.235 confirmed deaths due to the global pandemic reported by the dashboard of the World Health Organization (WHO, 2021). As a generation born in the latest quarter of the 20th century, we witnessed many things on our television screens and our physical environments due to the unprecedented scale of change in technology, wars, refugee crises around the world, and explorations on Mars. Humanity has experienced the Covid-19 pandemic recently, and it has brought restrictions to all parts of life by limiting people from reaching their everyday routines concurrently across the globe.

Education is one of the most affected domains by the pandemic. Most educational institutions from all levels were forced to close their doors to students to avoid transmission. Teachers and students had neither heard of nor experienced a kind of online education previously. However, the pandemic led to the shifts of face-to-face education contexts to either synchronous or asynchronous education contexts after overnight news throughout the world. As a result, all educational professionals started to conduct our lessons through the Internet and experienced, maybe for the first time during our teaching and learning lives, the total immersion in remote education during the pandemic. In this context, things may become complicated due to learners' different levels and competencies in foreign/second language education contexts. Teaching in online education contexts may become a problem, especially for those who are so-called digital immigrants. Prensky defines digital immigrants as "*Those of us who were not born into the digital world but have, at some later point in our lives, become fascinated by and adopted many or most aspects of the new technology are ... Digital Immigrants.*" (2001, p. 1-2). Most of the teachers, who are digital immigrants, currently teaching at various education institutions, either public or private, to different levels of students address those students who speak a totally different language, a digital one. As this is the case, we need to adopt digital skills and adapt our existing skills to the new digital environments. Many students may be from various backgrounds and foreign/second language levels in these new digital education contexts. At this point, a question that arises is whether it is possible to standardise online education environments.

Education mainly included a classroom setting and an instructor who delivered necessary content to learners in a classroom setting by utilising conventional and traditional methods (Summers et al., 2005). However, with the outbreak of the Covid-19 pandemic, education systems have to be changed drastically due to fundamental reasons. In the Covid-19 situation, schools, higher education institutions, private courses across the World needed to end traditional education and continue through online education and courses, which is somehow unprepared for the parties of the education system (Erarslan, 2021). The changed situation in the education system has affected students, teachers, administrators, and families in many ways. The United Nations Educational, Scientific and Cultural Organization (UNESCO) (2021) states that approximately 1, 5 billion students worldwide have been affected by this sudden change and more than 800 million students have difficulty adopting online education. English language teaching as a field is not an exception to the changed education system during the Covid-19 pandemic. Computer-Assisted Language Learning (CALL) has been utilised for language teaching and learning for more than 40 years, according to Bailey and Lee (2020). However, English language education and learning have altered significantly due to technological advancements, paving the path for online language learning. Thus, while the teaching of English via online or distance courses is not a novel phenomenon, the move to urgent online language instruction may provide specific issues for students and teachers (Erarslan, 2021).

When we think of foreign/second language skills teaching, the situation gets more complicated, especially in terms of speaking skills, a productive one. Organising learning/teaching processes and designing language activities may become problematic in setting common standards for teachers. Following validated standards and referencing recognized descriptors in online language education contexts may guide foreign/second language teachers and ease their preparation of activities. In this regard, the Common European Framework of Reference for Languages (CEFR) can be followed as a reference, and the descriptors presented in the CEFR Companion Volume (CEFR-CV) can provide shared insights for online foreign/second language education contexts. The CEFR-CV proposes descriptors for different language levels regarding "goal-oriented transactions" and "collaboration" addressing speaking skills. The focus of the current study is transactions and collaboration based on the CEFR-CV descriptors in online foreign/second language education environments.

DISTANCED ONLINE LANGUAGE EDUCATION DURING THE PANDEMIC

Higher education institutions were the pioneers in online language education by providing learners with distanced online education programs compared to other educational institutions (Tanyeli, 2009). The Covid-19 pandemic changed this phenomenon, and all levels and varieties of educational institutions adapted their programs to online education or switched to online education totally. The recent developments and trends in the digital area have already enabled professionals in education to design and enrich their materials following the latest trends. The Internet, multimedia tools, and Web 2.0 tools are some of the technology tools currently available in education contexts for teachers and learners (Liu et al., 2002; Yüce, 2019; Yüce, 2022). However, the rapidly changing trends and uses may bring many challenges, especially for teachers. When it comes to online foreign language teaching, the situation becomes harder as online language classes may involve learners from different levels and various backgrounds in a distanced manner. Indeed, several research studies carried out during the Covid-19 pandemic supported the aforementioned views in one way or another. For example, Allo's (2020) study in Indonesia reported that the Internet allowed them to follow their EFL lessons in a distanced manner. However, they also expressed that the online lessons need to be designed regarding materials used, assignments and directions given. In another study, Shaaban (2020) revealed that the participants needed the training to promote their skills of designing, developing, and preparing plans for EFL online classes. Atmojo and Nugroho (2020) reported that teachers conducted the lessons either synchronously or asynchronously in various ways through numerous platforms concerning school policies and that online learning did not meet their expectations in terms of preparation and planning. Hartshorn and Mcmurry's (2020) study in the United States showed that the speaking skills of the ESL students did not advance as much as their writing skills. Lee and Bailey (2020) expressed that the pandemic demonstrated challenges in transferring face-to-face lessons to online lessons for EFL instructors in terms of pronunciation and speaking. All these findings address the problematic nature of online foreign/second language education in terms of speaking skills and planning education processes.

Moving from this endpoint, the current study addresses the descriptors presented by the CEFR-CV in terms of "goal-oriented transactions and collaboration". The professionals of online foreign language teaching contexts can benefit from these descriptors in planning online transaction tasks and collaboration activities for the language learners in a standardised manner in online foreign language education environments. In this perspective, research indicates that online learning environments, which have been utilised during the Covid-19 pandemic, are not well designed to develop foreign/second language learners' English language speaking skills appropriately to CEFR companion volume. The materials, tasks, and activities used in online classrooms are not standardised to foster communicative competences for language learners. The current book chapter describes the CEFR framework, then two example activities are presented for foreign/second language teachers of English to prepare more standardised and appropriate speaking activities and tasks for their online language classrooms.

THE CEFR

The CEFR has become a globally recognized reference tool for learning, teaching, and assessing languages. Published originally in French and English languages in 2001 by the Council of Europe (CoE) and reachable now in more than 40 languages, the CEFR addresses protecting linguistic and cultural diversity, enhancing plurilingual and pluricultural education, and promoting intercultural understanding for countries all over Europe (CoE, 2020). The CEFR contains pedagogical principles and scales of proficiency descriptors for foreign/second language users. The CEFR was developed to foster mutual understanding among European countries primarily; however, its influence as a guide to shape language implementations from policy development to assessment practices in educational contexts was profound due to its coherent and comprehensive nature (Alderson, 2007; Byram & Parmenter, 2012; CoE, 2020; Girard & Trim, 1998; Hulstijn, 2007; Mirici, 2015; North, 2014). The scales presented in the CEFR involve descriptors categorising six language proficiency levels (Breakthrough and Waystage / A1 and A2; Threshold and Vantage / B1 and B2; and Effective Operational Proficiency and Mastery / C1 and C2) (CoE, 2001).

Figure 1. Common reference levels
(CoE, 2020; p.36)

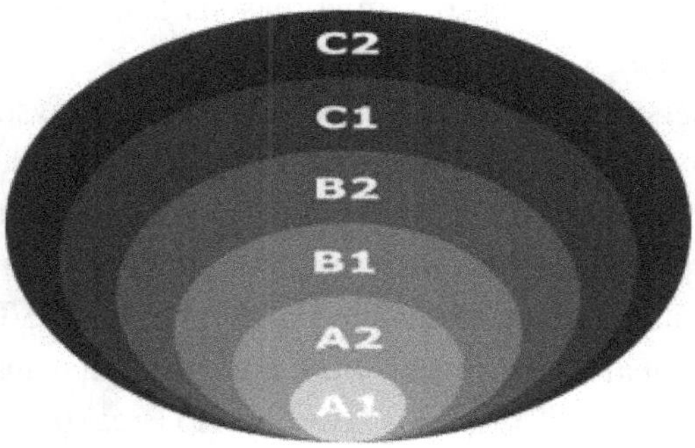

The following figure (Figure 1) presents the categorization of language levels in a broad perspective as follows:

The Common Reference Levels are presented in a holistic way for professionals, non-professionals, curriculum developers, and stakeholders to gain insight into their further language uses and practices. A summary of these levels is as follows:

Firstly, Proficient Users are labeled as C2 and C1. At C2 (Mastery) level, language users are expected to understand everything spoken or written easily. They can outline spoken and written information, direct disputes, and detail in organised presentations. They can express themselves immediately, very easily and accurately, putting emphasis on the slightest differentiation in meaning even in the most complicated circumstances (CoE, 2001). At the C1 (Effective Operational Proficiency) level, they are capable of comprehending a wide range of challenging, lengthier texts and recognizing hidden meanings. They are able to express themselves fluently and freely without having to look for words. They are able to employ language in a variety of ways for social, intellectual, and professional goals. They can write understandable, well-organised, thorough writing on complicated topics using organisational patterns, conjunctions, and cohesive devices in a controlled manner (CoE, 2001).

Secondly, Independent Users are labeled as B2 and B1. At the B2 (Vantage) level, language users can comprehend the primary thoughts of perplexing text on both concrete and conceptual themes, remembering specialised conversations for their subject areas. They can collaborate with a level of familiarity and immediacy that enables standard connection with local speakers very conceivable without strain for one or the other party. They can create clear, point-by-point content on a broad range of areas and clarify a perspective regarding a vital topic by presenting the benefits and weaknesses of different choices (CoE, 2001). At the B1 (Threshold) level, language users are capable of comprehending the primary concerns regarding primary contribution to ordinary and routine subjects experienced at work, education contexts, recreation, and so forth. They can manage most circumstances liable to emerge while going to a place where the target language is used as a means of communication. They can create associated basic texts on recognizable subjects or appeal to individual interests. They can express encounters and occasions, dreams, expectations, and desires and briefly give reasons and clarifications for feelings and plans (CoE, 2001).

Lastly, Basic Users are labeled as A2 and A1. At A2 (Waystage) level, language users are capable of comprehending expressions and routine speech connected with mainly used domains such as individual and family issues, neighbourhood, shopping, and workplace. They can maintain dialogue in basic and daily tasks, which necessitate a basic information exchange on routine issues. They are capable of describing their personal backgrounds, close environments, and issues that require instantaneous commitment (CoE, 2001). At the A1 (Breakthrough) level, language users can comprehend and benefit from ordinary expressions and primary phrases to reach their basic needs. They can introduce themselves and maintain dialogues by giving details about themselves and their immediate environments. They can maintain interaction in a basic manner on the condition that the interlocutors respond clearly and slowly by showing that they are eager to support (CoE, 2001).

The Common Reference Levels are introduced in an all-encompassing way for experts, non-experts, educational program designers, and partners to effectively acquire knowledge for their language uses and practices. In addition, these six language levels intend to assist language learners in figuring out their language skills (reading, writing, listening, and speaking), and language learners can search for descriptors in a detailed manner to self-assess their proficiency levels (CoE, 2001).

The CEFR is a globally accepted reference tool for learning, teaching, and assessing of foreign/second languages. It is a comprehensive tool for language education contexts. It provides validated scales involving proficiency descriptors for different levels of language users to guide their language competencies in various contexts. Language learners can easily self-assess their competencies by consulting the proficiency descriptors. Language teachers can design classroom activities based on the pedagogical principles and proficiency descriptors it presents. They can develop assessment tools with reference to the descriptors. Material designers can plan and develop language education materials in line with the CEFR descriptors in a standardised manner that can address multiple needs of students in language education contexts. Finally, policymakers can develop language education policies based on the CEFR in a restricted region or across a whole country to follow common ground globally to address their citizens' language learning needs. For all the aforementioned and many reasons, the use of the CEFR in language education contexts is well-established across the globe. In this regard, this study adopts the CEFR as a reference tool in designing the activities suggested in this chapter.

THE CEFR-CV AND ONLINE TRANSACTIONS AND COLLABORATION

The CEFR-CV was published in 2020 after its provisional version appeared in 2018 to update several scales of the CEFR and extend the CEFR by including new aspects (CoE, 2018; CoE, 2020). One of these aspects is online interactions. Online interactions differ from conventional classroom interactions conducted in a face-to-face manner. Conventional classroom interactions involve conveying gestures, mimics, and feelings besides oral expressions, which enable interlocutors to communicate effectively. In face-to-face interactions, teachers can easily address the contextual needs of learners by providing immediate feedback. In face-to-face classrooms, teachers can easily adapt classroom activities according to the levels of students from various foreign/second language backgrounds. However, online interactions are technology-based remote ones. They lack the affective factors that enable teachers to direct interactions effectively. They lack the gestures and mimics that enable teachers to decide whether conversations are accomplished. In addition, teachers may have difficulty understanding their students' foreign/second language levels and backgrounds to design correct language teaching materials. For these reasons, the descriptors of the CEFR-CV may provide an overview regarding online transactions and collaboration for foreign/second language teachers to address the differing needs of language learners from various backgrounds on a standard basis.

Online interactions involve conversations, discussions, transactions, and collaboration. This study focuses on online transactions and collaborations. The CEFR-CV proposes a scale for online transactions and collaborations which involves key concepts for profiting from various media and tools in online environments, and the concepts are:

- Purchasing goods and services online;
- Engaging in transactions requiring negotiation of conditions, in a service as well as client role;
- Participation in collaborative project work;
- Dealing with communication problems. (CoE, 2020, p. 86)

Our modern life involves interactions and transactions that need to be accomplished collaboratively to fulfil specific outcomes. Goal-oriented refers to the processes requiring cooperation among participants to achieve elaborated projects or tasks. In this regard, from filling simple online forms to solving problems by participating, coordinating, and conducting project works that necessitate competencies from simple to complex reactive and proactive participation can be sequenced among goal-oriented online transactions and collaboration. Collaborative tasks include coordinating a group in a project online, providing detailed instructions, evaluating proposals from the participants, and giving explanations to attain the joint tasks (CoE, 2020). The CEFR-CV presents 22 descriptors in total that can be referenced by language professionals in designing activities for online transactions and collaboration in terms of solving problems, filling forms, participating in and coordinating projects online (CoE, 2020). The following table (Table 2) gives language levels and sample descriptors for online transactions and collaboration:

Table 2. Descriptors for online transactions and collaboration

Levels	Descriptors
C2	Can resolve misunderstandings and deal effectively with frictions that arise during the collaborative process.
C1	Can co-ordinate a group that is working on a project online, formulating and revising detailed instructions, evaluating proposals from team members, and providing clarifications in order to accomplish the shared tasks.
B2	Can collaborate online with a group that is working on a project, justifying proposals, seeking clarification and playing a supportive role in order to accomplish shared tasks.
B1	Can interact online with a group that is working on a project, following straightforward instructions, seeking clarification and helping to accomplish the shared tasks.
A2	Can use formulaic language to respond to routine problems arising in online transactions (e.g. concerning availability of models and special offers, delivery dates, addresses).
A1	Can complete a very simple online purchase or application, providing basic personal information (e.g. name, e-mail or telephone number).
Pre-A1	Can make selections (e.g. choosing a product, size, colour) in a simple online purchase or application form, provided there is visual support.

*Taken from the CEFR-CV (CoE, 2020, p. 86, 87)

ENGLISH LANGUAGE SPEAKING SKILLS IN DIGITAL LEARNING ENVIRONMENTS

As one of the productive skills, speaking skills are generally perceived as the capability to express ideas, intentions, emotions, and thoughts with other language speakers in a context. In this respect, speaking is an interactive process that includes both speaker and listener along with the targeted message (Brown, 1994; Hughes, 2002). Speaking has a crucial role in communication which can be either interactional or transactional. Nevertheless, learning to speak in a second language is often perceived as the most vital of the language skills (Garbati & Mady, 2015). English language speaking skills have been taught through online environments since the emergence of the Covid-19 Pandemic. This situation has caused sudden, unexpected and radical changes in the teaching of English speaking skills. Both foreign language teachers and foreign language students have been trying to adapt to this compulsory situation they face since the beginning of 2020. Foreign language teachers continue to teach foreign languages in this process, regardless of whether they have technological literacy and proficiency. One of the most important points to focus on is whether the digital content, materials, and activities used by foreign language teachers, who are faced with a sudden change, are in accordance with the CEFR-CV. As the main focus of the current book chapter, teaching English language speaking skills in a digital environment in line with CEFR-CV has gained importance due to inadequate resources.

Most academic fields have been affected positively and continuously due to the constantly developing technology and ICT. In this respect, technology's integration into speaking skills teaching and utilising ICT in the speaking classroom has a crucial role in developing English language learners' communicative competence. Thus, language learners communicate heavily through technology (Kirovska & Simjanoska, 2019). On the other hand, language learners' speaking ability can be affected by various factors such as physiological, emotional, physical, and environmental factors positively or negatively (Çetin Köroğlu & Utku, 2018). Digital learning environments can foster flexibility and geographical barriers to developing language learners' foreign language speaking skills with respect to its application and use. Web-based language teaching and learning activities, computer-assisted language learning, blended learning, and online learning continue to facilitate and develop fields, enabling language learners to use their second or foreign language in authentic digital environments. Warschauer and Meskill (2000) point out that "the key to successful use of technology in language teaching lies not in hardware or software but in "humanware"; our human capacity as teachers is to plan, design, and implement effective educational activity (p.316)." In this respect, language teachers' technological literacy and capabilities play an important role in utilising these highly effective tools to promote language learners' speaking skills and interaction among students. Language teachers use various digital tools such as learning management systems (Edmodo, Geenio, Ecoach, Talentlms, etc.), online materials, and resources (Linght, Vocaroo, Audacity, Lingro, Voicethread, etc.), conferencing programs (Zoom, Google Meet, Hangouts, and etc). Computer-assisted language learning (CALL) needs to be focused on at this point that Warchauer (2000) focused on the evolution timeline in three stages. The first stage is structural CALL which aims to develop better accuracy throughout the learning process. In the first stage, little interaction takes place. The second stage is communicative CALL which focuses on learners' cognitive models. The third stage is integrative CALL which aims to integrate online platforms and multimedia into the learning process to develop interaction. In this respect, the third stage of CALL absolutely is the reflection of remote teaching during the Covid-19 pandemic. Foreign language speaking skill is a demanding task in nature that was discussed by Muanjayanah (2004). The problems were categorised under four headings as follows;

- Inhibition: Language learners are inhibited about speaking in class since they are generally worried and anxious.
- Nothing to say: Generally, language learners state that they have nothing to say about the given topic.

- Low or uneven participation: Few or dominant students lead the discussion in crowded classrooms.
- Mother tongue use: Learners switch to their mother tongue whenever possible because it is easy to use.

The problems may occur during online speaking classrooms because language learners generally state some other problems. Most students state that they have a weak internet connection or do not have a microphone to talk in online lessons. Another problem is that very few students are eager to talk or comment on the given topic. Research carried out by scholars show that speaking skill was the most neglected, and writing was the most enhanced skill during online lessons during the Covid-19 pandemic (Hartshorn & Mcmurry, 2020; Karataş & Tuncer, 2020). The reason for this result is that speaking was used to communicate during the lesson, which is generally teacher-led; on the other hand, students needed to use writing skills for their homework and assignments. Another study showed that educational technologies and online platforms had been used heavily by language teachers to deliver course content effectively, such as Zoom, Moodle, Google meet, etc., to develop intrapersonal communication during the pandemic (Erarslan,2021). Language teachers should take the same precautions to prevent the aforementioned problems during their online courses. The first problem is students' inhibition due to their speaking anxiety and shyness. To solve this problem, language teachers can apply collaborative speaking activities in their online lessons. By doing this, both shy and anxious language learners can actively participate in speaking activities and interact with other group members. Additionally, they can work on a given task to accomplish it. The second problem is that students generally state they have no idea about the topic, but if background information and necessary vocabulary are provided before the actual performance, they can think over the topic and create their speech. These speaking aids could easily be provided in online lessons because the Internet presents many resources. As discussed earlier, the third problem is that little participation occurs, or dominant students only participate orally in lessons. Language teachers can assign a task to each student or can create groups of students in digital lessons. By doing so, each participant needs to contribute to the process by interacting with others. The last problem proposed by Muanjayanah (2004) is the mother tongue use in classrooms. The use of mother tongue should not be allowed as much as possible by the teacher, but when it occurs, the teacher should find solutions to minimise it (Çetin Köroğlu, 2019; Çetin Köroğlu, 2021; Maxammatkulova, 2021).

GOAL-ORIENTED DIGITAL SPEAKING ACTIVITY SAMPLES

Willis (2007) defines task as "a goal oriented activity with a specific outcome where the emphasis is on exchanging meaning, not producing specific language forms" (p.36). This section presents two different goal-oriented digital speaking activities/ tasks suitable for the CEFR companion volume. The activities are designed in the form of goal-oriented for B1 and B2 levels. Additionally, different Web 2.0 tools are used to design the activities. For example, Voicethread (https://voicethread.com/myvoice/) and Flipgrid (https://info.flipgrid.com/) emphasised these activities. Hence, these Web 2.0 tools present various features to support language learners' speaking skills in the target language.

Speaking Activity One

Level: B2 (CEFR-CV)

Task: Hotel search & reservation for Christmas vacation (4 days)

Skills: Speaking, reading, listening, and minimal writing

Web 2.0 tools: Zoom, Voicethread and Booking website in the L2

Materials: information cards

Pre-set criteria: information cards for students

Cities need to be searched: North Pole, Bethlehem, Asheville, & Branson.

This speaking activity can be carried out in pairs or small groups online. Students need to search for four hotels to stay in for Christmas vacation. According to teachers' pre-set specific criteria, each hotel should be suitable for people.

This speaking activity was designed in line with the descriptor for B2 level *'Can collaborate online with a group that is working on a project, justifying proposals, seeking clarification and playing a supportive role in order to accomplish shared tasks'* (CoE, 2020, p. 86, 87). Accordingly, students can use the Zoom breakout rooms feature for collaboration and interaction when they continue their searches on booking websites. Additionally, they can interact with each other in the target language to decide on the hotels due to criteria. They can read hotels' comments and features and calculate budgets. Then they can utilise the chat function to write short messages to teachers about their preferences with their reasons and explanations.

After completing their task on Zoom, students can utilise Voicethred to create a speaking video as a product of their tasks. In this video, students can add their voices and pictures to videos. When they complete their product, they can easily post it into their online classroom which the teacher created. Other students can comment on it too.

Figure 2. https://www.booking.com/index.tr.html

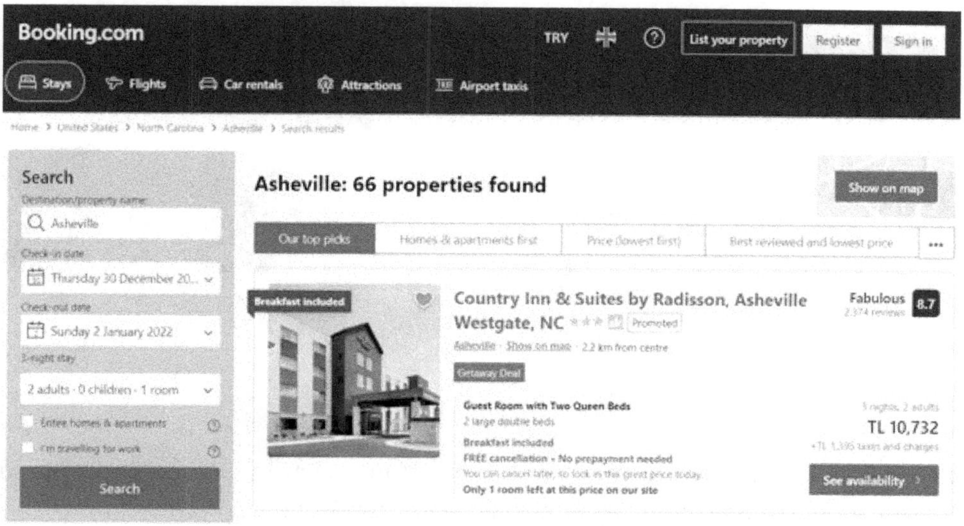

If one of the group members has difficulty in understanding instructions or makes a mistake on the online Project, other group members can help and clarify the problematic point through chat function and breakout rooms.

Speaking Activity Two

Level: B1 (CEFR-CV)

Task: Dishes & Famous chefs

Skills: Speaking, reading & writing

Web 2.0 tools: Flipgrid, Zoom, and Google Document

Materials: Videos, visuals, and laptop

Famous Chefs: Ferran Adrià, Gordon Ramsay, Gale Gand, Rick Bayless.

This speaking activity was designed in line with the descriptor for the B1 level; *'Can interact online with a group that is working on a project, following straightforward instructions, seeking clarification and helping to accomplish the shared tasks'* (CoE, 2020, p. 86, 87). *Accordingly,* this speaking activity can be carried out with small groups of students or individually. Language teachers can create groups of two people before the activity begins. The teacher assigns a famous chef to each group. Students need to find information about the chef and his/her signature meal.

Students can use the Zoom breakout rooms feature for collaboration and interaction when they continue their searches on Google. Additionally, they can interact with each other in the target language to decide on their presentation's content. For example, they can read the chef's biography, his/her success story, and signature meal. Then

Figure 3. https://info.flipgrid.com/

they can utilise the chat function to write short messages to teachers if they need clarification on instructions or seek some help with the task.

Afterwards, each group prepares an online presentation related to their assigned task in which they both present the chef's biography and the details about the meal. In this phase, an imaginary situation is created in which students act out like they present their presentation on a TV show. The teacher could act out like he/she is the TV show's presenter and asks questions about the students' presentation. Students use Flipgrid to share their video presentations.

After completing the goal-oriented task, the language teacher gives feedback and suggestions on students' performance synchronously by using Zoom meetings.

The aforementioned goal-oriented digital speaking activities are appropriate for B1 and B2 levels of CEFR-CV. The activities aimed to develop English language learners' online interaction skills in a group project, collaboration skills in group work by seeking clarification in a problematic situation, and peer supporting skills in a complicated task to achieve the goal of the task. The aims of the activities are determined due to CEFR-CV descriptors for Online Transactions and Collaboration. Thus B1 and B2 level descriptors mainly focus on interaction and collaboration among learners. It is believed that these goal-oriented online speaking activities will contribute to English language teachers' speaking task preparation process by presenting samples. Thus, online speaking skills teaching activities are rare and are not prepared due to CEFR-CV. Scholars state that the activities for teaching speaking skills should balance language input, structured output, and communicative output (Mounika & Thamanara, 2018). In goal-oriented speaking activities, language input was provided as content-oriented input because given tasks are prepared as project and group work. The language learners assigned to complete these tasks will need background information to accomplish them.

Another point is that the activities contain structured output and communicative output effectively. Thus, in the first activity, students are expected to make a hotel reservation for the Christmas holiday vacation due to pre-set criteria. The criteria were designed in a complicated way to make language learners communicate with each other through online learning environments. As the output of the first speaking activity, they need to create a video about their hotel reservation by presenting all it details and need to upload it to the Web 2.0 tool (Voicethread was used in this activity). As explained, the activity contains both structured output and communicative output in a balanced way. Similarly, the second goal-oriented speaking activity consists of content-related input, structured output, and communicative output. Thus, language learners are required to search for the given task and communicate with each other to complete the task. At the end of the negotiation among learners, they need to accomplish the task as groups. It is crystal clear that goal-oriented speaking activities provide rich content, a task completion process, and output. It can be said that these activities effectively develop language learners' speaking skills in many ways discussed above. Chandra (2004) states that "Technology's capacity to reach learners in any place and at any time has the potential to promote revolutionary changes in the educational paradigm" (p.19). It is quite possible to teach English speaking skills appropriately through an online learning environment for CEFR-CV. The two goal-oriented speaking activities were designed to show this possibility. Likewise, English language teachers can utilise web 2.0 tools and learning environments to design such speaking activities.

CONCLUSION

Foreign language teaching in online education contexts may be problematic for those language teachers who are used to teaching in conventional classrooms on a face-to-face basis. Designing tasks and activities serving educational purposes in accordance with the features of contemporary life for learners with various foreign language backgrounds may become critical for online language classes. To this end, the CEFR-CV can be taken as a reference point as it presents descriptors for all language proficiency levels, from C2 to Pre-A, for online transactions and collaboration, and foreign language teachers can benefit from these descriptors from planning to the assessment of activities in online language education contexts. Research showed that language learners have a positive attitude toward the innovative use of online materials (Hazaymeh, 2021; Memić-Fišić & Bijedić, 2017). The point is that the online materials should be prepared suitable for CEFR-CV to get more viable and sustainable development. The advent of technological tools and resources enriches language classrooms in many ways. First of all, these classrooms appeal to language learners more and lead them to better learning. With the utilisation of technology, language teachers can use various platforms and tools so that speaking skills teaching can easily be taught and developed easily with these applications. In this respect, language teachers should cleverly and creatively select and design speaking activities that are prepared due to CEFR-CV. Additionally, they need to be aware of students' interests and levels. Campana et al. (2021) state that various types of intervention are required to develop language learners' speaking skills in online environments in which learners receive feedback as a reward after they perform orally. It should be noted that utilising innovative online approaches to develop English language speaking skills is motivating and challenging for both language teachers and language learners. However, it seems that online teaching will lead education practice all around the World after the Covid-19 pandemic. The case is that online teaching is appropriate to the CEFR-CV to have a standard in applications. The current book chapter aims to shed light for language practitioners, administrators and language learners from these perspectives.

REFERENCES

Alderson, J. C. (2007). The CEFR and the need for more research. *Modern Language Journal, 91*(4), 659–663. doi:10.1111/j.1540-4781.2007.00627_4.x

Allo, M. D. G. (2020). Is the online learning good in the midst of Covid-19 Pandemic? The case of EFL learners. *Jurnal Sinestesia, 10*(1), 1–10.

Atmojo, A. E. P., & Nugroho, A. (2020). EFL classes must go online! Teaching activities and challenges during COVID-19 Pandemic in Indonesia. *Register Journal, 13*(1), 49–76. doi:10.18326/rgt.v13i1.49-76

Bailey, D. R., & Lee, A. R. (2020). Learning from experience in the midst of Covid-19: Benefits, challenges, and strategies in online teaching. *Computer Assisted Language Learning Electronic Journal (CALL-EJ), 21*(2), 176–196.

Brown, H. D. (1994). *Teaching by principles: An interactive approach to language pedagogy*. Prentice Hall Regents.

Byram, M., & Parmenter, L. (2012). *The common European framework of reference: The globalization of language education policy*. Multilingual Matters. doi:10.21832/9781847697318

Campaña Días, D. C., Porras Pumalema, S. P., Ávila Herrera., S. A., & Fierro López, D. V. (2021). Promoviendo habilidades del habla en ambientes online. *Conciencia Digital, 4*(1.1), 241-249. doi:10.33262/concienciadigital.v4i1.1.1556

Çetin Köroglu, Z. (2019). Interventionist Dynamic Assessment's Effects on Speaking Skills Testing: Case of Elt Teacher Candidates. *Advances in Language and Literary Studies, 10*(3), 23–31. doi:10.7575/aiac.alls.v.10n.3p.23

Çetin Köroğlu, Z. (2021). Using Digital Formative Assessment to Evaluate EFL Learners' English Speaking Skills. *GIST–Education and Learning Research Journal*, (22), 103–123. doi:10.26817/16925777.1001

Çetin Köroğlu, Z., & Utku, Ö. (2018). Yabancı dilde konuşma becerisinin ölçülmesinde dinamik ölçme. In Ö. Balci & F. Çolak (Eds.), *Her Yönüyle Yabancı Dil Üzerine Araştırmalar II* (pp. 77–87). Çizgi Yayınevi.

Chandra, R. (2004). *Technology in the Preparation of Teachers*. ISHA.

Council of Europe (CoE). (2001). *Common European framework of reference for languages: Learning, teaching, assessment*. Cambridge University Press.

Council of Europe (CoE). (2018). *The CEFR companion volume with new descriptors*. Language Policy Programme, Education Policy Division, Education Department. https://rm.coe.int/cefr-companion-volume-with-new-descriptors-2018/1680787989

Council of Europe (CoE). (2020). *Common European framework of reference for languages: Learning, teaching, assessment-Companion volume*. Strasbourg: Council of Europe Publishing. www.coe.int/lang-cefr

Erarslan, A. (2021). English language teaching and learning during Covid-19: A global perspective on the first year. *Journal of Educational Technology & Online Learning, 4*(2), 349–367. doi:10.31681/jetol.907757

Garbati, J. F., & Mady, C. J. (2015). Oral skill development in second languages: A review in search of best practices. *Theory and Practice in Language Studies, 5*(9), 1763–1770. doi:10.17507/tpls.0509.01

Girard, D., & Trim, J. L. M. (Eds.). (1998). *Learning and teaching modern languages for communication: Final report of the project group (activities 1982/87)*. Council of Europe.

Hartshorn, K. J., & Mcmurry, B. L. (2020). The effects of the COVID-19 pandemic on ESL learners and TESOL practitioners in the United States. *International Journal of TESOL Studies, 2*(2), 140–156. doi:10.46451/ijts.2020.09.11

Hazaymeh, W. A. (2021). EFL students' perceptions of online distance learning for enhancing English language learning during Covid-19 pandemic. *International Journal of Instruction, 14*(3), 501–518. doi:10.29333/iji.2021.14329a

Hughes, R. (2002). *Teaching and researching speaking*. Pearson Education.

Hulstijn, J. H. (2007). The shaky ground beneath the CEFR: Quantitative and qualitative dimensions of language proficiency. *Modern Language Journal, 91*(4), 663–667. doi:10.1111/j.1540-4781.2007.00627_5.x

Karataş, T. Ö., & Tuncer, H. (2020). Sustaining language skills development of pre-service EFL teachers despite the COVID-19 interruption: A case of emergency distance education. *Sustainability (Basel), 12*(19), 1–34. doi:10.3390u12198188

Kirovska-Simjanoska, D. (2019). Digital vs in-person learning environment in ESP classrooms: Let the students decide. *SEEU Review, 14*(1), 36–68. doi:10.2478eeur-2019-0004

Lee, A. R., & Bailey, D. R. (2020). Learning from experience in the midst of covid-19: Benefits, challenges, and strategies in online teaching. *Call-Ej, 21*(2), 176-196. http://callej.org/journal/21-2/Bailey-Lee2020.pdf

Liu, M., Moore, Z., Graham, L., & Lee, S. (2002). A look at the research on computer-based technology use in second language learning. *Journal of Research on Technology in Education, 34*(3), 250–273. doi:10.1080/15391523.2002.10782348

Maxammatkulova, I. N. (2021). Teaching Speaking in English Lessons in Elementary School: Problems and Solutions. *Academic research in educational sciences, 2*(7), 95-98.

Memić-Fišić, I., & Bijedić, N. (2017). Teaching materials for ESL distance learning. *Explorations in English Language and Linguistics, 5*(1), 40-54. https://hrcak.srce.hr/216834

Mirici, İ. H. (2015). Contemporary ELT practices across Europe and in Turkey. *International Journal of Language Academy, 3*(4), 1–8. doi:10.18033/ijla.333

Mounika, K., & Tahamarana, S. (2018). Teaching Speaking Skills Online: Prospects and Possibilities. Eltai Tirupathi, *Annual International Conference,* (pp. 1-6). IEEE.

Muanjayanah, A. (2004). *The implementation of communication language*. Bumi Aksara.

North, B. (2014). *The CEFR in practice*. Cambridge University Press.

Prensky, M. (2001). Digital natives, digital immigrants. *On the Horizon, 9*(5), 1–6. doi:10.1108/10748120110424816

Shaaban, S. S. A. (2020). TEFL professors' e-learning experiences during the Covid-19 pandemic. *European Journal of Foreign Language Teaching*, *5*(1), 82–97. doi:10.46827/ejfl.v5i1.3202

Summers, J. J., Waigandt, A., & Whittaker, T. A. (2005). A comparison of student achievement and satisfaction in an online versus a traditional face-to-face statistics class. *Innovative Higher Education*, *29*(3), 233–250. doi:10.100710755-005-1938-x

Tanyeli, N. (2009). The efficiency of online English language instruction on students' reading skills. *Procedia: Social and Behavioral Sciences*, *1*(1), 564–567. doi:10.1016/j.sbspro.2009.01.102

Warschauer, M. (2000). *CALL for the 21st Century*. IATEFL and ESADE Conference, Barcelona, Spain. http://www.gse.uci.edu/markw/cyberspace.html

Warschauer, M., & Meskill, C. (2000). Technology and second language teaching and learning. UCI. https://education.uci.edu/markw-tslt.html

Willis, D., & Willis, J. (2007). *Doing Task-based Teaching*. Oxford University Press.

World Health Organization [WHO]. (2020a). *Novel Coronavirus (2019-nCoV) SITUATION REPORT-1*. WHO. https://www.who.int/docs/default-source/coronaviruse/situation-reports/20200121- sitrep-1-2019-ncov.pdf?sfvrsn=20a99c10_4

World Health Organization [WHO]. (2020b). *Novel Coronavirus (2019-nCoV) SITUATION REPORT-22*. WHO. https://www.who.int/docs/default-source/coronaviruse/situation-reports/20200211- sitrep-22-ncov.pdf?sfvrsn=fb6d49b1_2

World Health Organization [WHO]. (2021). *WHO Coronavirus (COVID-19) Dashboard*. WHO. https://covid19.who.int/

Yüce, E. (2019). Possible problems in online foreign language teaching at a university context. *International Journal of Curriculum and Instruction*, *11*(2), 75–86.

Yüce, E. (2022). The immediate reactions of EFL learners towards total digitalization at higher education during the Covid-19 pandemic. *Kuramsal Eğitimbilim Dergisi [Journal of Theoretical Educational Science]*, *15*(1), 1-15.

ADDITIONAL READINGS

Yüce, E. (2019). Possible problems in online foreign language teaching at a university context. *International Journal of Curriculum and Instruction*, *11*(2), 75–86.

Yüce, E. (2022). The immediate reactions of EFL learners towards total digitalization at higher education during the Covid-19 pandemic. [Journal of Theoretical Educational Science]. *Kuramsal Eğitimbilim Dergisi*, *15*(1), 1–15. doi:10.30831/akukeg.939836

KEY TERMS AND DEFINITIONS

CEFR: Addresses protecting linguistic and cultural diversity, enhancing plurilingual and pluricultural education, and promoting intercultural understanding for countries all over Europe.

CEFR-CV: The cefr-cv was published in 2020 after its provisional version appeared in 2018 to update several scales of the cefr and extend the cefr by including new aspects

Chapter 7
A Novel Framework for Developing Digital Platforms for Engineering Students

KS Sastry Musti
https://orcid.org/0000-0003-4384-7933
Namibia University of Science and Technology, Namibia

Harmony Kuitakwashe Musiyarira
Namibia University of Science and Technology, Namibia

ABSTRACT

This chapter presents a novel framework for the design and development of digital platforms using mature rapid e-learning tools for teaching and learning purposes, specifically in engineering programs. A good number of recent works have been summarized and then the foundation for the chapter is provided. The development process for a simple rapid e-learning tool is outlined, and a 3-tier architecture for a simple digital platform is also presented. Then, the chapter presents a novel framework that uses rapid e-learning tools in the design and development process of digital platforms. Challenges associated with developing digital platforms and important steps in the strategic deployment of the suggested framework are illustrated.

DOI: 10.4018/978-1-6684-4940-0.ch007

INTRODUCTION

Universities and Higher Educational Institutions (HEI) across the world continue to design new range of learning mechanisms to support student learning processes. Particularly, post Covid-19 use of digital platforms has gained more prominence as due to the restrictions imposed in physical meetings and/or gatherings. Training requirements and standards to the students vary from faculty to faculty. Hands-on training is critical in the professional fields such as engineering and medicine. In other words, the core operations towards training future graduates involve using various methods of developing the content for learning, hands-on training, skills development, content delivery, formative and summative assessment etc.

Typically, teachers in engineering programs use various teaching methodologies in the traditional face-to-face classroom setting. Such approaches also include the regular classroom engagement followed by a well-structured laboratory training to provide hands-on training to the students. Due to technological advancements, restrictions imposed by pandemics such as Covid-19, demands of the contemporary operating conditions in reaching out to the students etc., digital life in the HEI operations is now occupying more space than before (Wang et.al, 2020). In the modern era, student learning is supported through several strategies and concepts such as using escape rooms, digital platforms and rapid e-learning etc. Several authors point to the need of adopting digital platforms in HEIs due to changing needs and times (Bo, 2011; Renée and Maria, 2022; Wang et.al, 2020; Lene et.al., 2020; Alice et.al 2021). Since these are relatively newer concepts, their definitions and usage patterns are not very well described yet. Though many distinct and/or combinational philosophies exist, the scope of discussion in this chapter is restricted to the treatment of digital platforms that can be developed using rapid e-learning tools for providing much required hands-on training to the engineering students. However, the benefits of escape rooms and rapid e-learning cannot be ignored, when they are used on a standalone basis. This warrants an appropriate treatment of these concepts to take advantage in developing digital platforms to the purpose. Literature is very clear about the ambiguity in defining these terms and their end-usage. Lene et.al.(2020) and Alice et.al (2020) have reviewed this aspect of ambiguity besides various aspects related to escape rooms based learning and assessment. The following paragraphs explain these three chosen concepts to provide proper background to this chapter.

Escape rooms are something that require students to participate in a game like environment on their own, without the teacher; and then understand a specific problem, resources, conditions and various possible paths to the solution – all entirely on their own (Alice et al, 2021). They are generally intended to remove the boredom in the learning; however modern day definitions and expectations of escape rooms vary widely (Lene et al., 2020).

The term digital platforms is generally used to describe a digital ecosystem that supports a few or several requirements such as content delivery, assessment of knowledge in both summative and formative modes, monitoring of learning activity etc. Typically, presence of the teacher is required to provide orientation about the platform and/or the content and/or overall process. This is the contrast between using a digital platform and an escape room. Sometimes, use of a standard or an in-house developed software application can also be considered as the use of a digital platform to train students on a specific topic or concept. Another term that used is digital laboratory, but a digital platform can be seen as a superset and a digital lab can be a subset in the wider teacher / learning spectrum (Fushshilat et. al., 2018). It is possible to design and develop a design laboratory with some or more attributes of a general digital platform also (Nepsha et. al, 2021). A well designed digital laboratory with its core functionality to impart the required training can be upgraded with a selected set of features of a digital platform such as content delivery, assessment and monitoring the user participation etc.

Just as escape rooms and digital platforms; the rapid e-learning also has varying forms of definitions and philosophies of understanding. To begin with, majority consider rapid e-learning as a process to build the course material rapidly. This process uses wide ranging design and delivery tools. For instance, it is possible to use a few simple PowerPoint slides (to explain the basics of the topic), one or two online resources (such as research papers, YouTube videos and/or websites with meta information for providing a contextual setting), a video session or two (using Zoom/ MS-Teams for discussion and/or analysis) followed by an assessment session (using any standard assessment tool be it on LMS or on Teams). All the above activities are different and yet, they all can be combined using any appropriate content delivery tool that can hold these composite resources together and deliver the content in an orderly (as programmed) manner. Several authoring tools such as Web 3.0, Virtual Reality tools or even a simple Adobe Flash / a single HTML website can serve as the delivery mechanism platform. The works - M.K.S. Sastry and Riaz Ali (2009), Sastry (2007) and Musti (2020a) have presented various technology platforms and their use in developing information systems and digital platforms. There are several obvious advantages of using rapid e-learning philosophy. They include faster absorption of information (read as knowledge) though in small fragments; minimized (or absence of) logistical issues with content in terms of portability and access; significant reduction in overall times and costs; higher overall productivity.

From the above, it can be seen that the three concepts: escape rooms, digital platforms and rapid e-learning have their own approaches, though all of them keep learning effectiveness, content delivery and student engagement in their core functional operation. Escape rooms are more targeted to minimize the presence of teacher (not the role of the teacher), thus aiming at independent learning. Digital platforms can potentially cater to the needs of specialized and focused hands-on training through complex simulations or computations with sets of data sets or composite information. Rapid e-learning in principle is more of a process to develop (or package) content with different tools and then deliver using an appropriate platform. Rapid e-learning is not specific to any specialization or specific field of education. Thus, it targets wider audience in a very broad-spectrum. Hence it is widely considered as a promising and futuristic approach due to several advantages associated. Though these philosophies are different and distinct, it is interesting to note that computer technology (or digital tools/ platforms) is the common backbone to design, develop and operate these concepts in a bid to meet the learning appetites of students of modern era. E-learning platforms are typically designed and operated by staff members with computer programming and system background. Due to the advancement and simplification of technological tools and platforms, rapid e-learning ecosystems can be developed and/or can be used to package the content even by the teachers themselves. On the other hand, digital platforms for training in complex engineering tasks can only be designed and developed by the teachers with specific knowledge and expertise in that area. It is important to note that there are no contributions that focus on using one of these concepts to develop the other, which is a clear gap. This chapter attempts to fill that very gap where in rapid e-learning tools can be used to develop digital platforms.

LITERATURE REVIEW

Over the years quite a lot of scholarly content is published in a bid to deal with the above mentioned approaches. Most of the works predominantly dealt with three major topics. The first is the design and development (or the overall process) of the content itself using a specific approach (Sang et. al, 2020; KS Sastry et al, 2020; Bo, 2011; Ahmed et. al, 2016 and Stahre et. al 2019). Second is the development of the technological platform and/or applying a specific technological tool or software to package the content (Antonio et al, 2012; Sáenz et. al, 2015; Martin et. al., 2015; and Musti and Van, 2022). And the third is about the user reactions through feedback to illustrate the learning effectiveness (Ahmed et al., 2016; Nedic and Nafalski, 2015; Sastry and Riza, 2009). However, it should be noted that there is no work that deals with combinational approach that might derive the advantages from these three approaches. Besides the above, definition of the terms and concepts, advantages and disadvantages of the approaches have also been presented.

Designing a single digital platform to train all the students in all the courses is nearly impossible due to the specialized nature of the content. Some courses may require display of 3D models, some courses may be purely mathematical (thus may require display of equations with standard symbols and notations), some programming courses may require display of processes and flowcharts to depict the logic used etc (Ahmed, 2016). Engineering courses generally require students to use a combination of concepts that include mathematics, engineering design, analytical approaches and in some cases applying a solution methodology that has a sequence of steps in an iterative manner (Sáenz et. al., 2015; Sastry and Riaz, 2009). However, it should be noted that design and development of digital platforms can be time-consuming process due to several reasons (Sastry and Riaz, 2009). This is in total contrast with philosophy of rapid e-learning. On the other hand, teacher is required (though not essential) to assist in the learning process. So, the question is how best a digital platform can be designed and developed with some of the chosen benefits provided by other two approaches. Another contrasting difference in general is the shelf-life. Most researchers perceive Rapid e-learning approach results in shorter shelf-life. Even some indicated that shorter life-time is the result of frequent customization of the content due to changing requirements. However, shelf-life of digital platforms is generally longer, however is subjected to degree of user acceptance.

Numerous software tools exist for student training in engineering that deal with wide-ranging topics such as – power engineering, energy systems, thermal systems, fluid dynamics, statistical analysis etc. There are several research papers that have dealt with individual software tools, design and development; engineering application of such tools etc. Hans-Kristan et al. (2018) has even listed as many as 75 different software products with overlapping features in the area of energy systems. This naturally leads to a certain degree of debate and confusion in adopting a single or multiple software tools to provide standardized hands-on training. Varying views of academicians, industry experts and most importantly licensing costs etc., can potentially influence the choice of the software tool that can be used as a digital platform. Platforms such as MATLAB and MS-Excel are very popular for learning engineering topics and even for developing prototypes. MATLAB, with its toolboxes can be used for wide ranging purposes including data storage, computation and analysis. At the same time, MS-Excel is a simple and yet a powerful platform that can provide a range of opportunities for the developers (Berger et al., 2009; KSS Musti, 2020b). Some of the important features (as related to development of learning tools for engineering) of MS-Excel include – holding the data in rows and columns, support for programming through VBA, support for plotting different types of graphs etc. On the other hand, dedicated and domain specific software solutions have their own role in the learning landscape. For example, System Advisory Model (SAM) is a versatile software tool that can be used to design and develop energy system to the specific requirements; and thus it is specific to energy systems domain. MATLAB is a commercial software and requires monetary investments towards procuring license(s) every year. SAM is a license free software (for now) and thus does not require any investment. It should be noted that several of such commercial and license-free software tools do exist to provide hands-on training; however, a very few only can act as digital platforms.

To explain the complexity of the world of software and information systems in engineering sciences, consider the problem of energy mix planning, which is a well-known optimization problem and is well treated in the literature (KSS Musti, 2020b). Many software packages are available to plan the energy mix as there are numerous, different computational approaches exist. As many as 75 different software solutions are studied by Hans-Kristan et al. (2018) and their work reports on the use of different computational models, economic planning strategies and analyzing/ optimization processes of various approaches. Hence, it can be understood that engineering studies and simulations in general, are not entirely simple tasks even with the availability of software solutions (Antonio et al., 2012).

The major difference in general, between a software tool and a digital platform in teaching and learning segment is that a standard digital platform also provides good means for summative and formative assessment on the very content provided by it. Virtual laboratory is another term that is used more or less synonymous to the term digital platform or a digital laboratory (Stahre et al, 2019; Fushshilat et. al, 2018). For consistency and clarity, this chapter uses the term digital platform. Typically, digital platforms in engineering will need different infrastructure to develop. Typically, they can be divided into three categories: predominantly hardware, predominantly software and combination of hardware and software. Though teachers in engineering departments are the potential decision makers about the type of digital platform for a specific course, developing any digital platform requires a thorough understanding of software engineering processes with a few cycles of end-to-end product development (Bo, 2011; Ahmed, 2016). Thus, the entire process naturally requires a careful assessment of infrastructural, human resource and time-frame requirements.

The other way is to design and develop simplified versions of full-scale software tools that can act as digital platforms. However, several challenges are associated with developing digital platforms from the scratch in a typical university environment, where a significant portion of job expectations include teaching, assessment, administration and other scholarly activities. In addition, many universities value research and community service as well. Since, a lot of efforts and time are required to be invested in digital platforms, several important questions need to be answered. Some of them include - How many digital platforms are required for each class or program? Who are involved? How many developers and managers (team leaders) are required? How to quantify the efforts realistically ? Do such in-house developed digital platforms can deliver the expectations? How long it will take to develop? What will be the value addition? University managements generally will not be able to motivate their staff strongly towards developing digital platforms from the scratch with their own echo systems due to various reasons, but mostly due to the fact that it is not easy to take a stand from the possible and wide-ranging answers that might evolve for some of the above mentioned questions.

From the above, it can be understood that

- there is a significant interest in modern learning approaches, specifically escape rooms, digital platforms and rapid e-learning
- information technology is the backbone for these learning approaches
- modern day requirements are the driving force in adopting new learning approaches
- there exists an opportunity to develop digital platforms
- there exists a debate between using commercial software tools as digital platforms vs developing them in-house
- several challenges do exist in developing digital platforms in-house

Based on the above, this chapter deals with the specific objective of proposing a novel framework for the design and development of futuristic digital platforms to impart hands-on skills to the future engineering graduates. In accomplishing the set objective, the chapter first provides rationale for developing digital platforms in-house through literature review to identify the striking features of escape rooms and rapid e-learning approaches. Then it proposes a novel framework for developing digital platforms considering expectations of the users, teachers and different levels of university management. Prominent challenges in the development and adoption process are highlighted and remedial measures are outlines wherever possible. Discussion section takes up various views that are supportive, conflicting and contradicting towards developing digital platforms and how the proposed framework can address such views. Then it points to the need of furthering the framework to provide thoughts to contemporary researchers.

Developing Rapid E-Learning Prototypes

Let us consider a simple example of calculating the distance, for building a prototype in MS-Excel. The well-known relation for the distance in terms of velocity, time and acceleration are given by

$$s = u * t + 0.5 * a * t * t$$

where s is the distance in meters, u is the initial velocity in meters/seconds, t is the time in seconds and a is the acceleration in meters/ second sq. For this situation,

Figure 1. A simple example for MS-Excel based rapid e-learning tool

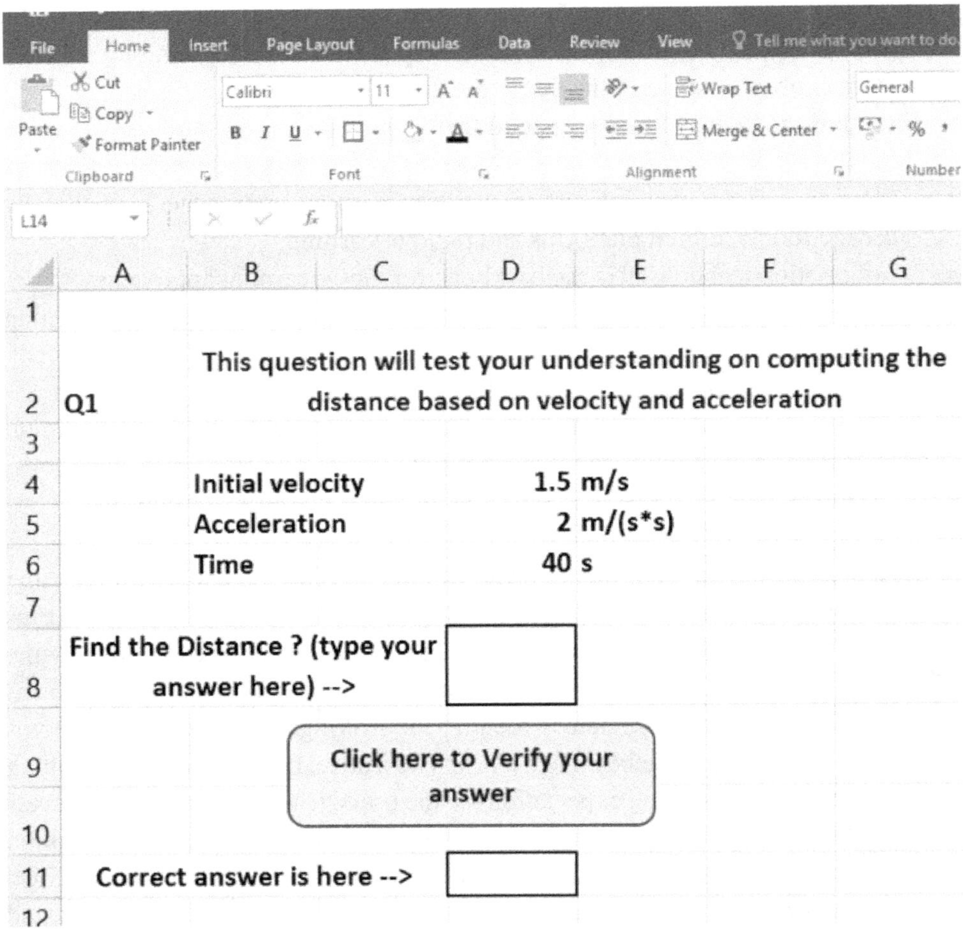

there are three different input variables viz., u, a and t and then one output variable which is the distance s itself. This is a well-known problem in elementary education and most question papers would present this in different ways. One of the common ways is - as a simple quantitative question where in students are typically expected to write the down the formula, then substitute the numerical values provided etc. On the other hand, the same question can be presented as an objective (or multiple choice) type question as well. In either case, students need to observe the values of the variables and their units and then proceed for the calculation. Now consider the task of develop a simple MS-Excel as shown in figure 1, for testing students in this case. The input variables should be mentioned clearly along with their respective units in a suitable layout as shown in figure 1 that does not require a lot of time to comprehend the question and/or the environment.

Figure 2. VBA code for developing a simple MS-Excel based rapid e-learning tool

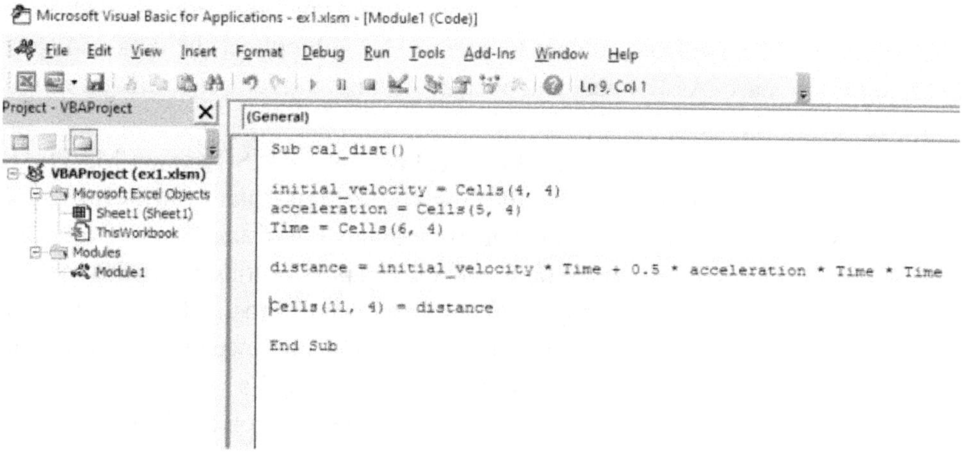

Let us first examine the nature of question. Mathematical equation is not provided, but the variables required for determining the distance are provided along with their respective units. It is very straight forward for the students to answer; and even boxed cell wherein they have to type their calculated answer. There is a button, that is self-explanatory; answer will be displayed on clicking this button.

Let us now examine the design. In a way, this is a rigid type where in input variables are specified and output is simply the distance. In normal written type assessment, any three out of the four variables can be given and the students can be asked to determine the fourth one. Then the students need to substitute the known and then determine the unknown. Whereas this design is rigid since the input variables are fixed. Though there are different ways of developing this prototype, two most common ways will be discussed here. First using a macro written in Visual Basic for Applications (VBA). The second approach is to use the cell formula, however it is not suitable as the moment values are available for input variables, the answer appears automatically. Thus, such a design cannot challenge the students in any way. VBA macro along with the code is shown in figure 2.

This simple concept does not really require MS-Excel prototype or a digital platform. However, it serves as a good example in understanding how such a concept can be realized in a digital platform. In a typical digital platform, there will be three layers - a database layer, Application Program Interface (API) and a standard User Interface (UI). Now, the question number, question itself, value of variables and units etc. can be inserted into database layer. The formula or the logic of the code in VBA can be re-programmed in the respective Application Program Interface (API). UI will provide the display. The advantage here is that the API can be programmed in such a way that the same question can be presented with different sets of data to the students. In other words, text of the question remains the same, but values of the parameters change from student to student. UI will collect the data and store back in the database. Assessment can be done through a small program that can be deployed in the database itself.

What is important in the process is that maturity of the MS-Excel or MATLAB based prototype itself. Before moving the prototype to digital platform, the prototype should be very well tested in a comprehensive manner. For instance, what are all the various concepts, questions, assessment modes, and possibilities etc. In fact, design requirements need to be well-thought out before proceeding to the digital platforms. For instance, distance can be calculated in another way, using acceleration, initial and finial velocities alone. However, that uses another formula [s = (v*v – u*u)/(2*a)]. If this needs to be tested, then preferably, a separate question needs to be used in the MS-Excel and so in the digital platform as well. So, the developers should first identify the requirements and understand various concepts and possibilities and then program carefully. This also means, the concept of distance computation has different approaches based on the variables used; and thus different questions with changing sets of variables and formulae etc. can be formulated. Though it is possible to present the concepts and explain the computational processes, it is not possible to demonstrate all the different approaches due to obvious time constraints. This is where rapid e-learning using simple prototype helps readily. With a well-designed MS-Excel or MATLAB tools, students can do the required self-study in their own comfort zones without having to worry about the presence of the teacher or peers in the class, as the rapid e-learning tool with a proper design can quickly provide the expected solution instantly.

Matured Rapid E-Learning Tools

As stated earlier, the distance computation example is too simple, but a good candidate for understanding the overall process. Different courses in engineering certainly offer wide ranging opportunities for developing digital platforms, and thus offer excellent prospects for deploying rapid e-learning processes in the first place using simple prototypes. Thus, it is important to take a look at some of such learning tools and digital platforms, to see if a connection can be established between them in terms of development cycles and processes. Some of the matured MS-Excel tools are illustrated in the table 1. Based on user experience and the richness of the content offered by these tools, it can be understood a lot of time and efforts would have been spent by the respective developers to shape up these tools to a level of maturity.

Table 1. Summary of a few selected matured MS-Excel based tools

Details of the MS-Excel tools	Purpose and Reference
Microsoft Excel-Based Tool Kit for Planning Hybrid Energy Systems (developed by Asian Development Bank)	This tool can be used to size and analyze various configurations of power plants based on renewable energy resources. The tool helps in arriving at an appropriate energy mix to provide reliable, adequate, and affordable energy.
Power system load flow analysis using Microsoft Excel–Version 2 (Ricardo and Musti, 2019)	This tool takes the standard input for the load flow analysis and then carries out the computations using four different well-known methods and then solutions are compared with one another. Tool provides intermediate calculations to assist students in their learning process. Tool is free to download without any restrictions and all source code is available.
EV Charging Financial Analysis Tool (2022), improved by Atlas Public Policy; originally developed by Cadmus Group in partnership with the Center for Climate and Energy Solutions	The EV Charging Financial Analysis Tool equips users with critical information on the financial performance of electric vehicle charging projects. The Microsoft Excel-based tool is capable of evaluating a variety of business arrangements, including sophisticated public-private partnerships. The tool uses the discounted cash flow method to evaluate the financial performance of a charging project through a variety of revenue streams over the lifetime of the charging equipment. The tool is highly flexible, with over 100 inputs and supports customizable sensitivity variables.
Musti, K. S., & Van der Merwe, M. (2022). A Novel MS Excel Tool for Multi-Criteria Decision Analysis in Energy Systems.	This MS-Excel tool presents 4 different multi-criteria decision analysis methods based on a set of input variables that cannot be compared with one another. The sheet also provides a comparison of all the four methods in a separate sheet. The tool comes with two sample systems for ready use and faster understanding. Tool is free to use and users can create their own problems with their own input data sets; and then use the tool to study the outputs. https://data.mendeley.com/datasets/zjckp3b259/1 available online, last accessed July 2022

In rapid e-learning philosophy, learning effectiveness and is the key. For this, the learning tools (either MS-Excel or MATLAB prototypes) need to be very simple. In reality, students look for - value proposition, usability, user-friendliness when using such learning tools. Thus, the design of the tool itself should be such that, it does the job in a simple and friendly manner; and does not require students to spend more time in understanding the tool itself. Value proposition of a learning tool is something that is often ignored. If the tool can be used even after the program is completed, then naturally it will enjoy longer shelf-life. In other words, students may tend to use the tool even after they complete programs as the tool may be capable of designing engineering systems or may be useful in undertaking planning studies and/or analysis of large systems etc. For a classroom tool to attain such a maturity takes time and efforts by the developers. On the other hand, developers (typically teachers) should be aware of the contemporary developments, field operating conditions so that they can further improve the tool in gradual manner. Sometimes, it is good to include practising engineers and consultants in testing process through

Table 2. Summary of a few selected digital platforms

Author(s) and Year of contribution	Details of the digital Platform
Renée and Maria (2022); Reitan and Eirik (2020); Bo (2011); Magin and Reizes (1990); Fushshilat et. al.(2018); Veldkamp et. al.(2021)	These contributions explain various reasons why digital platforms, escape classrooms should be developed for use in HEIs; and prospects of using such learning mechanisms
E. Prieto-Araujo et al (2013); Nedic and Nafalski (2015); M.K.S. Sastry and Riaz Ali (2009); Boudreaux (2018); Martin et. al.(2015); Nepsha et. al.(2021); Gangat et. al.(2018); Antonio et. al.(2012); K. S. Sastry Musti et. al.(2020)	Digital platforms for teaching concepts of Renewable energy, Power Systems Engineering, smart grid and electrical engineering systems

short-term training or even workshops for their feedback. In other words, proof of acceptability by wider audience is the key in the process of maturity of any rapid e-learning tool or process.

Digital Platforms

Over the years, several authors made contributions on digital platforms. Different aspects such as development processes, conceptual models, overall architecture (for various purposes) and even for specific applications. Since the discussion in this chapter focuses on learning in an academic setting and that too in engineering programs, it is important to consider digital platforms that can be potentially used for training the students and engineers. On the other hand, many authors have brought some compelling reasons why digital platforms should be developed for use in HEIs. Table 2 shows a few selected digital platforms that are reported in the literature thus far.

From the above, it can be seen that there is a significant interest in developing digital platforms to assist the learning processes in HEIs. Tables 1 and 2 indicate that a lot of interest in this area can be seen among the researchers in the fields of pure education and also in engineering and thus use of digital platforms in the near future can be imminent. Table 2 also indicates that different digital platforms need to be developed as there are different courses and/or areas where students need to be trained and assessed.

One important question is – what is the rationale behind developing a digital platform, when rapid e-learning tools can be developed and improved for training the students. Digital platforms typically are based on databases that are kept in a central server. Rapid e-learning tools are desktop applications and thus it is difficult to collate individual student actions and responses. In other words, assessment is not automated and even there is a possibility of students editing the content; though such

Figure 3. Individual prototypes and architecture of a simple 3-layer digital platform

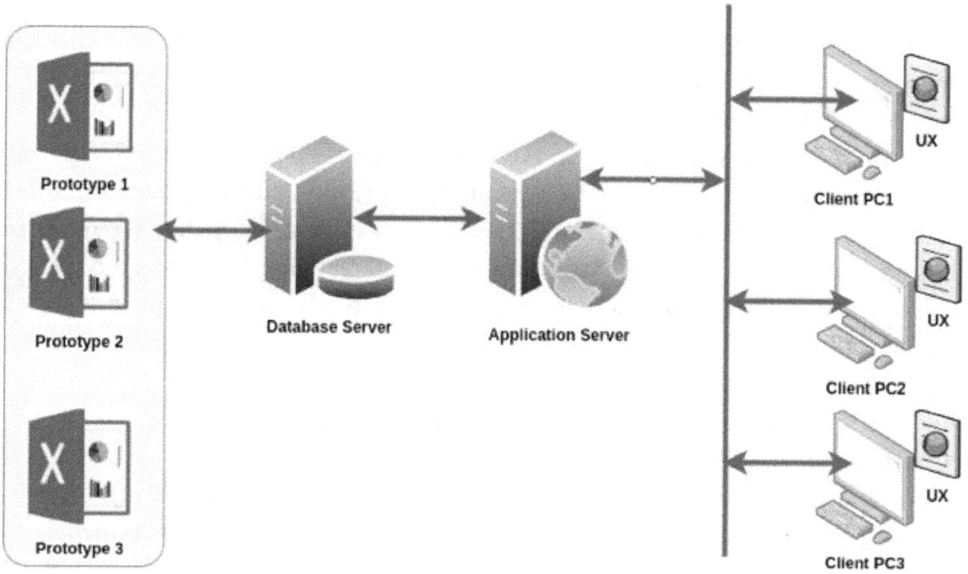

attempts can be restricted through programming. On the other hand, digital platforms have numerous capabilities such as - randomize the content that is presented to students; shuffle the sequence of the questions; collect the responses and even stop the learning and/or assessment process beyond a set instant of time. Data integrity, transparency and scalability are the hallmark indicators of digital platforms and thus it is important to develop such platforms to better serve the students.

A simple, but standard 3-tier architecture is suggested for deploying the digital platform as shown in figure 3. The first tier will have the database layer. Though several database products are available, usage of open-source database MySql is recommended since it reduces a lot of overheads and also it is now considered as an excellent product to provide high quality database services, that are more or less same as commercial databases such as Oracle. Typically, digital platforms for teaching and learning purposes in any HEI, that too within an academic unit can be designed for 400 to 500 students per course. In reality, student registration in core engineering will be under 500 per course, though there may be exceptions. Thus, MySql will be able to meet all the requirements, which means HEIs need not have to budget for a commercial product. PHP is also an open-source platform and this can be used for developing API based Apache service in the middle tier, where the application server will manage all the interfacing calls. UI can be developed using simple HTML screens along with Java-scripting. Thus, open-source platforms can be effectively used for developing digital platforms.

A Novel Framework for Developing Digital Platforms

Development of digital platforms for learning and assessment in HEIs is not new and in fact, several researchers (Yuen, 2021; Renée 2022; Sastry and Riaz, 2009) contributed on this aspect.

From the above sections, it can be seen that simple rapid e-learning tools can be developed quickly. Then such tools can be improved to develop a well-defined learning resource. Further, such resources can be used to develop digital platforms. It is possible to link these resources through careful planning and concerted efforts. A Novel Framework for developing a typical digital platform using rapid e-learning tools is proposed in terms of a few major steps.

- Design and develop a low fidelity desktop prototype
- Test the prototype and modify as required
- Deploy the product to the classroom usage and student self-study purposes
- Collect student feedback, specifically in terms of required improvements
- Further develop the prototype to reach a stage what is called as medium fidelity prototype
- Deploy the product to the classroom usage and student self-study purposes
- Collect student feedback, specifically in terms of required improvements
- Finalize the prototype to reach a stage what is called as high fidelity prototype
- Design and develop database based on the desktop prototype
- Develop required API
- Develop required UI
- Test the database driven digital platform on the local network

Though the suggested framework looks simple, some of the steps may involve significant efforts over longer time periods. However, it should be understood that the process from the low fidelity prototype to the end product (which is the digital platform) is indeed a software engineering project by itself, and the steps only outline major aspects and do not provide the intricate details. Thus each step in the above process needs to be understood from the software engineering processes for any typical project development. The intention behind providing major aspects (and not the details) is to stay only suggestive and not as prescriptive; since internals of digital platform development vary from course to course as the content varies.

Figure 4 illustrates the overall process of development of digital platforms using rapid e-learning tools. Consider a typical course in engineering that has more intense content in engineering principles, application of mathematics and system approach. Different chapters in that course may need different rapid e-learning tools that may require different design and UI. Considering the work of (Ricardo and Musti, 2019)

Figure 4. Rapid e-learning tools feeding into the development of digital platform

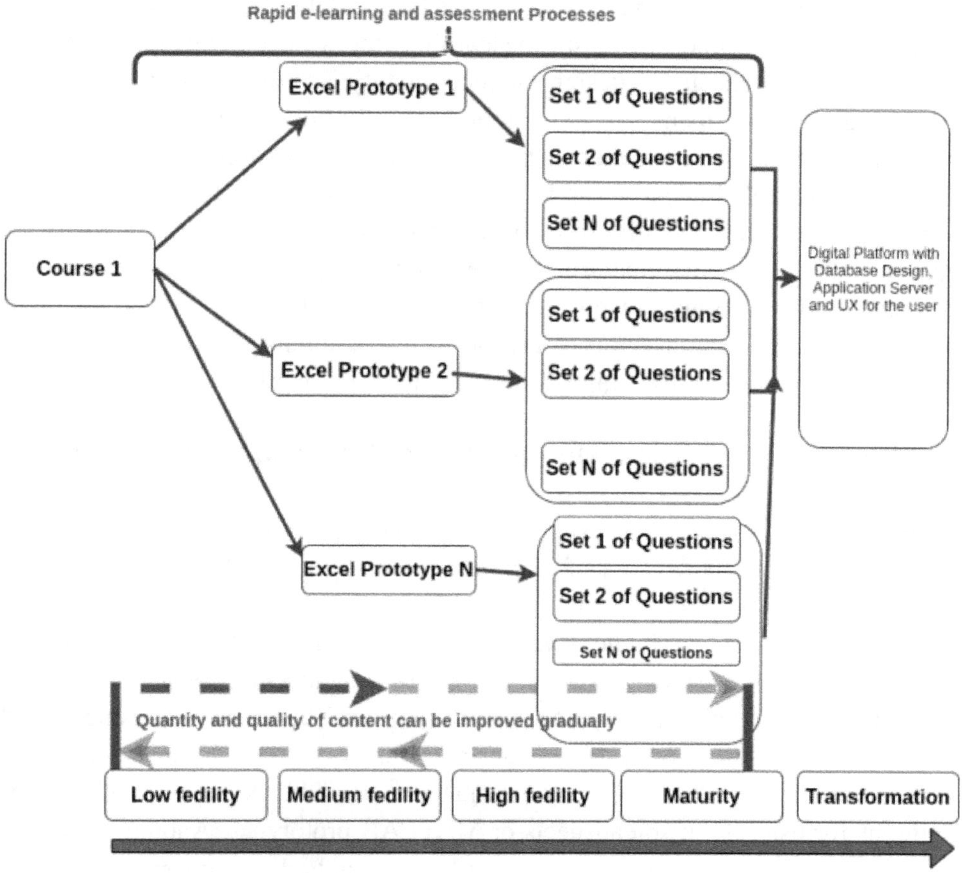

for example: the MS-Excel tool developed by Ricardo and Musti (2019) has ability to study different power flow algorithms for planning studies based on a single set of data. It should be noted that these algorithms are different from one another and in fact, are taught in different chapters in a power system planning course. These algorithms require application of engineering principles, mathematics and programming logic. When the basics are taught in the class, students can retreat into their comfort zones if they are equipped with properly designed rapid e-learning tools for independent and further learning; and even self-assessment. This approach essentially provides the students with so called escape classrooms as they are equipped with a tool that can be used to enhance the knowledge acquired from classroom teaching. Each prototype may offer the relevant content for learning and a range of questions that are embedded into the tool itself. Now, there can be N different rapid e-learning tools as shown in figure 4.

Extending this ideology for other courses, it is possible that several different rapid e-learning tools that may exist. It should be noted that these tools need to very simple as they are supposed to assist the learning process. In other words, such tools should not be complicated by design and functionality. There are two important parts – learning and assessment. The tools should be designed for both parts as students would prefer to self-test to gain confidence. In the first iteration of development, a very simple (rough draft) tool can be used that has a lower fidelity. Over the time, more features/ content can be added to further improve so that fidelity increases gradually so that a state of maturity can be attained. Now, at this point of maturity; core content for learning as well as input and output data sets for assessment will be clearly defined without errors in any form. Once attaining such state of maturity, then efforts for developing digital platforms can be put in place.

Challenges in a Typical University and/or Academic Setting

Generally, high and middle level administrative personnel will be looking for opportunities to adopt strategies for forward moving. Rapid e-learning and escape classrooms provide powerful pathways in creating futuristic, student friendly learning environment and yet with higher level of academic engagement. However, the most critical and important elements are the teachers and students, between which the teaching and learning occurs. Any tool, and/or approach can be naturally questioned by the peers who may not be entirely aware of the advantages of rapid e-learning. Even some may be in favor of using automated tools and thus may express counter opinions for using such spreadsheets or MATLAB prototypes. Another opposing view comes the philosophy of using industry standard, commercial software, particularly in engineering programs. Some may even suggest the software platform that is generally used in the local industry as there may be higher chances of students gaining job if they are trained on the same platform. However, stand and commercial software platforms can be expensive to use. Also they are not typically meant for student usage. In other words, they are purpose built for engineering design studies and analysis in the industrial setting; and thus will not be able to assist the student in the learning process of basic and core engineering concepts. Also, such packages will not provide questions and answers to support student self-study process. Hence, senior management at the department or faculty level need to gently explain the importance and benefits of adopting rapid e-learning process and thus pave the path for development of prototypes in the first place. Continuous improvement of the prototype and periodical student feedback is utmost essential in setting the positive tone for continuation of the overall process up to the realization of digital platforms.

Shortage of Human Resources and Inadequate Laboratory Infrastructure

The processes of hiring and retaining highly qualified faculty is always a challenging task even for established universities. Shortage of well-qualified and trained faculty and inadequate funding can be generally seen in most places. Engineering programs always require latest laboratory equipment and infrastructure due to recent technological trends and developments in the market. This aspect is typical to engineering programs and hands-on training is one of the integral part of outcomes and expectations of quality and accreditation processes across the world. This is a big challenge in the sense, teachers (and students) are left with limited time and resources. So answering the questions - how to develop and/or who will develop the required digital platforms can be very difficult. Of course, rapid e-learning provides convincing answers to this question. Firstly, prototypes do not take very long time to develop, if planned carefully on the lines of the course content that an individual teacher offers. Fortunately, learning and assessments are interlinked and this aspect needs to be well utilized. The prototype should be designed in such a way that it can be used for self-study purposes and also for one of the internal assessments of the course; let us say with a weighting up to 10 or 15% - such as a laboratory test or in-class mini-exam or even a surprise test. There are different ways to accomplish this. Both MS-Excel and MATLAB can be programmed to generate random numbers and thus it is possible to create same questions but with different input data sets as explained earlier. This approach in fact can be very friendly to both students and teachers. Firstly, students would have practiced more or less same questions in their so called escape sessions with the rapid e-learning tool. During the examination they may be asked to do the similar or slightly modified questions, but essentially on the same platform; where in the assessment is done automatically. This saves a lot of time for the teacher(s) to evaluate and then provide the feedback etc. Students naturally appreciate this as this is an automated process without any human involvement in the assessment process. Also, waiting for the marks is avoided as well.

Who Will Develop the Prototype?

First time development from the scratch involves some critical brainstorming and careful planning of the content, questions and assessment process within the prototype. However, once developed, rapid e-learning tools (or the prototypes) provide great flexibility to both students and teachers. There are different standard types and ways to design and develop prototypes. Prominent among them are the low, medium and high fidelity type prototypes, and these represent the stage and/or scale of development from the scratch to the final intended target. Low fidelity prototype is a first rudimentary draft for which development involves low cost, lesser time and efforts. On the other hand, high fidelity prototype would have gone through a certain degree of maturity through consistent efforts and costs and time. Since time and resources are limited, at the beginning low fidelity type prototype can be used and the same can be modified further in the due course of time. Importantly, students can be actively involved in the development, testing and feedback processes, if the course and/or field of study is very complex. Two important factors motivate this approach. First one is the opportunity learn the programming with MATLAB and/or MS-Excel. Typically, training with MATLAB or VBA macro programming takes about 2 or 3 hours hands-on, after that most students typically learn independently. Now, the task of developing prototype can be assigned to groups of students in a class to develop macros for various purposes in the very course; and of course this task can be treated as an assignment with a small weighting towards the overall assessment. This works very well, if the learning in the course and/or topic involves complex mathematics and/or lengthy design processes. Based on our own experiences, students appreciate if the content in the tool connects them to the prescribed textbook and/or standard learning resources. For instance, a few questions from prescribed books can be incorporated without any change; and a note may be included next to those questions to refer to the specific section/page of the book. Similarly, there are numerous ways to connect and engage the students with the learning tool and also the recommended books, just as in rapid e-learning and escape classroom processes.

What Is in it for the Higher and Middle Level Management?

The answers can be readily seen from the above discussion. Effective teaching and learning process; Improved student satisfaction; Higher academic engagement etc. These are some of the benefits cited in adopting the rapid e-learning and escape classrooms. However, the focus on this chapter is how best such prototypes can be further used to build digital platforms to automate the process and in turn to serve wider student population. One of the challenges in using the MS-Excel or MATLAB based platforms is to collect the responses (answers) submitted by the students. This is not a problem with rapid e-learning or the escape classroom approach and in fact, it is due to the very technological drawback as both MS-Excel and MATLAB are essentially desktop tools and cannot communicate to a centralized server on their own. Hence, the automation of the assessment part becomes time consuming and due to this, even some may rule out the very idea of the overall approach itself. This is where databases and/or digital information systems provide excellent solution(s). It is for this very reason of full scale automation that includes both learning and assessment parts; digital platforms need to be developed as soon as desktop prototypes mature to the desired level. This is where the role of middle and higher level managements is very critical. Information systems or digital platforms require a centralized server with client nodes. This infrastructure needs to be provided to the enthusiastic faculty members and departments. Typically, each department in most well-ranked universities will have their own local server to cater to the localized needs such as hosting technical / research/ developmental projects; projects related to teaching and learning etc. Existing computer laboratory with appropriate networking facilities also can be used for this purpose with or without the internet. Internet is required to accommodate off-site students. For product development local network is quite adequate.

Discussion

Figure 3 clearly indicates the presence of both hardware and software for developing digital platforms. The path of realization to a successful digital platform requires concerted efforts over the time. There can be several challenges in establishing digital platforms. The article titled 6 challenges to address when building a smart, digitalized laboratory (Biosistemika, 2021) states that

Firstly, higher and middle level managements need to be having a positive view of adopting modern learning practices such as rapid e-learning, digital platforms and escape classrooms. Several authors have indicated that the support of top level leadership is essential. (Biosistemika, 2021) explains the importance of digitalization and digital transformation in developing smart, digital platforms. It further states that

"Digital transformation only happens when leadership recognizes the strategic importance of making profound organizational changes to the company that is customer-driven rather than technology-driven"

It is important to note that some of the concluding remarks made by (Biosistemika, 2021):

- *Digital transformation is a complex process, but it will increase the value of your laboratory and company. The world is moving into the digital era, and laboratories will need to digitalize.*
- *Digitalization does not have to happen all at once. It is better to do it step-by-step, but with a strategy behind it to support it.*
- *Your investment in digitalization will not only pay off in the long run, as there are also short-term savings that you will experience.*
- *Digital culture will be a very important part of your digital transformation, and it takes time to get fully established.*

Secondly, localized computing facilities need to be established so that prototyping and further developing of the rapid e-learning tools can take place seamlessly. Thirdly, senior staff need to motivate both faculty and students in productive engagement towards adopting such learning approaches. Fourthly, a handful of early adopters of these niche practices need to be given required time and space to create rapid e-learning tools and use in teaching and learning processes. While a few individual teachers may be in a position to develop, a majority may have diverse opinion (read as resistance) about using such practices. Like any new approach, rapid e-learning philosophy also may take its own time to descend into practice. To infuse its use, wider acceptance of the tools developed by early adopters is the key. Hence, it is important to establish a conducive ecosystem for such developments.

Scope for Further Work

The three areas – escape classrooms, digital platforms and rapid e-learning tools do offer a wide ranging opportunities to the researchers in the field of higher education. Aspects such as - costs, efforts, end-use, end-benefits, learning effectiveness and student satisfaction etc., as related to these three areas need to be studied carefully considering real-life constraints as cited in previous sections. Quality indicators for learning effectiveness when using such rapid learning tools need to be identified and then how such indicators can be determined also needs to be worked out. On the case study and/or application front, design and development of specific systems need to be explored so that others can adopt such developmental processes. Importantly, comprehensive survey needs to be undertaken within the HEIs on the prospects of using such learning and assessment mechanisms.

CONCLUSION

Modern landscape of learning is more digitalized than before. HEIs need digital platforms to carry out their core operations. However, developing digital platforms is not only complex, but also time consuming. This chapter first illustrated the key issues related to the use of niche tools and recent developments. Process of developing a MS-Excel based rapid e-learning tool is illustrated with a simple example. Then a few examples of matured learning tools and digital platforms are outlined. Then the chapter proposes a novel framework for developing digital platforms at the conceptual level using rapid e-learning tools. Design and ecosystem for a simple, laboratory class digital platform is also presented. Challenges, wide ranging opinions and possible opposing views are captured through simple questions and remedial approaches were suggested wherever applicable. Overall, the chapter makes a strong case for developing digital platforms in HEIs.

REFERENCES

Ahmed, R., Hughes, P. G., Friedl, E., Ortiz Figueroa, F., Cepeda Brito, J. R., Frey, J., Birmingham, L. E., & Atkinson, S. S. (2016). A Novel Simulation Technician Laboratory Design: Results of a Survey-Based Study. *Cureus*, *8*(3), e534. doi:10.7759/cureus.534 PMID:27096134

Alice, V., Knippels, M.-C. P. J., & van Joolingen, W. R. (2021). Beyond the Early Adopters: Escape Rooms in Science Education. *Frontiers in Education*, *6*, 622860. doi:10.3389/feduc.2021.622860

Antonio Molina Bonilla, A. C. Santos, M. Castro Gil, D. Borge Diez and J. Vazquez Espierrez. (2012). Virtual Lab platform for distance learning courses in engineering technologies for the use of renewable energies. Proceedings of the 2012 IEEE Global Engineering Education Conference (EDUCON), (pp. 1-7). IEEE. 10.1109/EDUCON.2012.6201082

Berger, N., Arent, M., Arnowitz, J., & Sampson, F. (2009). *Effective Prototyping with MS-Excel*. Elsevier. doi:10.1016/B978-0-12-088582-4.X0001-7

Biosistemika, (2021). *6 challenges to address when building a smart, digitalized laboratory*. Biosis Temika. https://biosistemika.com/blog/6-challenges-when-building-digitalized-laboratory/,

Boudreaux, J. (2018). Design, Simulation, and Construction of an IEEE 14-Bus Power System. [Master's Theses, LSU]. doi:10.31390/gradschool_theses.4801

Fushshilat, I., Rahmat, A., Somantri, Y., & Haritman, E. (2018). Laboratory management: Digital laboratory information system (DLIS) concept. *IOP Conference Series. Materials Science and Engineering*, *434*, 012286. doi:10.1088/1757-899X/434/1/012286

Gangat, Y., Grondin, D., Issoufaly, T., Coquillas, N., Benne, M., & Chabriat, J. (2018). Simulation & Emulation platform for smart grid technologies. *2018 International Conference on Control, Electronics, Renewable Energy and Communications (ICCEREC)*, (pp. 122-128,) IEEE. 10.1109/ICCEREC.2018.8711994

Li, B. (2011). Design and implementation of Web-based laboratory management system in colleges and universities. *2011 3rd International Conference on Computer Research and Development*, (pp. 468-471). IEEE. 10.1109/ICCRD.2011.5764176

Magin, D. J., & Reizes, J. A. (1990). Computer simulation of laboratory experiments: An unrealized potential. *Computers & Education, 14*(3), 263–270. doi:10.1016/0360-1315(90)90009-V

Martin, S. S., Chebak, A., & Barka, N. (2015). Development of renewable energy laboratory based on integration of wind, solar and biodiesel energies through a virtual and physical environment. *2015 3rd International Renewable and Sustainable Energy Conference (IRSEC),* (pp. 1-8). IEEE. 10.1109/IRSEC.2015.7455086

Musti, K. S., & Van der Merwe, M. (2022). A Novel MS Excel Tool for Multi-Criteria Decision Analysis in Energy Systems. In N. Jain, J. Maherchandani, N. Agrawal, & T. Gupta (Eds.), *Optimal Planning of Smart Grid With Renewable Energy Resources* (pp. 83–109). IGI Global. doi:10.4018/978-1-6684-4012-4.ch003

Musti, K. S. S. (2015). An effective approach for teaching database course, International Journal of Learning. *Teaching and Educational Research, 12*(1), 53–63.

Musti, K. S. S. (2020a). Management Information Systems for Higher Education Institutions: Challenges and Opportunities. In Quality Management Implementation in Higher Education: Practices, Models, and Case Studies (pp. 110-131). IGI Global, doi:10.4018/978-1-5225-9829-9.ch006

Musti, K. S. S. (2020b). Quantification of Demand Response in Smart Grids. *IEEE International Conference INDISCON,* (pp. 278-282). IEEE. 10.1109/INDISCON50162.2020.00063

Nedic, Z., & Nafalski, A. (2015). Development of an online renewable energy laboratory. *Proceedings of 2015 12th International Conference on Remote Engineering and Virtual Instrumentation (REV),* (pp. 136-139). IEEE. 10.1109/REV.2015.7087279

Nepsha, F., Shubin, N., Andrievsky, A., & Golovin, A. (2021). Development of Energy Management System Based on a Digital Platform. 2021 Ural-Siberian Smart Energy Conference (USSEC), (pp. 120-124). IEEE. 10.1109/USSEC53120.2021.9655765

Prieto-Araujo, E., Cheah-Mañé, M., Villafafila-Robles, R., Gomis-Bellmunt, O., & Junyent-Ferré, A. (2013). Development of a laboratory platform for testing new solutions to integrate renewable energy sources in power systems. *2013 15th European Conference on Power Electronics and Applications (EPE),* (pp. 1-10). IEEE. 10.1109/EPE.2013.6634674

Ramkhelawan, R. & Musti. K. (2019). *Power system load flow analysis using Microsoft Excel–Version 2.* Spreadsheets in Education 12.1.

Renée, D. (2022). Link and Maria Gallardo-Williams, We Should Keep Developing Digital Laboratory Resources in the Postpandemic Era. *Journal of Chemical Education*, *99*(2), 519–520. doi:10.1021/acs.jchemed.1c01197

Ringkjøb, H.-K., Haugan, P. M., & Solbrekke, I. M. (2018). A review of modelling tools for energy and electricity systems with large shares of variable renewables. *Renewable & Sustainable Energy Reviews*, *96*, 440–459. doi:10.1016/j.rser.2018.08.002

Sáenz, J., Chacón, J., De La Torre, L., Visioli, A., & Dormido, S. (2015). Open and Low-Cost Virtual and Remote Labs on Control Engineering. *IEEE Access: Practical Innovations, Open Solutions*, *3*, 805–814. doi:10.1109/ACCESS.2015.2442613

Sang, Y., Liu, P., & Liao, L. (2020). Experimental Design of the Mechanical Design Course in Distance Education. 2020 IEEE 2nd International Conference on Computer Science and Educational Informatization (CSEI), (pp. 248-251). IEEE. 10.1109/CSEI50228.2020.9142512

Sastry, M. K. S. (2007). Development of an academic information system for effective education management. *International Journal of Management Education*, *1*(3), 276–286.

Sastry, M. & Riaz, A. (2009). The design and development of a virtual laboratory for power system modelling and load flow analysis to promote innovative learning. *International Journal of Innovation and Learning*, *6*(2), 178-191. doi:10.1504/IJIL.2009.022812

Sastry Musti, K. S., Iileka, H., & Shidhika, F. (2020). Industry 4.0-Based Enterprise Information System for Demand-Side Management and Energy Efficiency. In Novel Approaches to Information Systems Design (pp. 137-163). IGI Global, doi:10.4018/978-1-7998-2975-1.ch007

Stahre Wästberg, B., Eriksson, T., Karlsson, G., Sunnerstam, M., Axelsson, M., & Billger, M. (2019). Design considerations for virtual laboratories: A comparative study of two virtual laboratories for learning about gas solubility and colour appearance. *Education and Information Technologies*, *24*(3), 2059–2080. doi:10.100710639-018-09857-0

Taraldsen, L. H., Haara, F. O., Lysne, M. S., Jensen, P. R., & Jenssen, E. S. (2020). *A review on use of escape rooms in education – touching the void*. Education Inquiry. doi:10.1080/20004508.2020.1860284

Veldkamp, A., van de Grint, L., Knippels, M.-C. P. J., & van Joolingen, W. R. (2020). Escape education: A systematic review on escape rooms in education. *Educational Research Review*, *31*, 100364. doi:10.1016/j.edurev.2020.100364

Wang, X., Chen, W., Qiu, H., Eldurssi, A., Xie, F., & Shen, J. (2020). A Survey on the E-learning platforms used during COVID-19. *2020 11th IEEE Annual Information Technology, Electronics and Mobile Communication Conference (IEMCON)*, (pp. 0808-0814). 10.1109/IEMCON51383.2020.9284840

Yuen, T. (2021). Low Cost Simulation Lab for Teaching Control Theory Concepts, advances in intelligent systems and computing (Vol. 1314). Springer. doi:10.1007/978-3-030-67209-6_22

Chapter 8
Evaluation and Quality Assurance for Rapid E-Learning and Development of Digital Learning Resources

C. V. Suresh Babu
Hindustan Institute of Technolgy and Science, India

B. Rohan
Hindustan Institute of Technology and Science, India

ABSTRACT

E-learning has turned into an undeniably significant instructing and learning mode in instructive organizations and corporate preparation. To guarantee that quality is settled in the use of innovation to accomplish instructive objectives, it is basic to follow the quality checking strategy all through the phases of e-learning asset plan, creation, and conveyance. From a pattern of training of endeavoring to assess numerous e-learning programs, one of the most serious issues has ended up being taking care of the quantity of factors which possibly influence on the viability of the program and concluding what are reliant, free, and unessential factors in a given circumstance. The evaluation of e-learning project has cultivated a more complete construction. This study demonstrates the authoring tool which is used to create the digital learning content and evaluation criteria, and how the quality of e-Learning resources is maintained, and finally the future development of digital learning resources.

DOI: 10.4018/978-1-6684-4940-0.ch008

INTRODUCTION

E-learning is a method for getting the hang of utilizing computerized or web-empowered innovation like PCs, tablets, or cell phones. Web based learning, frequently known as e-learning, considers remote admittance to organized learning or any ideal course by means of a computerized gadget with the help of dependable web network. An understudy can utilize e-figuring out how to get to learnings or bits of knowledge on any chosen subject carefully from any area in the globe. E-learning, frequently known as web-based learning, contrasts significantly from customary learning methods in that the last option require the genuine presence of the two teachers and understudies. The school system encountered a significant change because of the Covid pandemic. The prerequisite of social disconnection and the worldwide highly sensitive situation incited instructive organizations to close for a vague period, which prompted the improvement of e-learning. This key change in schooling demonstrated straightforward and achievable even in the center of the emergency in light of the fact that to the accessibility of contemporary innovation and development.

Mentors from one side of the planet to the other have involved in eLearning and considered it as a vital stage. It appeared to be impossible that everybody would have prior admittance to data. Geographic limits made it hard for instructors and understudies to migrate to different countries. Predictable training has been made conceivable by this latest development. Applications for portable e-learning can cultivate better cooperation and culturally diverse impetuses among understudies and instructors. In the present computerized age, accentuating the benefit of eLearning education is urgent. Another technique for educating is as of now utilizing on the web educational plans and vivid learning conditions. The possibility that more people ought to start eLearning and contact an eLearning application advancement business is additionally right.

An individual used to have the option to learn one exchange and do it until the end of their lives but there will be an absence of a lot of need for change or headway. That is not the circumstance any longer. In the present economy, most of people won't just maintain a few sources of income, yet many will likewise change occupations many times over their life expectancy, requiring a significant change in information and ranges of abilities. Indeed, even the people who work similarly situated for a really long time at a time discover that they should continually work on their abilities to stay aware of the requirements of the market. The requests organizations make of prepared work force differ alongside innovation. The utilization of Fast eLearning advancements and approaches is presently turning out to be increasingly better known in the corporate area because of this moving climate.

It's as of now not adequate to simply make corporate learning accessible in the high-speed universe of today. To fulfill the needs of workers' hands on learning, it should be given quickly. Quick e-learning can assist in circumstances with preferring that.

Rapid e-learning, as the name recommends, includes the making of e-learning materials quick. Be that as it may, top notch doesn't need to be forfeited for facilitated producing. To keep the interest of time-squeezed workers, e-discovering that is made rapidly ought to by the by be convincing. There are a few prescribed procedures for supporting fast turn of events, such, to specify a couple, taking on a creating device with no expectation to learn and adapt and having well-informed authorities produce their own informative materials (Acheson, 2008).

E-learning research is turning out to be more well-known because of the speedy development of e-learning. The quality confirmation of e-learning has drawn the most consideration among all the review issues. A delivered eLearning course's issues and missteps are consistently found through a method called quality assurance. QA might be characterized as an eLearning organization's affirmation to its clients that they will be totally happy with their acquisition of labor and products. The objective of eLearning quality confirmation is to expand the proficiency, adequacy, and efficiency of your web-based course. Notwithstanding, on the grounds that it is difficult to recall each and every quality check, the most common way of eLearning quality confirmation is somewhat troublesome. Accordingly, intensive investigation and suitable testing are fundamental to guaranteeing the exhibition of different parts and conveying an eLearning course that is both fulfilling and alluring. In this way, a progression of purposeful evaluations is utilized to ensure the nature of courses, and e-learning ought to be the same.

BACKGROUND

The Historical Backdrop Of E-Learning

The expression "e-learning" has possibly been in presence beginning around 1999 when the word was first used at a CBT frameworks class. Different words likewise started to jump up looking for an exact depiction, for example, "internet learning" and "virtual learning". Nonetheless, the standards behind e-learning have been legitimate since forever ago, and there is even proof which proposes that early types of e-learning existed as far back as the nineteenth hundred years (Cross, 2004).

A Timeline of Historical E-Learning

A long time before the web was shipped off, distance courses were being proposed to give students tutoring on unambiguous subjects or capacities. In the 1840′s Isaac Pitman showed his students shorthand through correspondence. This sort of meaningful forming was expected to additionally foster creating speed and was notable among secretaries, writers, and other people who did a huge parcel taking or making. Pitman, who was a guaranteed instructor, was sent completed jobs by means of mail and he would then send his students more work to be finished using a comparable structure.

In 1924, the essential testing machine was envisioned. This contraption allowed students to test themselves. Then, in 1954, BF Skinner, a Harvard Educator, planned the "showing machine", which engaged schools to manage tweaked direction to their students. It wasn't long after 1960 at any rate that the primary PC based planning program was familiar with the world. This PC based planning program (or CBT program) was known as PLATO-Tweaked Reasoning for Automated Instructing Exercises. It was at first planned for students going to the School of Illinois, yet ended up being used in schools generally through the area.

The essential web learning systems were genuinely basically set up to pass information on to students anyway as we entered the 70s eLearning started to end up being wiser. In Britain, the Open School rushed to take advantage of e-learning. Their plan of guidance has everlastingly been fundamentally revolved around learning a decent way off. Already, course materials were passed by post and correspondence with guides was on through mail. With the web, the Open School began to offer a greater extent of instinctive educational experiences as well as faster correspondence with students through email, etc.

Advancement in Todays eLearning

With the presentation of the PC and web in the late twentieth hundred years, e-learning apparatuses and conveyance techniques extended. The primary Macintosh in the 1980′s empowered people to have PCs in their homes, making it simpler for them to find out about specific subjects and foster specific ranges of abilities. Then, at that point, in the next 10 years, virtual learning conditions started to genuinely flourish, with individuals accessing an abundance of online data and e-learning open doors.

By the mid-90s, a few schools had been set up that conveyed course online just, capitalizing on the web and carrying training to individuals who wouldn't beforehand have had the option to go to a school due to geological or time limitations. Innovative headways likewise assisted instructive foundations with decreasing the expenses of distance learning, a saving that would likewise be given to the understudies - carrying training to a more extensive crowd.

In the 2000's, organizations started utilizing e-learning out how to prepare their representatives. New and experienced laborers the same presently had the chance to refine their industry information base and grow their ranges of abilities. At home, people were allowed admittance to programs that offered them the capacity to acquire online degrees and enhance their lives through extended information.

How Does E-Learning Work? Does Education Consider It Important?

Up until the mid-2000s, schooling occurred in a study hall with an educator responsible for the cycle. This is as yet the situation with regards to web-based learning in the instructive setting. Whatever else was, best case scenario, theoretical, and actual presence was an easy decision. At the point when the web showed up, all the other things followed. E-learning is a rapidly creating industry, the effects of which we can follow back to the 1980s and, shockingly, quite a while before that (as distance learning and broadcast courses) - these will be discussed later in this computerized boo.

Now that sensible e-learning game plans exist for the two laptops and web, it simply takes a respectable e-getting the hang of creating devices for guidance to be worked with from fundamentally wherever. Development has advanced such a ton of that the geological opening is spread over with the use of instruments that make you feel like you are inside the homeroom. E-learning offers the ability to share material in many associations like accounts, slideshows, word reports, and PDFs. Coordinating web-based courses (live online classes) and talking with educators through visit and message conversations is moreover a decision open to clients.

There is a lot of different e-learning systems (likewise called Learning The board Structures, or LMSs for short) and techniques, which believe courses to be conveyed. With the right gadget, various cycles can be electronic like a course with set materials and normally look at tests. E-learning is a sensible (and much of the time free) game plan which outfits the understudies with the ability to fit progressing around their lifestyles, effectively allowing even the most dynamic person to extra a livelihood and gain new capacities. Unquestionably the main progressions in tutoring have happened since the farewell of the web. These days understudies are proficient in the usage of mobile phones, message illuminating and using the web so participating in and running a web-based course has transformed into a clear illegal relationship. Message sheets, electronic diversion and different technique for online correspondence grant understudies to keep in touch and look at course-related matters, while obliging a sensation of neighborhood. In the fast universe of e-learning, the open advances to make a course up 'til now unfathomable are persistently changing, and course fulfilled can and should be revived quickly to give students the very latest information. This is especially huge if the e-getting planning is being given to laborer's in a space were keeping awake with the most recent on industry upgrades is totally crucial. This is one motivation behind why various associations are by and by offering planning through e-learning - various reasons consolidate low costs and the limit with respect to laborers to focus on intentionally and place. For the most part, customary learning is exorbitant, consumes a huge piece of the day and the results can change. The meaning of e-learning is as of now a given truth and it can offer an elective that is a ton speedier, more affordable and perhaps better.

Learning vs. Training: What Is the Distinction?

Understanding the distinction among learning and training is significant. Obviously, they are inseparably connected, yet they are exceptional parts of any instructive cycle. Training is the giving of data and information, through discourse, the composed word or different techniques for exhibit in a way that educates the learner. Learning is the most common way of retaining that data to expand abilities and capacities and utilize it under various settings.

Anything that the objectives, the nature of the learning will depend to a great extent on the nature of the training, thus the job of trainer is vital as it can massively affect the result of a course for the student.

In order to understand what makes an e-learning environment effective, let's examine each of these features.

1. **The Characteristics of learning:** As referenced above, learning is the most common way of engrossing data and holding it determined to expand abilities and capacities to accomplish objectives - yet it's more than that. Realizing is what we go through when we need to be prepared for vague and startling circumstances and the two are not fundamentally unrelated. While you truly do figure out how to accomplish something explicit, you are additionally accidentally furnished with the information as well as abilities to confront future difficulties. Fundamentally, learning is tied in with preparing an individual to handle the present issues, yet setting him up/her to imaginatively concoct ways of handling the upcoming issues.
2. **The Characteristics of Training:** On the other hand, training places more of an emphasis on the creation of new talents or skill sets that will be employed. When a new employee joins a firm, they go through training to learn how to carry out daily tasks, understand how their department functions, and understand how job-specific equipment work in order to fulfil their obligations.

> In essence, training is not intended to change an individual's behavior; rather, it aims to instruct an employee or student on how to do a task so they can do it independently.

In a perfect world, an e-learning environment will use both learning and preparing standards all through its educational program. This permits educators/mentors to furnish their students with the instruments to handle recent concerns, foster long lasting abilities, enhance their critical thinking abilities and use assets overall quite well.

ISSUES AND CHALLENGES IN E-LEARNING

Problems With Technology

The e-learning brings critical difficulties up in the innovative exploration region. For improvement of e-learning assets that meet the client's prerequisite should be tended to. The innovative difficulties of e-learning can be considered as two key innovative exploration regions.

Improvement of New Forms of Learning People Group and Interactive Learning

In e-learning conditions association, participation and local area assume a significant part to help learning. The improvements in the space of e-learning conditions give new types of connection for growth opportunity. It produces new connections among student and PC and furthermore structure another learning local area. Main points of interest include:

- New types of multimodal point of interaction to help learning.
- New strategies to comprehend and uphold learning networks.
- The advancement of frameworks to help versatile networks of students.
- Personalization methods that meet client individual requirements and current action.
- Procedures to advance and support cooperation.
- Revelation of new learning networks.
- Support for time-to-time evaluation administrations.

Growing New Knowledge Facilities for e-Learning

e-learning climate needs to help the fast expansion in the size and assortment of information by fitting semantic administrations. The semantic administrations produce an encompassing semantic setting for learning support. Research that requirements to deal with:

- Advancement of learning and thinking hypotheses for unsure and inadequate information.
- Support for the advancement of enormous scope learning offices.
- Support for a powerful educational experience.
- Support for data sharing across various learning offices.
- Improvements of lightweight information catch procedure for advancement of deep-rooted learning.
- Improvement of learning support administrations according to the necessity of various areas and clients.

Challenges In E-Learning Research

Flow e-learning research unites instructive, specialized and hierarchical worries inside a more extensive arrangement of socio-social elements. These elements impact the exploration plan in e-learning framework. Understanding these more extensive social and social issues is critical to the research networks associated with e-learning and will have a critical job in illuminating future practices. In counseling the INDIA research local area, various examination issues arisen:

Interdisciplinary, and the idea of various voices, is a characterizing normal for the area. How do different exploration points of view impact the general region? How do issues in the act of various disciplines contrast in the reception and utilization of learning innovations?

Access and consideration, incorporates issues around the broadening investment plan. What are the hindrances to incorporation and what are the issues encompassing the degree of the computerized partition?

Change, and its relationship to learning advancements. How does change affect upon inspirational issues? What are the drivers and reasonings for change? What are proper procedures for overseeing changes and systems for their execution?

Assembly and interoperability, regarding investigation of various types of intermingling (authoritative, innovative, instructive, sectoral, institutional, and so on). How well do they grasp issues of globalization and adaptability norms to help interoperability? These are intricate connections. An ongoing spotlight is likewise on normalization across the instructive, specialized, authoritative and human perspectives versus study of union.

Intelligence and social collaboration: How do the intuitiveness of various apparatuses connect with, or influence upon, the nature of the medium? How is intuitiveness communicated at various degrees of associations, and how have authoritative limits and practical groupings obscured as a result of new innovations? What potential do the new innovations need to improve correspondence and cooperation and furthermore making new networks and organizations?

Issues in Rapid eLearning

In the present high-speed world, it's as of now insufficient just to make corporate learning accessible. It should be created rapidly to stay aware of representatives' advancing requirements at work. That is where fast e-learning can make distinction.

As its name suggests, rapid e-learning is the method involved with creating e-learning content rapidly. However, fast creation doesn't need to come to the detriment of value. As a matter of fact, quickly created e-learning ought to in any case be connecting with to hold the focusing ability occupied workers. There are a few prescribed procedures for working with quick turn of events, such as utilizing a composing instrument with zero expectation to learn and adapt and having educated authorities make learning content themselves, to give some examples.

We'll investigate the issues and difficulties looked by rapid eLearning:

- Quick Circle back Compromises Quality

Quick improvement is typically inseparable from an eliminated and-glue position. You're working rapidly, which leaves more space for human blunder. In any case, the right fast eLearning apparatus highlights resources, for example, video clasps, pictures, and illustrations you can integrate into your web-based preparing exercises, that advance your eLearning preparing content as opposed to lessening quality. The condition is that you should explain the internet preparing goals and make a reasonable improvement course of events. Like that, you stay on time without depending on easy routes. There must likewise be an in-house master or SME available for QA.

- Absence Of Content Variety:

Each web-based course appears to be identical and has similar exercises. The main thing different is the substance that you plug into the placeholders. This disadvantage is the aftereffect of asset misallocation. The fast-writing apparatus has resources you can use to make different substance that takes care of everybody's work prerequisites and ability holes, as well as their own inclinations. Utilize worked in assets in various ways to extend your spending plan and further develop web-based preparing adaptability. For instance, one video recording contains 5 clasps you can reuse for different internet instructional classes. The altering apparatus permits you to split it up and add illustrations. Despite the fact that it could require some "out-of-the-container" thinking, the rapid eLearning programming transforms obsolete assets into assorted web-based preparing content.

- Discreet Real-World Applications:

Numerous associations expect that rapid eLearning is saved for hypothetical information. For example, fostering a consistence course loaded with rules and guidelines. The eLearning writing programming makes upkeep a breeze, so it's expected for subjects that require regular updates or changes. In any case, fast creating apparatuses can work with genuine application, particularly those that highlight reproduction and situation formats.

- Working on a challenging subject is a challenge:

For rapid eLearning creation, some themes or tasks are not appropriate. They entail challenging ideas or concepts that can necessitate extensive financial outlay and full-length eLearning courses. You must thus use the resources at your disposal to figure out how to make it simple to understand for online learners. Chopping up larger eLearning content into more manageable eLearning modules is one of the most efficient methods to do this. Organize the subject content, for instance, into distinct eLearning modules and activities that each cover a particular activity or ability.

- Utilizing Fewer Resources:

Many people who work in the field of eLearning encounter this conundrum. However, it's extremely harder for rapid eLearning developers that are working with a limited eLearning budget. It's possible that you don't have the resources or the tools required to make an excellent eLearning course.

- Repetitions Result from Rapid eLearning Development:

Rapid eLearning programmes have, at some point, come to be equated with boring eLearning templates. Fast turnaround times are frequently associated with uninteresting eLearning materials that do not motivate and engage students.

AUTHORING TOOLS

What Is an Authoring Tool?

A piece of software called an authoring tool allows you to create digital learning content. This could be as basic as generating a paper in Microsoft Word or as sophisticated as using a graphic design programme. The user of eLearning authoring software can create and manipulate multimedia assets for the content's intended purpose. Authoring tools are used to generate digital learning content, or 'eLearning,' in the learning and development field. Instructional designers in L&D teams typically utilize eLearning authoring tools to develop training materials for their staff. Compliance, onboarding, hard and soft skills, and other topics may be covered during this training. eLearning authoring software might be quite complex and specialized, or it can be very basic. After this post pandemic eLearning plays a vital role in the educational industry. Many web applications are developed like byju's learning, unacademy learner app, vedantu live learning app, etc., which have been introduced in online platforms for students.

There are no two content writing tools that are the same. There are a range of programme alternatives created by various software businesses that cater to various eLearning demands. Some programmes are designed for non-specialists who need to develop eLearning quickly and want to use pre-made templates for simple content, interactions, and quizzes, while others are designed for specialists who want to create highly customized content, such as adaptive learning experiences, simulations, or custom gamification. Regardless of the features and capabilities provided, authoring tools all serve the same purpose: they generate eLearning courses for end users through content creation, content management, and content standards.

Course creation software is available in a variety of sizes and forms. Before you get started, it's critical to know what kind of learning software you'll need. Several learning management systems (LMS – software for distributing digital learning content) provide writing tools as standard. These are frequently quite simple, limiting writers who are just starting out in the field of design. 'Standalone' course writing software, on the other hand, is designed specifically for the creation of digital learning, offering instructional designers additional flexibility in creating high-quality, personalized material (Haghshenas, Khademi, and Kabir, 2012).

SCORM

You may hear individuals talk about 'SCORM versions' or ensuring that a course is 'SCORM compliant' when you go into eLearning. But, in practice, what does this imply? What exactly is the SCORM?

SCORM is an acronym for Shareable Content Object Reference Model. It's a method of creating an eLearning course that can be accessed from any learning management system (LMS) (as long as the LMS is SCORM-compliant, of course). SCORM establishes the common set-up that allows eLearning to be read by any LMS, similar to how DVDs are constructed in a standardized manner so they can be read by any DVD player (Jones, 2022).

SCORM is in charge of two things: content packaging and run-time.

1. Material packaging specifies how a piece of content should be delivered physically. SCORM defines how learning content should be organized within a file so that it may be launched, interpreted, and monitored correctly.
2. How the learning object "talks" to the LMS is defined by the run-time communication or data exchange. This is how instructions between the learning material and the module are conveyed, such as "request the learner's name" and "inform the LMS that the learner scored 85 percent on this exam."

SCORM specifies how eLearning content should be packed into a "Package Interchange File," which is a transferable ZIP file. This is referred to as a SCORM file. It's this file that needs to be set up in accordance with SCORM standards, including the core files that allow it to interface with the LMS properly. There are so many different types of authoring tools and LMS platforms, without a standard, authoring tools and platforms would be unable to communicate with one another. Content standards such as SCORM help to enable seamless integration.

Need and Criteria for Evaluating Best Authoring Tool

The following are the top five reasons to utilize an authoring tool:

1. Allows you to tailor your information and learn in a more people-centered way;
2. Allows you to work successfully with your team, allowing writers, SMEs, and stakeholders to cooperate in a fluid manner;
3. Makes it simple to deploy eLearning courses in several places and rapidly and easily change material to meet with new laws;
4. Enables you to continuously enhance your eLearning by evaluating statistics and collecting feedback on how well your material works;
5. Allows you to easily adjust to new demands and create eLearning material to support them.

What factors do you consider when selecting a writing tool for your personal training or organizational needs? It is critical to comprehend the demands and requirements of your unique training project in order to make the best option. Most writing tools have their own distinct set of features and capabilities that cater to various training requirements. In order to discover what features and capabilities you might require, ask questions about your project, such as:

- At what degree of competence will you be working with the software?
- What type of e-learning programme do you wish to develop?

With a better understanding of the proposed e-learning project, the characteristics and capabilities of software may be examined to ensure that the appropriate tool is selected.

The following are the criteria for evaluating best authoring tool:

1. The output of an eLearning programme should be of high quality.
    - Customizability level
    - The ability to pick from a variety of forms
    - Instructions for design are already included in the product.
    - Possibilities for branching out
2. Rapidity and efficacy:
    - How fast can you create high-quality eLearning?
    - Productivity-enhancing features
    - Options for collaboration to speed up the feedback process
    - Ease of collaborating with numerous authors on a project at the same time
    - Experience level necessary for an author to successfully use the platform
3. Scalability:
    - What is the ease of reusing, editing, and scaling your eLearning content?
    - Producing eLearning material at scale at a low cost
    - The ability to import and export
    - Choices for translation

History of Authoring Tools

In the early 1960s, the first computer-based instruction was written using general-purpose programming languages (e.g., FORTRAN, BASIC, Assembly). The first author languages, such as IBM's Course writer and the PLATO system's Tutor, arose in the middle of the 1960s. New author languages arose alongside the advent of new CBI systems. More commands were introduced to the author languages as the systems' hardware capabilities (e.g., color, sound, touch, graphics, typefaces, etc.) grew (Khademi, Haghshenas, and Kabir, 2011).

There were other attempts to create "generic" authoring languages that could run on a variety of machines and so improve courseware portability. PILOT, PLANIT, and NATAL are some examples of generic author languages. Despite a number of valiant initiatives, generic author languages have not resulted in considerable courseware exchange across multiple systems.

Following author languages, the creation of the first authoring system, APT for the TICCIT system, was the next important advance in authoring tools. In many ways, APT and TICCIT were significant milestones. It was the first CBI system built entirely on instructional concepts and research. It also implemented learner control in the system's software and hardware. It established a pedagogical framework to which the author had to adhere, as did all succeeding writing systems. The delivery ecosystem has evolved substantially, even though the nature of authoring tools hasn't. There were no cellphones or tablets ten years ago. We just had to deal about PCs and laptops, which are effectively the same devices when it comes to playing back eLearning content.

Table 1. Present best e-learning authoring tools

eLearning Software	Type of Solution	Quality of Output	Speed and Efficiency	Scalability
1.Elucidat	eLearning authoring platform	High	Fast	High
2. Adobe Captivate	Standalone authoring tool	High	Slow	Low
3. Articulate Storyline	Authoring suite	Medium	Slow	Low
4. Articulate Rise	Online authoring tool	Low	Fast	Medium
5. Gomo	Online authoring tool	Medium	Fast	High
6. Lectora	Standalone authoring tool	Medium	Slow	Medium
7. Adapt	Online authoring tool	Low	Fast	Medium
8. DominKnow	Online authoring tool	High	Average	Medium
9. Easygenerator	Online authoring tool	Low	Fast	Low
10. iSpring Suite	Authoring suite	Medium	Average	Medium
11. Evolve	Online authoring tool	Medium	Fast	Medium
12. Camtasia	Video authoring software	Medium	Medium	Low

(Source: The Best eLearning Authoring Tools, Platforms & Software January 21, 2022 by Steve Penfold)

Our server-based design was never envisioned utilizing a browser ten years ago. It would have been a disaster in terms of usability if it hadn't been for the. Today, creating attractive and highly functioning drag-and-drop user interfaces in a browser without the need of plug-ins is pretty simple. Online publishing has become both cost-effective and pleasant because to cloud computing, cheaper storage costs, and increasing bandwidth. So, are stand-alone eLearning programmes no longer viable? The answer is no, based on today's most popular eLearning technologies. But, in 10 years, will I have to eat my words once more?

I'm going to predict that they'll be dead this time. While there are still some desktop products that will last a few more years, you can guarantee that the manufacturers that offer them are pouring their resources into the development of server-based, responsive eLearning solutions. It will be fascinating to observe who—or what—comes out on top in the history of writing tools (Quah and Ng, 2022).

Cloud-Based Authoring Tools

Content authoring tools are no exception to the rule of rapid technological evolution. New and upgraded writing tools are coming to market with a variety of features and capability for every need, in order to stay up with new types of learning, such as mobile or app-based learning. eLearning authoring tools can be cloud-based or desktop-based, with the latter becoming more prevalent. Cloud-based authoring tools enable for smooth, synchronous collaboration with other developers or stakeholders while providing the same fundamental features and capabilities as the desktop version (Masud and Huang, 2012).

Benefits of cloud-based authoring tool over desktop authoring tools:

- There is no need to download or set up anything. Log in from anywhere, on almost any device, and get started.
- Without you having to do anything, new features and releases are automatically rolled out.
- Multiple contributors can work on the same project at the same time, with all of their modifications preserved, reducing project schedules and eliminating long handovers.
- Images, movies, and other resources can be uploaded once and then saved in the tool's asset library for all authors to use. You can replace photos in bulk with one click using Elucidat's expanded asset library.
- Reviewers with 'review only' access can log into the tool and review the course as if they were a learner.
- Everyone is working towards one version of the truth. The capacity to track and store different versions of a project during the development process.

With so many possibilities, determining your goals and priorities is the first step toward making an informed decision between desktop and cloud-based authoring tools. It's a lot easier to test different tools against your criteria when you know exactly what you're searching for.

QUALITY ASSURANCE IN RAPID ELEARNING DEVELOPMENT

One of the major worries of L&D executives is quality assurance in the production of quick eLearning! Totally in agreement? Now let's examine how outstanding standard and efficient fast eLearning work hand in side.

The word "quality assurance" might have implications that emphasize the idea of responsibility at the cost of quality as progress, making it a contentious concept. In actuality, quality as accountability contributes nothing to learning in higher education since it cannot aid in the development of a process-related understanding, which is important to comprehend how to enhance processes (Boehle, 2005).

It is important to think about a few key questions in order to comprehend the model in ways that place it in the context of managing quality assurance for eLearning:

- What crucial elements or steps in the process (the design and delivery of the course) are being examined?
- What mechanisms are put in place to enable universities to regularly assess and enhance the way they incorporate eLearning into what was formerly a face-to-face experience?

Figure 1. A condensed quality feedback loop to comprehend quality standards and systems

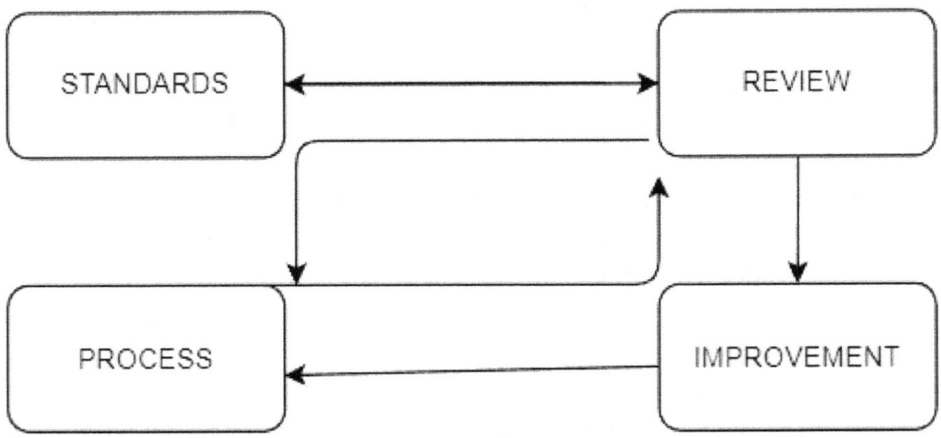

- What are some of the tactics utilized to keep the process cohesive so that eLearning is continuously reviewed in the course creation and teaching?

It is well known that creating top-notch eLearning courses may require a lot of time and work. Errors are more likely to go unnoticed when several teams are working together. This is possibly the cause of L&D executives' assumption that quality would be sacrificed in the hasty production of eLearning, a solution for an efficient and speedy implementation of eLearning. However, strong quality checks and testing are necessary to guarantee the quality of quick eLearning, or any eLearning development technique for that matter. Because even the slightest flaw in the functionality, design, or content can have an adverse effect on the business. As a result, a perfect course is essential to guaranteeing consistency (which keeps learners' attention) and a seamless learning experience. How are your rapid eLearning courses quality assured, though?

Here are 5 techniques for evaluating the quality of fast eLearning courses.

1. Business Style Guide:

The main resource that will assist the development team (whether internal or external to an eLearning provider) in ensuring consistency and uniformity in the courses developed by various individuals at various periods is your corporate style guide. They outlined the requirements for the design of the created eLearning courses. Delivering polished and professional eLearning courses will be very challenging without a style guide. Because separate teams would take their own approaches, it's also likely that courses in a curriculum may wind up appearing radically different. The following common and recognized principles for digital learning are laid out in style guidelines, which is why they are crucial for quality assurance:

- draughts of templates
- writing format (including tone, sentence structuring)
- spelling, such as in American or British English
- using symbols, lists, numbers, typefaces, etc.
- Word choice (capitalization, commas, etc.)
- Graphic design components and anything else you want the development team to follow.

Shortly put, a style guide acts as a point of reference for the team developing your fast eLearning courses.

2. Checklists:

"We sincerely apologize if the finished product had any mistakes."

"We meticulously examined the courses, yet we somehow overlooked certain components."

Do these justifications from your quick eLearning development team truly make you dread hearing them? Maybe the group didn't create quality checklists after all. Checklists are essential if you want to offer speedy eLearning courses without any errors at all! Instructional designers, visual designers, developers, and other teams who are engaged in the design and development of eLearning might all have their own checklists. These checklists provide a comprehensive picture of what each team has to double-check before delivering the completed quick eLearning course. Checklists are designed to make sure each successive stage in quick eLearning production is immaculate, from the welcome and summary slides through SCORM Cloud testing.

3. Design and Development in Agile

Are you still using the ADDIE paradigm for design and development at your company (or your eLearning provider)? If so, I do not need to describe the scope of modifications that could be required towards the conclusion of the development cycle. Quality assurance is put on hold when high-level feedback implementation approaches the project's conclusion in favor of getting it done. Additionally, you will have to spend more money and put in more time and effort as a result.

By using a more agile design and development method, you may, however, avoid all the last-minute craziness (including extra expense, time, and efforts) and achieve excellent quick eLearning courses. Compared to the traditional ADDIE model, the Agile approach or SAM (Successive Approximation Method) displays a higher level of openness. After each milestone, the eLearning team presents an iteration of a project for review, allowing the team and stakeholders to identify problems and fix them before moving forward. Therefore, you can be confident that the finished product will be faultless and high-impact, just as you had hoped.

4. Online Evaluation Tools

Reviewing storyboards in the eLearning industry used to entail recording feedback and comments in Word documents, PowerPoint presentations, and even Excel sheets.

Numerous issues with this traditional procedure frequently have a detrimental effect on the calibre of e-learning courses.

Consider this:

- maintaining a record of many feedback papers from various SMEs
- Making sense of conflicting comments from several reviewers
- ignoring small suggestions while addressing significant ones

and other factors that can have an impact on the calibre of the courses.

The use of online review tools and applications, such as ReviewLink, Review360, and ReviewMyElearning, aids in the resolution of all these problems. As a result of the online tools, the development team is better able to concentrate on quality assurance.

- version control and contextual feedback
- The reviewed courses are accessible online
- centralized coherence of feedback

In addition to receiving courses of the highest calibre, you also significantly reduce your overall time commitment.

5. SCORM Cloud testing

Technology compliance is as crucial to ensure the quality of quick eLearning courses as design and development. After all, what use are high-quality courses if you're Learning Management System (LMS) can't track student progress via them?

Therefore, testing your courses on SCORM Cloud prior to the official launch is crucial. This aids in assessing how well your courses will operate on your LMS or learning platforms and comply to eLearning technical standards like SCORM, xAPI, or cmi5 (Jones, 2022).

To put it simply, SCORM Cloud enables you to:

- Test your eLearning course's compatibility with your LMS.
- Get detailed analytics and reports
    - Bookmarking
    - Score: the outcomes of the evaluation.
    - Status of the course: passed/failed, begun/yet to begin, finished/in-progress
    - student attempts

Overall, a test run will guarantee that your quick eLearning courses are high-quality and error-free in terms of technology.

Overall, efficient quality assurance procedures result in reduced rework and speedier finalization in rapid eLearning development. In addition, improving the learning experience rather than correcting mistakes is the main goal. The lack of a strong quality assurance procedure is most important since it is equivalent to intentionally endangering learners' interest and attention, and (at worst) turning them off.

EVALUATION APPROACH

Any e-Learning course or programme that emphasizes ongoing improvement must have evaluation as its central component. So basically, what is evaluation and why it's necessary is the most common questions asked several times. Different techniques to plan, organize, and carry out evaluation initiatives are known as evaluation methodologies. Some methods of evaluation improve on current techniques while others assist in problem solving. By evaluating e-Learning, we can better grasp its advantages and disadvantages, as well as its quality, effectiveness, and potential for improvement.

The majority of people think that evaluation happens after e-Learning is finished. Wrong! Evaluation takes place prior to the e-Learning (needs analysis), plan the e-Learning. Formative evaluations are conducted during online learning to identify areas for development, and summative evaluations are conducted afterward to assess results (Kapounová, 2007).

Why Do We Require New Evaluation Models and Procedures for Online Learning?

The improvement of e-learning items and the plan of e-learning potential entryways are two areas of guidance and setting up that are becoming the speediest. E-learning is propelling even more rapidly paying little regard to the state of affairs appropriated —through the web, media, instinctive television, or PC based planning. The absence of dependable logical assessment, notwithstanding, has restricted how we might interpret this state of the art preparing methods. Is internet learning effective? What conditions? For what kinds of understudies? How do different understudies respond? Do different ICT stages contrast fundamentally from each other? Does the sociocultural climate matter? Is there a beneficial profit from speculation while executing ICT-based preparing considering the expenses? What are individuals' perspectives about VET experts?

E-learning is one of the fields that gets the most noteworthy cash for Research and development. We should foster dependable e-learning assessment models and advances that are adaptable in utilization however produce reliable results if we have any desire to capitalize on this venture.

The stream research base for surveying e-learning is missing, regardless of the way that new focus has worked on its appraisal. Driving appraisal studies is basic in view of the extraordinary straightforward costs of making e-learning programs (The American Culture for Preparing and Improvement 2001).

One of the greatest supporters of state-of-the-art e-learning drives in European VET, the Leonardo da Vinci 1 program, was the subject of the Capitalization report, which additionally named the shortfall of orderly assessment as the principal shortcoming of e-learning drives. The reaction by a sizable piece of the local area of e-learning designers and professionals, notwithstanding, has been a developing distraction with programming and stages. While some have been frantically looking for replies to the inquiry "What works and what doesn't work?" and searching for ways of working on the nature of e-realizing, this reaction has been from some. Learning and instructional method definitely stand out. Upgrading the nature of e-learning and directing and affecting future approach and practice improvement can both be achieved with the production of models and techniques for assessing e-learning (Rughoobur-Seetah and Hosanoo, 2021).

What Does the Research On E-Learning Evaluation Tell Us?

Contextual Investigations of Specific E-Instructional Classes

These are fundamentally American, illustrative instead of logical or prescriptive, focused on the "virtual study hall" idea, and set essentially in advanced education settings rather than those for professional preparation. Furthermore, they habitually just cover a restricted scope of themes, including IT, dialects, and designing fields. (This isn't to contend that simply these fields benefit from e-learning; rather, it is to say that these fields are overrepresented in assessment reports.)

Relative Investigations With Conventional Training

There are a couple (however shockingly barely any) orderly investigations that are upheld by observational information and contrast the viability of e-learning and conventional learning. Those that truly do exist are commonly limited scale concentrates on that as often as possible utilize a coordinated. Planning two by two is broadly utilized in profoundly unambiguous circumstances of web-based realizing, where the e-learning approaches are specific and the outcomes can't be summed up.

Devices and Instruments for Assessment of E-Learning

There is an overflow of writing specifying devices for the assessment of e-learning. In any case, these are predominantly separated into two kinds. Right off the bat there are many on-line information gathering instruments for evaluating, normally, the UI qualities of programming (for example understudy discernment polls) or also, there are gadgets to record and examine utilization by term and recurrence of sign in, pages got to, client profile and so on. A significant number of these are modern in their plan and resourcefulness however need direction on understanding and examination.

Profit From Speculation (Return for Money Invested) Reports

There are shockingly couple of return on initial capital investment reports, taking into account the gigantic interests into e-advancing at all levels. Most of those that exist draw fundamentally from industry-based models furthermore, are composed according to a HRD point of view. The end is unavoidably that the venture was savvy and addressed esteem for money however frequently the reserve funds are characterized in proficiency as opposed to adequacy with no long-haul influence examination that assesses accidental results and outcomes. It is additionally challenging to think about figures across reports in light of the fact that the qualifications between net also, gross expenses, capital and income costs, uprooting of existing assets, costs over the long run and so on are frequently obscured or missing. Numerous returns for money invested type assessment reports seem, by all accounts, to be legitimizing venture instead of assessing it and more outfitted to a group of people of investors as opposed to specialists.

Comparison Models

There have been a few endeavors to produce sets of rules for quality guaranteeing e-learning. Notwithstanding, these will generally be slanted towards proposing quality norms for e-learning frameworks and programming which frequently dismiss key factors in the more extensive learning climate or depend on rules related with assessing conventional growing experiences (and which ignore the innovation) or rules related with estimating student accomplishment through customary instructional methods. An unexpected issue is that the planners of these benchmarking frameworks are frequently locked in to a specific model of e-realizing which limits their adaptability.

Item Assessment

By a wide margin the best number of 'hits' on assessment of e-learning are reports portraying (and lauding the temperance's of) specific instruction programming. By far most of these reports are dispatched or distributed by the product engineers. This isn't to scrutinize the handiness of these reports or essentially to question their legitimacy yet assessment of 'decontextualized' programming is definitely not an OK substitute for the thorough assessment of eLearning frameworks.

Execution Assessment

Scriven's (2000) in the USA, utilizes the term execution assessment' for what might, in European terms, be called understudy appraisal. While the facts really confirm that an assessment of understudy execution is a strong sign of the viability of e-learning, it is in no way, shape or form the only one. Besides, a study of reports on execution assessment with regards to e-learning were mostly worried about on-line devices and instruments for analyzing information-based student execution and could subsequently be sorted under that heading. Handbooks for the assessment of e-learning There is a rising number of handbooks for e-realizing which center basically around assessment. The assessment techniques and apparatuses vary generally. What they truly do share practically speaking is that they perceive the significance of assessment what's more, many recommend that assessment ought to be a necessary piece of any e-learning drives or improvement. In such manner, they incline toward the board model of assessment; the essential point of the assessment is to give criticism to impact e-learning execution and future turn of events.

Handbooks for the Assessment of E-Learning

There is a rising number of handbooks for e-realizing which center fundamentally around assessment. The assessment techniques and devices vary generally. What they truly do share for all intents and that's what purpose is they perceive the significance of assessment also; many suggest that assessment ought to be a necessary piece of any e-learning drives or improvement. In such manner, they incline toward the executive's model of assessment; the essential point of the assessment is to give criticism to impact e-learning execution and future turn of events. A large number of the handbooks seem to have been created by schooling counsels and warning 11 administrations and offices. They are as often as possible very fundamental and come up short on hypothetical methodology. An amazing number refer to The Assessment Cookbook also, seem to have acquired large numbers of their thoughts from this powerful distribution. More stressing is the innovation focused approach that large numbers of the aides uphold.

Issues and Holes

To start with, the positive things which have arisen structure the writing survey. There have all the earmarks of being a developing acknowledgment of the significance of assessment. This appears to be connected to worries that e-learning is not prevailing in the manner that had been normal. Assessment is expected to acquire a superior comprehension of the issues and issues with respect to learning. There is likewise a rising spotlight on assessment procedures and an acknowledgment that the assessment of e-learning is complicated and requires the improvement of new models and approaches.

Assessment and Evaluation

Anyway, there remains disarray between assessment and evaluation. Somewhat this can be made sense of by various understandings of assessment in various nations and by the phonetic disarrays between the two processes. Notwithstanding, I think it goes further than this. There gives off an impression of being an over dependence on appraisal or accomplishment as the premise for assessment. Saying this doesn't imply that that student accomplishment isn't an assessment factor. In any case the presumption that on the off chance that something has not been evaluated it has not been learnt is doubtlessly wrong. Besides, such a methodology misses casual endlessly learning excluded in the evaluations.

Program and Strategy Assessment

The second hole in the writing audit is program and strategy assessment. Each country and most huge organizations have dynamic arrangement driven projects to create e-learning. In any case, there are not many program level assessment reports, yet less models or on the other hand hypothetical methodologies for assessing eLearning strategy. This is both astounding and stressing. Without assessment, how would we know which strategy approaches are working what's more, which are not? I stay dubious that e-learning is simply seen by strategy producers as a 'beneficial thing' and that cash is being contributed with minimal comprehension of where or why

Models and Speculations of Assessment

Development of Assessment Hypothesis

Assessment as a conventional movement that we would perceive, has existed for a shockingly significant time-frame. Quite possibly of the earliest recorded was the assessment of the adequacy of lime-juice in forestalling scurvy in mariners - authorized by the English naval force in the eighteenth 100 years! The French make even prior guarantee and say that the Norman armed forces directed an assessment of the general viability of the crossbow and the longbow. Tragically, the government decided to use the crossbow based on the findings of the assessment, and the rest is, as they say, history! Nevertheless, since the 1960s, evaluation has only recently become a recognized field of scientific review. The claim that evaluation is probably clear was first made as a training field, and the hypothesis was derived from it. As it progressed, disagreements over definitions, wording, morals, etc. brought about philosophical concerns in close proximity.

Why would that be an issue? For what reason should specialists require a hypothetical structure? A "good" hypothesis will essentially state the assumptions it is basing its reasoning on as well as the assumptions it is making. Various hypotheses make unique presumption and create models that will be founded on various pre-originations and meanings of assessment, which thus lead to altogether different practices.

Models and Devices for Assessment of e-Learning in Higher Professional Training

The student benchmarking instrument created for the assessment of e-learning in higher professional training is a shopper device in request to assess the utilization of Virtual Learning Conditions (VLE). It depends on an on-line survey remembering things for the examination of the VLE involved by the educators in their courses. The Student Assessment instrument is centered around the direction or platform educators give inside the VLE and depends on constructivist standards.

The SPEAK Model and Device

SPEAK is a model and device for the self-assessment of learning in a gathering and local area setting. Working with group is planned both conversation and self-assessment and to give aggregate information for program assessment. The SPEAK framework has been intended to consolidate various between related capabilities inside a sensible structure (Attwell, 2006).

- Vital Preparation: creating data to help both staff and the executives to make informed choices.
- Assessment: progressing inward survey; cross project occasional evaluations; with an office for outer data sources.
- Information: organizing in view of sharing data between establishments, nations,districts and subjects.

The SPEAK model has been created as an electronic instrument conveyed by a Compact disc ROM. Information can be accumulated and inquiries through a server application.

Figure 2. Schematic of the SPAK evaluation framework

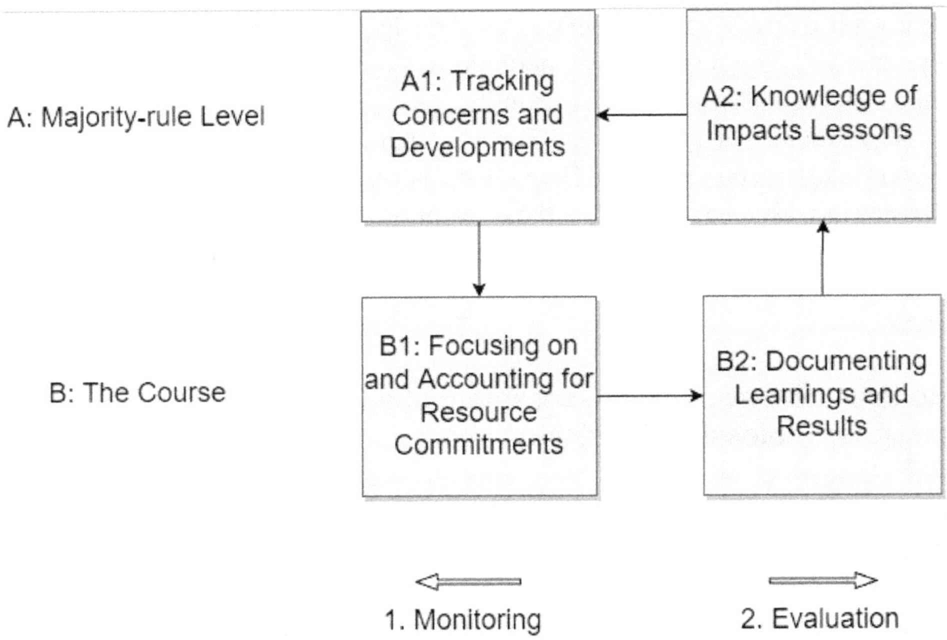

PDPP Model

This paradigm includes planning, development, process evaluation, and product evaluation in its four-phase approach to e-learning course assessment. This evaluation technique is used to improve both the quality assurance and the eLearning resources (Zhang and Cheng, 2012).

During the planning phase, it is important to take into account the market demand, viability, target student demographic, course objectives, and budgetary considerations. When assessing development, it's important to take into account the following: flexibility, student-student interaction, teacher/tutor assistance, technical support, and assessment. The process evaluation includes technical support, Web site usage, learning engagement, learning assessment, learning support, and flexibility. When reviewing a product, it is important to take into account elements like student satisfaction, teaching effectiveness, learning effectiveness, and product sustainability. There are 26 components in the e-learning evaluation model (see Figure 2). Figure 2 demonstrates how a feasibility and market demand study come first in the planning evaluation of e-learning courses. Market demands describe the knowledge and skill requirements for target student groups' future jobs. Employer viewpoints on the fundamental requirements of their employees must also be taken into account if the courses are relevant to the workplace. If a course is going to be exported to another nation, it is important to research the import laws, regulations, and levels

Figure 3. The PDPP e-learning course evaluation model
(Source: Zhang, W., & Cheng, Y. L. (2012). Quality assurance in e-learning: PDPP evaluation model and its application. International Review of Research in Open and Distributed Learning, 13(3), 66-82)

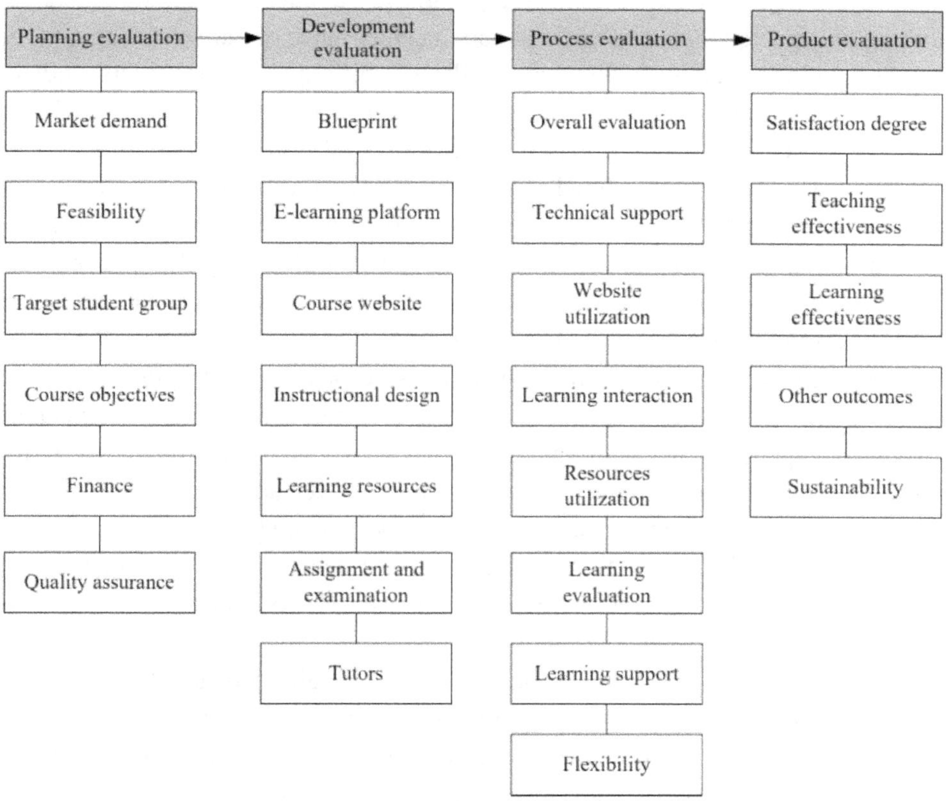

of technical assistance there. The target student population, the course objective, the financial situation, and the quality control mechanism must all be studied after that. Age range, educational attainment, employment history, hours worked, study time availability, learning motives, and job requirements are all considered in the analysis of the target student groups. Analyzing the partner institution's quality assurance system is necessary if the exported course is to be released in conjunction with local educational institutions.

E-learning course development evaluation entails dissecting each element of the course development process, including the course outline, e-learning platform, course website, instructional design, learning resources, assignments and exams, and tutors.

The degree of student happiness, the effectiveness of the instruction and learning, and any additional outcomes that might be achieved are all measured in the product evaluation. The outcomes of the aforementioned analyses will ultimately determine the viability of courses.

FUTURE IMPROVEMENTS IN DIGITAL LEARNING RESOURCES

As innovation proceeds to develop and guzzle itself in our regular routine, today is nothing unexpected that, it likewise shapes a center piece of our schooling system. It is determined that by 2050, there will be 2 billion more upskillers/students worldwide, driving training to turn into a $7 trillion+ industry. Throughout the course of recent years, the schooling business saw an entirely different part in computerized advancing as the pandemic spread across the world, driving classes to move on the web. Simultaneously, it is clear that eventual fate of instruction is computerized. New advances in innovation, for example, AR and cloud-based learning offer understudies an opportunity to rapidly stay up with the latest with our steadily impacting world, as well as bring students across the world nearer.

E-learning is digging in for the long haul. As PC possession develops across the globe e-learning turns out to be progressively suitable and available. Web association speeds are expanding, and with that, open doors for more mixed media preparing strategies emerge. With the massive improvement of versatile organizations in the beyond couple of years and the expansion in working from home, taking every one of the wonderful highlights of e-learning out and about is a reality with cell phones and other convenient gadgets. Advances, for example, online entertainment are likewise changing training continually.

Learning is often costly, time-consuming, and results-dependent. Since many years ago, e-learning has been making an effort to enhance our learning process and make it more efficient and quantifiable. As a result, a variety of technologies are now available that may be used to develop interactive training programmes, standardize the learning process, and/or include informal components into otherwise formal learning processes. We can clearly see the future of e-learning and how learning tools will be developed by examining a number of e-learning trends:

The focus of **micro-learning** is on the creation of small-step micro-learning activities in digital media settings, which are already part of the everyday lives of knowledge workers in the present. A learner's daily routines might include several activities. Microlearning frequently leans toward push technology through push media, which lessens the cognitive burden on the learners, in contrast to "conventional" e-learning methodologies. Therefore, for didactic designs, it is crucial to consider the choice of micro-learning objects as well as the speed and timing of micro-learning activities. Since the learning process is integrated into the end-everyday user's activities, micro-learning represents a significant paradigm change that eliminates the need for separate learning sessions. Long courses may be overkill on mobile devices, where this is also ideally suited.

Gamification is the utilization of game reasoning and game mechanics in a non-game setting to draw in clients and tackle issues.

Personalized Learning is the fitting of teaching method, educational plan and learning conditions to address the issues and yearnings of individual students. Personalization is more extensive than just individualization or separation in that it bears the cost of the student a level of decision about what is realized, when it is advanced and the way things are learned. This may not demonstrate limitless decision since students will in any case have focuses to be met. Nonetheless, it might give students the chance to learn in manners that suit their singular learning styles and numerous insights.

The Far Future of Digital Learning: Automatic Learning

In a notable scene from the film The Matrix, Neo rests in a cutting-edge dental specialist's seat and lashes on a wild cluster of cathodes, downloading a progression of combative techniques preparing programs into his mind. Subsequently, he wakes up and expresses the words nerds have been citing from that point forward: "I know Kung Fu."

This sort of programmed learning could seem like a tragic future for some yet it is where we are going. Furthermore, in spite of the moral inquiries that might emerge, the advantages could be significant at numerous levels whenever utilized appropriately. This is the carefully guarded secret: you pick an errand that requires superior execution from your visual cortex like getting a ball. Then you go get somebody who's a master at getting a ball, place them in a fMRI machine and record what's happening in their mind while they envision getting a ball. Then, at that point, you have your ball-getting project, and you're prepared to learn. Following stage: put yourself into the fMRI machine, and apparatus it to actuate that supportive of ball-getting symbolism that you recorded before in your cerebrum utilizing neurofeedback. This doesn't even require your attention while it's happening. Your cerebrum, however, gets comfortable with that example - which basically learning is: the mind getting comfortable with new examples.

Research has shown that this fMRI design playback can cause enduring improvement in assignments that require visual execution. In principle, a kind of mechanized learning is a possible result and what e-learning in the far-off future might seem to be.

Moreover, other than the way that procuring computerized abilities coordinates intimately with an advanced type of learning since both are carefully disposed and can happen for all intents and purposes, the eventual fate of work will seemingly drive more advanced incorporation, as additional mechanization and further developed innovations will increment around advanced advances. This will make digital learning basic coming soon for work, as a greater amount of these abilities can undoubtedly be mastered carefully and on the web.

Additionally, the capacity to effectively reskill and update such abilities is one more basic calculate the eventual fate of work. We ought to doubtlessly anticipate more changes and progressions in different computerized abilities, including other modern upsets and developments to come. Nonetheless, the capacity to handily refresh such abilities, as habitually on a case-by-case basis, is another main consideration, and here, the Automatic learning will assume a major part. This dynamism braces one more key advantage of eLearning coming soon for work, as eLearning will assist no sweat and comfort to refresh and move new abilities quickly.

CONCLUSION

eLearning is a present and developing peculiarity in the realm of corporate preparation. It "is turning into a more unavoidable and trained practice as it battles with and takes care of issues normal to all e-Learning plan and conveyance exertion. The business world is developing more serious and more reliant upon innovation. Subsequently, powerful preparation is turning out to be significantly more critical to both enormous and independent companies. PC based learning arrangements, eLearning, is assuming a huge part in gathering that challenge. eLearning, both the apparatuses and the techniques, misses the mark concerning a considerable lot of the principles advanced inside the educational plan local area. It urges an engineer to easy route both the examination and configuration periods of the improvement cycle. Most eLearning courses miss the mark on profundity and quality that one would anticipate from an expertly grown course. By the by, eLearning is a developing reality in the corporate world. A few significant gatherings are held every year that are centered around Fast eLearning. Various programming organizations, for example, Articulate, have zeroed in their whole plan of action on eLearning. Considerably bigger programming organizations like Adobe have zeroed in critical assets on creating and advancing rapid eLearning devices. Every year these instruments involve an expanded portion of the preparation advancement programming being bought and utilized by corporate preparing offices.

eLearning plays a critical part to play in satisfying the preparation needs of the present corporate world. The requirement for quickly created preparing materials that are open to a geologically different populace will keep on developing. "As online encounters become more typical and all the more genuine in individuals' lives, we want to attempt to ensure they are adding to our personal satisfaction, and not reducing it". Those in the field of educational plan need to resolve this issue by tracking down ways of taking on and work on the apparatuses and techniques that contain Quick eLearning. we have also discussed various evaluation approaches in eLearning. Quality Assurance (QA) is one of the last steps and most significant stage in the eLearning improvement to convey a top notch, mistake free and very much performed courses.

eLearning won't ever be a field of training totally different to itself; rather it will keep on mirroring the endeavors of coaches, educational creators, and programming designers to develop the instruments and strategies utilized for eLearning. These progressions will keep on significantly affecting the field of Educational Plan, driving the requirement for continuous re-assessment of the job of the educational architect in both the corporate and scholarly universes.

REFERENCES

Acheson, S. W. (2008). *Rapid eLearning: its impact on instructional design in the corporate world.* University of Northern Iowa.

Attwell, G. (2006). Evaluating E-learning: A Guide to the Evaluation of E-learning. *Evaluate Europe Handbook Series*, *2*(2), 1610–0875.

Boehle, S. (2005). Rapid e-learning. *TRAINING-NEW YORK THEN MINNEAPOLIS THEN NEW YORK*, *42*(7), 12.

Cross, J. (2004). An informal history of eLearning. *On the Horizon*, *12*(3), 103–110. doi:10.1108/10748120410555340

Haghshenas, M., Khademi, M., & Kabir, H. (2012). E-learning and authoring tools: At a glance. *International Journal of Research & Reviews in Applied Sciences*, *10*(2), 259–263.

Jones, E.R. (2022). *Implications of SCORM and emerging e-learning standards on engineering education*. GSW.

Kapounová, J. (2007). *Approaches to the evaluation of eLearning*. E-learning and distance learning.

Khademi, M., Haghshenas, M., & Kabir, H. (2011, September). A review on authoring tools. In *Proceedings of the 5th International Conference on Distance Learning and Education, IPCSIT* (*Vol. 12,* pp. 40-44). IEEE.

Masud, M. A. H., & Huang, X. (2012, May). A novel approach for adopting cloud-based e-learning system. In *2012 IEEE/ACIS 11th International Conference on Computer and Information Science* (pp. 37-42). IEEE. 10.1109/ICIS.2012.10

Rughoobur-Seetah, S., & Hosanoo, Z. A. (2021). An evaluation of the impact of confinement on the quality of e-learning in higher education institutions. *Quality Assurance in Education*, *29*(4), 422–444. doi:10.1108/QAE-03-2021-0043

Chapter 9
The Rapid E-Learning Method:
A Guide to Developing Interactive Materials Development

Mohammad Issack Santally
https://orcid.org/0000-0003-3745-2150
University of Mauritius, Mauritius

Yousra Rajabalee
https://orcid.org/0000-0003-4885-610X
Mauritius Institute of Education, Mauritius

Ashvin Beetul
University of Mauritius, Mauritius

ABSTRACT

Rapid e-learning is a method to develop and deploy quality interactive learning materials in a shorter time span, and to address learning needs in different contexts—academic, professional, or commercial. Resources developed via rapid e-learning methods can be used in educational institutions from pre-primary to tertiary levels. They can also be used for professional training, short courses, or more advanced training that leads to alternative qualifications or micro-credentials that are recognised in the workplace. Often, they can be used as agile content to train sales officers on a new product on the market. In such situations, their relevance and lifespan are limited. Rapid e-learning allows for maximum flexibility in terms of re-use of learning materials and modification of content provided it is carefully planned and designed. One has to also design accessibility to ensure inclusiveness in the educational delivery approach. In this chapter, the authors provide an overview of the rapid e-learning method and its application to the development of interactive learning materials.

DOI: 10.4018/978-1-6684-4940-0.ch009

INTRODUCTION

Rapid e-learning is a design and development approach that enables the creation of digital learning materials quickly and efficiently. It is an alternative to traditional e-learning development approaches that often take months of work to produce just one course. In contrast, rapid e-learning methodologies allow for faster turnaround time, which can be particularly beneficial when it comes to creating educational content in fast-paced industries such as business or healthcare. The benefits of rapid e-learning are numerous. One significant advantage is that it can significantly reduce the cost and time required to produce high-quality courses (Dunkleberger 2011). This is due in part because rapid e-learning tools often involve pre-built templates, assets, and multimedia elements that make it easier to create engaging content quickly. It also allows organizations to roll out valuable training programs much more quickly than traditional methods. Using rapid e-learning tools, you can create various types of learning materials. Some examples include software simulations, video-based micro-courses, interactive PDFs, infographics, animated presentations as well as quizzes and assessments with real-time feedback.

In summary, designers and developers may use these tools when they have highly specific learning outcomes in mind for their audience or group requirement needs for mass deployments' utilization efficacy goals. Rapid E-Learning allows the production of high-quality digital education resources with users' desired properties without sacrificing effectiveness or engaging visual media at a lesser expense compared to other means of training material production.

One of the main constraints in the e-Learning field is that the design, development, and deployment of high-quality learning resources are very time-consuming and quite costly. There have been many attempts to produce informational materials quite quickly, but with resources that lack quality and are not engaging for learners. Rapid e-Learning is a term that has emerged from the concept of rapid development as applied to the software development industry (Parlakkılıç, 2014). The key is to acquire the ability to develop and deploy high-quality interactive multimedia e-learning courses, which are generally short to medium-length learning units in a minimum amount of time (Brandon 2005).

AN OVERVIEW OF THE RAPID E-LEARNING METHOD

The aim of a rapid approach is to move from the normal and traditional production cycle for developing course contents or training materials, down to approximately 30% less time. Anything longer than this basically fails the definition of a rapid e-learning project (Parlakkılıç, 2014). Below is a brief schema showing the phases

Figure 1. Phases of a rapid e-learning project

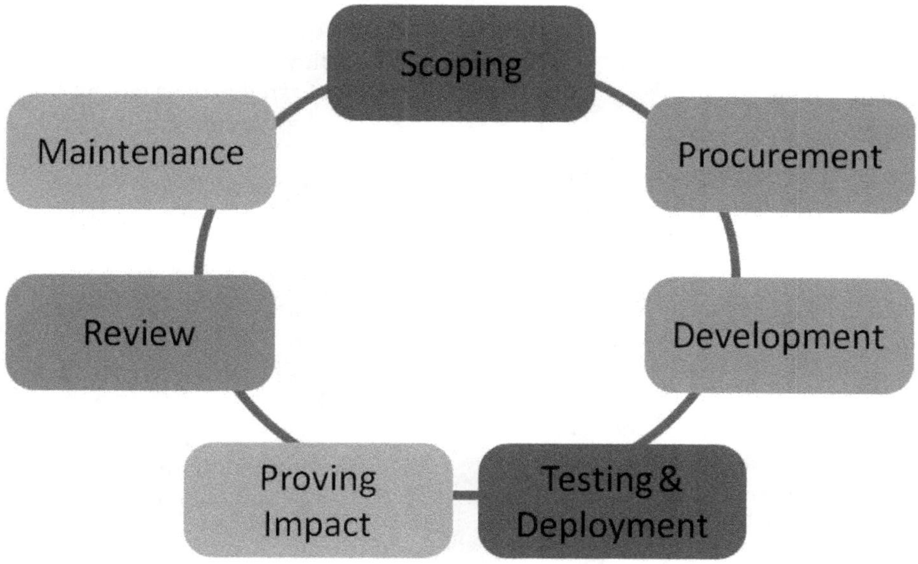

of a rapid e-learning project and in general, a project will have to undergo all these phases to reach its delivery.

However, while rapid development emphasizes reduced time and effort spent on analysis and design phases, they are still very crucial, especially in projects where it is important to meet requirements in a short time frame (Parlakkılıç 2014). The goal of a "rapid" development cycle is to produce the content as quickly as possible. This means the adoption of iterative development and continuous sign-off. The creation of graphics and rich assets are slightly lagged in their delivery. They are produced in a step parallel to the instructional design work, filling draft images and rough mock-ups with real images and interactions. The model below illustrates how rapid e-learning development can be integrated into the design of distance e-learning environments (Rajputh et al. 2016).

With reference to the model above, the first two steps are important in any distance education course and are usually referred to as self-instructional materials. Rapid e-learning assumes that content for a particular course is available in PDF, Word documents, or even printed manuals. But however, the course might be in any format, whether it is web-based or on CD, the rapid e-learning methodology helps a course developer to apply good e-learning design techniques to create professional and interactive courses rapidly that will be delivered to end-users. The idea is to develop informational content quickly, which will help learners to learn and apply skills and knowledge efficiently. Hence, the rapid e-learning methodology will help you as a

Figure 2. Rapid e-Learning process
(Rajputh et al. 2016)

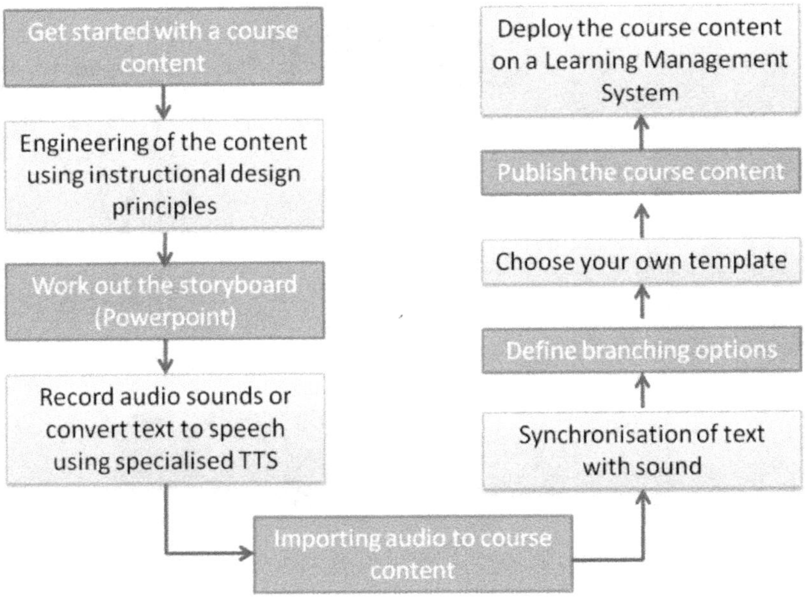

developer or education technologist to use proper instructional design techniques, to develop courses that will guide learners' attention and create better understanding.

TIPS FOR EFFECTIVE RAPID E-LEARNING DESIGN

Mayer describes multimedia learning as the building of mental representations from words (spoken or printed text) and pictures (such as illustrations, photos, animation, or video). From a pedagogical point of view, the use of multimedia for teaching and learning has many advantages. Multimedia captures the learners' attention through three main elements, and these are interactivity, personalized instruction, and the dimension of reality that can be added to the learning tasks (Mayer 2001).

Content development for e-Learning purposes can be in any different forms but the onus is to engage the learners in their learning process and help them use the learning content in meaningful ways. In this context, it is of utmost importance to properly design the course to make it the right one.

Ensuring learner engagement through effective design can be challenging and time-consuming without proper planning. As such, creating and planning an e-Learning course can be a lengthy process, whether from start or modifying of a

Table 1. CLEARS approach

Clarify learning objectives	Clearly describe the learning objectives and outcomes you hope to attain before starting to develop the contents. This will ensure that these contents are engaged and pertinent to the targeted audience.
Limit complexity	With the focus that the creation of learning materials rapidly and effectively is the main objective of rapid e-learning, complex interactions and too advanced design components are not recommended, as the processing may be time-consuming and may not really improve the expected learning outcomes.
Employ templates	Several rapid e-learning softwares provide ready-made themes or templates that can be personalised to suit specific needs. Making use of these templates surely contributes to speeding up the development process and also ensuring a professional end result.
Add multimedia	Captivating elements in multimedia can improve the learning experience and assist in knowledge retention. Examples include video clips, animations, photos, and interactive elements. These components should be used wisely though, so as not to overload or divert from the main content.
Repeat Tests	During any e-learning production process, the testing phase is essential to ensure that the contents are of high quality and effective. Before launching the finished product, think about running short-term experimental tests repeatedly during the development process to get maximum input from stakeholders.
Scrutinize data for continual progress	After launching of material, it is vital to monitor learner engagement indicators including completion rates, quiz results, and feedback comments. Such analytics information will be useful to deduce which part of the contents that need to be enhanced for future publishing.

current task. It demands know-how which many experts presumably have and want to acquire even further, and time to be spent for the development, which many do not have. As such, to avoid wasting time and resources, many developers cannot afford to include complex features in their e-Learning courses, as it is crucial to start the course effectively and under a tight deadline. Thus, to create clear and effective rapid e-learning, the CLEARS approach has been developed as per the following:

To create course content, a variety of authoring tools are available. These tools fall into two categories: open-source and proprietary software. A few differences between open-source and proprietary tools are explored below before moving on to an overview of rapid e-learning authoring tools.

OPEN-SOURCE V/S PROPRIETARY TOOLS

Open-source software is a type of software where the source codes which are used to create and edit the software is available on the internet freely. Such software allows users to edit the source code and then put it in a form that suits them best. For example, users can change the look and feel, and functionalities as per their needs directly from the source code. On the other hand, the source code for proprietary software is usually kept as a private asset of the company and no member of the public is allowed to make any changes to the codes. However, they can send their views about the product to the company and the company itself will make the amendments with the help of its qualified programmers.

Open-source software can be downloaded from the internet free of charge, and most of them have two common things: they can be used without a license fee, and anyone is allowed to edit or add any functionalities not yet implemented by the original developer. However, proprietary software needs to be purchased. Some companies provide a trial version for free, easily available on the internet with the option to upgrade to the full version after the trial expires. These types of software are usually more reliable in terms of stability, functionality, and usability.

The following offers some questions as guidelines based on a SECURE approach, when an authoring software for rapid e-learning need to be selected:

Table 2. SECURE approach

No.	Criteria	Question
1	**S**implification	Is it simple to use and navigate the software? - The development process can be simple to use when there is a user-friendly interface and also reducing the learning curve.
2	**E**ase of access	Does the software offer choices for producing WCAG 2.0 compliant accessible content, ensuring that students with infirmities can easily access and utilize the training contents?
3	**C**ross-platform compatibility	Is the material produced using the tool compatible with many platforms, Operating Systems (such as Windows, Mac OS, Android, and iOS) and devices (such as desktops, laptops, tablets, and smartphones)?
4	**U**ser engagement	Does the tool include interactive aspects that engage students and promote knowledge retention, such as quizzes, games, simulations, or other multimedia components?
5	**R**apid progress	Can the software produce material rapidly and effectively? - To speed up development, look for characteristics like ready-made templates, drag-and-drop capability, and themes with editing capabilities.
6	**E**fficient purchase	What are the prices for buying or subscribing to the software? Are there supplementary fees for maintenance or for the updates of the tool?

A solution can be selected based on what satisfies the unique requirements of an organization in terms of usability, rapid development, interactivity possibilities, multi-platform compatibility, accessibility compliance requisite, and financial implications as a whole by comparing authoring software using these norms.

OVERVIEW OF OPEN-SOURCE AUTHORING TOOLS

There are different open-source tools that can be used specifically to design e-learning courses and a brief overview of a few of them has been given as follows:

eXe (http://exelearning.net/)

eXe is a free e-learning tool that allows you to create presentations that can be exported to XHTML or HTML5. You can use text, images, or video clips to mount your resource and then publish it to a different format. It can also be integrated into a Learning Management System like Moodle.

Things that you can do with eXe Learning:

- Develop content in XHTML or HTML5
- Create a website with many pages which are inter-related (pages can be made responsive as well)
- Add interactive content (questions and activities)
- Export to different format (ePub3, IMS/SCORM, XLIFF)

XERTE Online Toolkits (https://www.nottingham.ac.uk/xerte/toolkits.aspx)

Another example of an open-source authoring tool is XERTE Online Toolkits which is a browser-based tool, and it allows you to create interactive learning resources using a web browser. It can be used very easily, and rapidly and the content can be delivered to HTML5 with responsive design to all devices. It provides simple online tools that anyone can use effectively to create online interactive materials. Initially, flash-based content was delivered as it was the best option at the time of the creation of the project, however, flash is now replaced with XHTML and HTML5.

PROPRIETARY RAPID E-LEARNING AUTHORING TOOLS

E-Learning development is multi-faceted, and it provides you with a panoply of rapid e-learning authoring tools that can help you to build effective e-learning courses using a lot of creativity, to engage your learners. Consequently, instead of simply applying a mechanical instructional design approach to your courses, you can use the features of the rapid e-learning tools to enhance your visual design and present your subject contents in creative ways, without overloading your learners cognitively.

The following is a brief overview of the different authoring tools you can use to develop your course rapidly.

ARTICULATE STORYLINE

Articulate Storyline is a powerful e-learning authoring tool that allows developers to easily create interactive and engaging e-learning content. It offers a range of features, including pre-built templates, slide master layouts, and design themes to help users create professional-looking courses quickly. One of the key features of Storyline is its user-friendly interface, which makes it easy for even non-technical users to create complex and interactive courses. The software offers drag-and-drop functionality, so you can easily add text, images, audio, video, animations, and interactions. Another benefit of Articulate Storyline is its ability to create responsive e-learning content that adapts to any screen size. This means that learners can access courses on their desktops or mobile devices without any loss in quality or functionality. Storyline also offers robust assessment tools like quizzes and surveys with customizable feedback options that allow instructors to evaluate learner progress effectively. There are other advanced features such as triggers and conditional actions that can be used to increase interactivity levels in eLearning lessons. Overall, Articulate Storyline is an all-in-one solution for building high-quality e-learning courses that engage learners and deliver real-world learning experiences.

ISPRING

iSpring is an authoring tool, and it works on Microsoft Office platforms. It offers a 30-day trial before use and it has a free version as well, with limited features. It consists of different features you can create video lectures, interactive assessments with different types of activities, record screens and teach through videos, e-learning interactions and convert PowerPoint into e-learning courses. With iSpring you can convert your PowerPoint presentations to Flash/HTML5, create quizzes and you can share your presentations and files online. You can enhance your PowerPoint with audio and video narrations, quizzes, characters, dialog simulations, etc. Anything you do with iSpring will automatically be responsive to make it viewable on any platform (Windows, IOS, Android, etc). You can also add a presenter to your slides by either adding a readymade video or recording a live video. Your presentation can be made more efficient by creating polls, surveys, and drag-and-drop activities. The material can be published to LMS which can be viewed on different screen sizes as the player is very adaptive and works everywhere.

DESIGNING INTERACTIONS IN RAPID E-LEARNING

The transformation of face-to-face activities into self-paced interactive e-learning activities requires careful planning. Therefore, by incorporating multimedia features such as images, videos audio, text, etc. can provide learners with a suitable design that effectively supports them in their educational journey. Following the appropriate steps which incorporate defining goals and choosing appropriate design and interaction techniques coupled with accessible digital multimedia elements help convert existing content into engaging interactive e-learning ready for self-paced environs of digital learners everywhere.

Figure 3. Steps in designing interactive contents

The design of interactive content for rapid e-learning development tasks can be accomplished through the utilization of what we have termed as the SCOPE model.

With the SCOPE steps, developers can add interactive features that serve the general learning objectives of the business while retaining a tight development timeframe.

DESIGNING FOR ACCESSIBILITY IN RAPID E-LEARNING

To ensure that everyone has access to the content equally, accessibility for learners with impairments must be considered while developing multimedia interactive learning resources. The following are some suggestions for meeting the needs of accessibility requirements:

Table 3.

1	Alt text for images	Use alternative text (alt-text) to describe images. By doing so, it will be easier for students using screen readers or other assistive technologies to interpret visual elements.
2	Captions/transcripts for A/V	To accommodate students who have hearing impairments, offer caption content videos, write out a transcript of the lecture, add speakers' names, describe any background noises and include all sound effects and music.
3	Assistive tech compatibility	Screen readers should be used to test e-learning materials, and compatibility with assistive technology like screen magnifiers and Braille output devices should also be guaranteed.
4	Plain language	Do not use jargon or complex words. To make it easier for people who might have lesser literacy to grasp, keep wordings brief, clear and to the point.
5	Keyboard navigation	Whenever necessary, allow users to browse interactive resources without a mouse.
6	WCAG-compliant contrast	To ensure that users who are colourblind or have vision disabilities may access learning resources, contrast between the colour of the foreground text and the background should match WCAG criteria for Colour Contrast at least at level AA (yet ideally AAA).

Implementing these strategies in your multimedia interactive learning materials early in the design process can improve accessibility for diverse learners, making their values reflected in your program design while conforming with high-quality instructional design best practices overall.

QUALITY ASSURANCE AND EVALUATION OF YOUR RAPID E-LEARNING COURSE

The main purpose of rapid e-learning is to deliver quality interactive multimedia learning content in the least possible time (Rajputh et al. 2016). Before publishing a course designed using the rapid e-learning method, the developer and reviewers need to go through the whole content, to identify any mistakes, technical glitches, navigational issues, gaps in the flow of content, and the linkages between units among others. The quality assurance process is an essential foundation for verifying and reviewing the design and the illustrations used to ensure that the necessary standards are being maintained. Furthermore, evaluating the effectiveness of your rapid e-learning course is critical to determine if it's meeting its intended objectives. Here are some ways to evaluate your course's effectiveness:

1. Conduct assessments - Assessments like quizzes, tests or surveys help measure knowledge retention and understanding of the topic. Create formative and summative assessments to determine if learners have met the learning objectives.
2. Use analytics - Most e-learning authoring tools provide analytics features that enable you to track learner progress and completion rates. Analyzing this data can help identify areas where learners struggle or succeed.
3. Solicit feedback - Conduct post-course surveys asking participants about their learning experience, what they liked or disliked, or ideas on how to improve the course for better user engagement.

By evaluating your rapid e-learning course using these methods, you'll get valuable insights into its effectiveness and be able to make necessary changes for optimal outcomes that meet the requirements both of short-term goals and prevailing trends toward digital education.

REFERENCES

Brandon, B. (2005). *Exploring the definition of rapid e-learning.* eLearning Guild. http://www.elearningguild.com/pdf/4/rapid_elearning_whitepaper_3-2-05.pdf

Dunkleberger, R. (2011). Rapid E-learning – Accomplishing more with less. *E-learning Concepts and Techniques, Institute for Interactive Technologies.* Bloomsburg University of Pennsylvania, USA. http://iit.bloomu.edu/spring2006_ebook_files/chapter2.htm#h2_3

Mayer, R. (2001). *Multimedia Learning*. Cambridge University Press. doi:10.1017/CBO9781139164603

Parlakkılıç, A. (2014). Rapid E-Learning and Desktop Virtualization In Education. *International Conference on Computer Science, Computer Engineering, and Social Media*, Thessaloniki, Greece.

Rajputh, R., Rajabalee, Y., Soni, J., & Koheeallee, N. (2016). Interactive Materials Development using the Rapid e- Learning Method - Examples from the Field. *Proceedings of the Commonwealth of Learning PCF8 Conference*. Oasis. https://oasis.col.org/bitstream/handle/11599/

Compilation of References

Abbad, M. M., Morris, D., & de Nahlik, C. (2009). *Looking under the Bonnet: Factors Affecting Student Adoption of E-Learning Systems in Jordan.* The International Review of Research in Open and Distance Learning.

Abo Mokh, A., Shayeb, S., Badah, A., Ismail, I., Ahmed, Y., Dawoud, L., & Ayoub, H. (2021). Levels of Technostress Resulting from Online Learning among Language Teachers in Palestine during Covid-19 Pandemic. *American Journal of Educational Research*, *9*, 243–254. doi:10.12691/education-9-5-1

Acheson, S. W. (2008). *Rapid eLearning: its impact on instructional design in the corporate world.* University of Northern Iowa.

Ahmed, Y., Ismail, I., Abo Mokh, A., & Hamarsha, M. (2020). *Exploring the effectiveness of technology integration on students' motivation and engagement during Covid-19 from teachers' perspectives: A case study*. İlköğretim Online. . doi:10.17051/ilkonline.2020.04.176

Ahmed, R., Hughes, P. G., Friedl, E., Ortiz Figueroa, F., Cepeda Brito, J. R., Frey, J., Birmingham, L. E., & Atkinson, S. S. (2016). A Novel Simulation Technician Laboratory Design: Results of a Survey-Based Study. *Cureus*, *8*(3), e534. doi:10.7759/cureus.534 PMID:27096134

Al-Attar, R. H. (2019). *The effectiveness of using scenario-based learning strategy in developing EFL eleventh graders' speaking and prospective thinking skills* [Unpublished master's thesis, The Islamic University of Gaza].

Alderson, J. C. (2007). The CEFR and the need for more research. *Modern Language Journal*, *91*(4), 659–663. doi:10.1111/j.1540-4781.2007.00627_4.x

Alderson, J. C., & Banerjee, J. (2001). Language testing and assessment (Part 1): State-of-the-art review. *Language Teaching*, *34*(4), 213–236. doi:10.1017/S0261444800014464

Alice, V., Knippels, M.-C. P. J., & van Joolingen, W. R. (2021). Beyond the Early Adopters: Escape Rooms in Science Education. *Frontiers in Education*, *6*, 622860. doi:10.3389/feduc.2021.622860

Alkhateeb, M. A. (2018). The effect of using performance-based assessment strategies to tenth-grade students' achievement and self-efficacy in Jordan. *Cypriot Journal of Educational Sciences*, *13*(4), 489–500. doi:10.18844/cjes.v13i4.2815

Allen, M. (2009). Authentic assessment and the internet:Contributions within knowledge networks. In *Proceedings of World Conference on E-Learning in Corporate, Government, Healthcare, and Higher Education* (pp. 1505-1510). Chesapeake, VA: AACE.

Allo, M. D. G. (2020). Is the online learning good in the midst of Covid-19 Pandemic? The case of EFL learners. *Jurnal Sinestesia, 10*(1), 1–10.

Allport, D. (1971). Parallel encoding within and between elementary stimulus dimensions. *Perception & Psychophysics, 10*(2), 104–108. doi:10.3758/BF03214327

Almazova, N., Rubtsova, A., Kats, N., Eremin, Y., & Smolskaia, N. (2021). Scenario-based instruction: The case of foreign language training at Multidisciplinary University. *Education Sciences, 11*(5), 1–18. doi:10.3390/educsci11050227

Alpay, E., & Gulati, S. (2010). Student-led podcasting for engineering education. *European Journal of Engineering Education, 35*(4), 415–427. doi:10.1080/03043797.2010.487557

Antonio Molina Bonilla, A. C. Santos, M. Castro Gil, D. Borge Diez and J. Vazquez Espierrez. (2012). Virtual Lab platform for distance learning courses in engineering technologies for the use of renewable energies. Proceedings of the 2012 IEEE Global Engineering Education Conference (EDUCON), (pp. 1-7). IEEE. 10.1109/EDUCON.2012.6201082

Archibald, L. M. D., & Gathercole, S. E. (2006). Short-term and working memory in specific language impairment. *International Journal of Language & Communication Disorders, 41*(6), 675–693. doi:10.1080/13682820500442602 PMID:17079222

Areekkuzhiyil, S. (2019). Assessment practices in higher education. *University News, 57*(11), 18–20.

Arkorful, V., & Abaidoo, N. (2015). The role of e-learning, advantages and disadvantages of its adoption in higher education. *International Journal of Instructional Technology and Distance Learning, 12*(1), 29–42.

Arslan, P. Y. (2012). A Review of Multimedia Learning Principles: Split-Attention, Modality, and Redundancy Effects. *Mersin Üniversitesi Eğitim Fakültesi Dergisi, 8*(1), 114–122.

Artino, A. R., La Rochelle, J. S., & Durning, S. J. (2010). Second-year medical students' motivational beliefs, emotions, and achievement. *Medical Education, 44*(12), 1203–1212. doi:10.1111/j.1365-2923.2010.03712.x PMID:21091760

Atmojo, A. E. P., & Nugroho, A. (2020). EFL classes must go online! Teaching activities and challenges during COVID-19 Pandemic in Indonesia. *Register Journal, 13*(1), 49–76. doi:10.18326/rgt.v13i1.49-76

Attwell, G. (2006). Evaluating E-learning: A Guide to the Evaluation of E-learning. *Evaluate Europe Handbook Series, 2*(2), 1610–0875.

Avci, D. E., & Bayrak, E. B. (2013). Investigating teacher Candidates' Opinions related to scenario-based learning: An action research. *Elementary Education Online, 12*(2), 528–549.

Ayres, P., & Sweller, J. (2005). The split-attention principle in multimedia learning. The Cambridge handbook of multimedia learning, 2, 135-146.

Ayres, P., & Van Gog, T. (2009). State of the art research into Cognitive Load Theory. *Computers in Human Behavior*, *25*(2), 253–257. doi:10.1016/j.chb.2008.12.007

Bachman, L. F. (2007). What is the construct? The dialectic of abilities and contexts in defining constructs in language assessment. In J. Fox, M. Wesche, D. Bayliss, L. Cheng, C. E. Turner, & C. Doe (Eds.), *Language testing reconsidered* (pp. 41–71). University of Ottawa Press. doi:10.2307/j.ctt1ckpccf.9

Bailey, D. R., & Lee, A. R. (2020). Learning from experience in the midst of Covid-19: Benefits, challenges, and strategies in online teaching. *Computer Assisted Language Learning Electronic Journal (CALL-EJ)*, *21*(2), 176–196.

Baleni, Z. (2015). Online formative assessment in higher education: Its pros and cons. *Electronic Journal of e-Learning*, *13*(4), 228–236.

Banerjee, H. L. (2019). Investigating the Construct of Topical Knowledge in Second Language Assessment: A Scenario-Based Assessment Approach. *Language Assessment Quarterly*, *16*(2), 133–160. doi:10.1080/15434303.2019.1628237

Beetham, H., & Sharpe, R. (Eds.). (2013). *Rethinking Pedagogy for a Digital Age: Designing for 21st Century Learning*. Routledge. doi:10.4324/9780203078952

Bennett, R. E. (2015). The changing nature of educational assessment. *Review of Research in Education*, *39*(1), 370–407. doi:10.3102/0091732X14554179

Bennett, S., Maton, K., & Kervin, L. (2008). The 'digital natives' debate: A critical review of the evidence. *British Journal of Educational Technology*, *39*(5), 775–786. doi:10.1111/j.1467-8535.2007.00793.x

Berger, N., Arent, M., Arnowitz, J., & Sampson, F. (2009). *Effective Prototyping with MS-Excel*. Elsevier. doi:10.1016/B978-0-12-088582-4.X0001-7

Biosistemika, (2021). *6 challenges to address when building a smart, digitalized laboratory*. Biosis Temika. https://biosistemika.com/blog/6-challenges-when-building-digitalized-laboratory/,

Boehle, S. (2005). Rapid e-learning. *TRAINING-NEW YORK THEN MINNEAPOLIS THEN NEW YORK*, *42*(7), 12.

Bonwell, C. C., & Eison, J. A. (1991). Active Learning: Creating Excitement in the Classroom. ASHE-ERIC Higher Education Report, School of Education and Human Development, George Washington University, Washington DC.

Borstorff, P. C., & Lowe, S. L. (2007). Student Perceptions and Opinions toward e-Learning in the College Environment. *Academy of Educational Leadership Journal*, *11*, 13–30.

Boud, D. (2000). Sustainable assessment: Rethinking assessment for the learning society. *Studies in Continuing Education, 22*(2), 151–167. doi:10.1080/713695728

Boud, D., & Falchikov, N. (2006). Aligning assessment with long-term learning. *Assessment & Evaluation in Higher Education, 31*(4), 399–413. doi:10.1080/02602930600679050

Boudreaux, J. (2018). Design, Simulation, and Construction of an IEEE 14-Bus Power System. [Master's Theses, LSU]. doi:10.31390/gradschool_theses.4801

Brandon, B. (2005). *Exploring the definition of rapid e-learning.* eLearning Guild. http://www.elearningguild.com/pdf/4/rapid_elearning_whitepaper_3-2-05.pdf

Brown, C., & Czerniewicz, L. (2010). Debunking the 'digital native': Beyond digital apartheid, towards digital democracy. *Journal of Computer Assisted Learning, 26*(5), 357–369. doi:10.1111/j.1365-2729.2010.00369.x

Brown, H. D. (1994). *Teaching by principles: An interactive approach to language pedagogy.* Prentice Hall Regents.

Bryant, B. R., Bryant, D. P., & Smith, D. D. (2019). Teaching Students with Special Needs in Inclusive Classrooms. Sage Publications.

Bsharat, T. R., & Behak, F. (2020). The impact of microsoft teams' app in enhancing teaching-learning english during the Coronavirus (COVID-19) from the English teachers' perspectives' in Jenin city. *Malaysian Journal of Science Health & Technology, 7.*

Burkholder, C. (2020). Looking within and looking around: On cellphilming with pre-service Social Studies teachers in Prince Edward Island. In K. C. Schmitz, M. Cotnam-Kappel, & N. Grant (Eds.), *Infiltrating, interrupting, investigating: Radical youth pedagogy in education* (pp. 167–178). DIO Press.

Burkholder, C., & Chase, A. (2021). Exploring the creative geographies of work with pre- service social studies teachers: Exposing intersections of time and labour in New Brunswick, Canada. *McGill Journal of Education, 55*(3), 1–20. https://mje.mcgill.ca/issue/view/573. doi:10.7202/1083423ar

Burkholder, C., & Frawley, A. (2019). Revisiting and disrupting uncritical diversity narratives through autoethnography and cellphilming. *LEARNing Landscapes, 12*(1), 63–76. doi:10.36510/learnland.v12i1.979

Byram, M., & Parmenter, L. (2012). *The common European framework of reference: The globalization of language education policy.* Multilingual Matters. doi:10.21832/9781847697318

Cain, K., & Oakhill, J. (2006). Profiles of children with specific reading comprehension difficulties. *The British Journal of Educational Psychology, 76*(4), 683–696. doi:10.1348/000709905X67610 PMID:17094880

Calk, R., & Patrick, A. (2017). Millennials through the looking glass: Workplace motivating factors. *Journal of Business Inquiry, 16*(2), 131–139. http:www.uvu.edu/woodbury/jbi/volume16

Campaña Días, D. C., Porras Pumalema, S. P., Ávila Herrera., S. A., & Fierro López, D. V. (2021). Promoviendo habilidades del habla en ambientes online. *Conciencia Digital, 4*(1.1), 241-249. doi:10.33262/concienciadigital.v4i1.1.1556

Canale, M. (1983). From communicative competence to communicative language pedagogy. In J. C. Richard & R. W. Schmidt (Eds.), *Language and Communication* (pp. 2–14). Longman.

Canale, M., & Swain, M. (1980). Theoretical bases of communicative approaches to second language teaching and testing. *Applied Linguistics, 1*(1), 1–47. doi:10.1093/applin/1.1.1

Cano, S., Collazos, C. A., Aristizabal, L. F., Moreira, F., Peñeñory, V. M., & Agredo, V. (2018). Designing Collaborative Strategies Supporting Literacy Skills in Children with Cochlear Implants Using Serious Games. *Advances in Intelligent Systems and Computing, 746*, 1317–1326. doi:10.1007/978-3-319-77712-2_126

Carter, T. (2018). Preparing Generation Z for the Teaching Profession. *SRATE Journal, 27*(1), 1–8.

Çetin Köroglu, Z. (2019). Interventionist Dynamic Assessment's Effects on Speaking Skills Testing: Case of Elt Teacher Candidates. *Advances in Language and Literary Studies, 10*(3), 23–31. doi:10.7575/aiac.alls.v.10n.3p.23

Çetin Köroğlu, Z. (2021). Using Digital Formative Assessment to Evaluate EFL Learners' English Speaking Skills. *GIST–Education and Learning Research Journal*, (22), 103–123. doi:10.26817/16925777.1001

Çetin Köroğlu, Z., & Utku, Ö. (2018). Yabancı dilde konuşma becerisinin ölçülmesinde dinamik ölçme. In Ö. Balci & F. Çolak (Eds.), *Her Yönüyle Yabancı Dil Üzerine Araştırmalar II* (pp. 77–87). Çizgi Yayınevi.

Chan, G. L., Santally, M. I., & Whitehead, J. (2019). Portrait of a Deaf Mauritian Student: How I propose to use educational games to ease up struggles faced in French elementary classes. *Pan-Commonwealth Forum 9 (PCF9), 2019*. http://hdl.handle.net/11599/3254

Chandler, P., & Sweller, J. (1991). Cognitive load theory and the format of instruction. *Cognition and Instruction, 8*(4), 293–332. doi:10.12071532690xci0804_2

Chandler, P., & Sweller, J. (1992). The split-attention effect as a factor in the design of instruction. *The British Journal of Educational Psychology, 62*(2), 233–246. doi:10.1111/j.2044-8279.1992.tb01017.x

Chandler, P., & Sweller, J. (1996). Cognitive load while learning to use a computer program. *Applied Cognitive Psychology, 10*(2), 151–170. doi:10.1002/(SICI)1099-0720(199604)10:2<151::AID-ACP380>3.0.CO;2-U

Chandra, R. (2004). *Technology in the Preparation of Teachers*. ISHA.

Chan, G. L., Santally, M. I., & Whitehead, J. (2022). Gamification as technology enabler in SEN and DHH education. *Education and Information Technologies, 27*(7), 9031–9064. doi:10.100710639-022-10984-y PMID:35345601

Choi, E. (2014). Second language learning through drama: Practical Techniques and Applications. Joe Winston (Ed.). New York, NY: Routledge. 2012. TESOL Journal, 5(4), 792–795.

Churches, A. (2008). Bloom's digital taxonomy. *Bloom's Revised Digital Taxonomy Map*, 6-8. Bloom.

Cooshna-Naik, D. (2018). *Undergraduate students' experiences of learning with digital multimodal texts*. [Unpublished doctoral dissertation], University of KwaZulu-Natal, Durban, South Africa

Cope, B., & Kalantzis, M. (2015). *The things you do to know: An Introduction to the pedagogy of multiliteracies*. doi:10.1057/9781137539724_1

Council of Europe (CoE). (2001). *Common European framework of reference for languages: Learning, teaching, assessment*. Cambridge University Press.

Council of Europe (CoE). (2018). *The CEFR companion volume with new descriptors*. Language Policy Programme, Education Policy Division, Education Department. https://rm.coe.int/cefr-companion-volume-with-new-descriptors-2018/1680787989

Council of Europe (CoE). (2020). *Common European framework of reference for languages: Learning, teaching, assessment-Companion volume*. Strasbourg: Council of Europe Publishing. www.coe.int/lang-cefr

Cross, J. (2004). An informal history of eLearning. *On the Horizon, 12*(3), 103–110. doi:10.1108/10748120410555340

de Freitas, S. (2018). Are Games Effective Learning Tools? A Review of Educational Games. *Journal of Educational Technology & Society, 21*(2), 74–84. https://www.jstor.org/stable/26388380

Di Mascio, T., Gennari, R., Melonio, A., & Vittorini, P. (2013). Designing games for deaf children: First guidelines. *International Journal of Technology Enhanced Learning, 5*(3/4), 223. doi:10.1504/IJTEL.2013.059493

Di Pietro, R. J. (1987). The scenario principle in the teaching of Italian literature. *Italica, 64*(3), 365–376. doi:10.2307/478496

Dörnyei, Z., & Thurrell, S. (1991). Strategic competence and how to teach it. *ELT Journal, 45*(1), 16–23. doi:10.1093/elt/45.1.16

Doyle, E., Buckley, P., & McCarthy, B. (2021). The impact of content co-creation on academic achievement. *Assessment & Evaluation in Higher Education, 46*(3), 494–507. doi:10.1080/02602938.2020.1782832

Dublin, L. (2003). If You Only Look Under the Street Lamps... Or Nine e-Learning Myths. *The eLearning Developers' Journal*. E-learning Guild. http://www.elearningguild.com/pdf/2/061603MAN.pdf

Dunkleberger, R. (2011). Rapid E-learning – Accomplishing more with less. *E-learning Concepts and Techniques, Institute for Interactive Technologies.* Bloomsburg University of Pennsylvania, USA. http://iit.bloomu.edu/spring2006_ebook_files/chapter2.htm#h2_3

Eitan, N., & Harel, D. (2011). Adaptive behavioral programming. Paper presented at *the tools with Artificial Intelligence (ICTAI), 2011 23rd IEEE International Conference.* IEEE. 10.1109/ICTAI.2011.109

El Mawas, N., Bratu, M., Caraman, D., & Muntean, C. (2019). Investigating the Learning Impact of Game-based Learning when Teaching Science to Children with Special Learning Needs. *30th Annual Conference of the Society for Information Technology and Teacher Education SITE.* HAL. https://hal.archives-ouvertes.fr/hal-02251329

Elsom, J. (2009). A creative assessment strategy to improve student motivation and engagement in biochemistry. In J. Barlow, G. Louw, & M. Price (Eds.), *Social Purpose and Creativity: Integrating Learning in the Real World.* University of Brighton Press.

Erarslan, A. (2021). English language teaching and learning during Covid-19: A global perspective on the first year. *Journal of Educational Technology & Online Learning, 4*(2), 349–367. doi:10.31681/jetol.907757

Errington, E. (2019). *As close as it gets: Developing professional identity through the potential of scenario based learning.* Life Wide Education. http://www.lifewideeducation.uk/uploads/1/3/5/4/13542890/c3._edward_errington.pdf

Errington, E. (2005). *Creating learning scenarios: A planning guide for adult educators.* Cool Books New Zealand.

Errington, E. P. (2010). Preparing graduates for the professions: Achieving employability through the exploration of near-world scenarios. *The International Journal of Interdisciplinary Social Sciences: Annual Review, 5*(5), 1–10. doi:10.18848/1833-1882/CGP/v05i05/51723

European Commission. (2001). *The eLearning Action Plan: Designing tomorrow's education.* EC. http://www.elearningeuropa.info

Faucette, P. (2001). A pedagogical perspective on communication strategies: Benefits of training and an analysis of English language teaching materials. *Second Lang. Stud., 19*, 1–40.

Febrilia, I., Warokka, A., & Abdullah, H. H. (2011). University students' emotional state and academic performance: New insights of managing complex cognitive. *The Journal of Learning in Higher Education*, 1–15. doi:10.5171/2011.879553

Florian, L. (2021). The Universal Value of Teacher Education for Inclusive Education. In A. Köpfer, J. J. W. Powell, & R. Zahnd (Eds.), *Handbuch Inklusion international / International Handbook of Inclusive Education* (1st ed., pp. 89–106). Verlag Barbara Budrich. doi:10.2307/j.ctv1f70kvj.8

Fook, C. Y., & Sidhu, G. K. (2014). Assessment practices in higher education in United States. *Procedia: Social and Behavioral Sciences, 123*, 299–306. doi:10.1016/j.sbspro.2014.01.1427

Fry, K. (2001). E-learning markets and providers: Some issues and prospects. *Education + Training*, *43*(4/5), 233–239. doi:10.1108/EUM0000000005484

Fushshilat, I., Rahmat, A., Somantri, Y., & Haritman, E. (2018). Laboratory management: Digital laboratory information system (DLIS) concept. *IOP Conference Series. Materials Science and Engineering*, *434*, 012286. doi:10.1088/1757-899X/434/1/012286

Gangat, Y., Grondin, D., Issoufaly, T., Coquillas, N., Benne, M., & Chabriat, J. (2018). Simulation & Emulation platform for smart grid technologies. *2018 International Conference on Control, Electronics, Renewable Energy and Communications (ICCEREC)*, (pp. 122-128,) IEEE. 10.1109/ICCEREC.2018.8711994

Garbati, J. F., & Mady, C. J. (2015). Oral skill development in second languages: A review in search of best practices. *Theory and Practice in Language Studies*, *5*(9), 1763–1770. doi:10.17507/tpls.0509.01

Garner, R., Brown, R., Sanders, S., & Menke, D. J. (1992). Seductive details" and learning from text. *The role of interest in learning and development*, 239-254.

Garner, R., Gillingham, M. G., & White, C. S. (1989). Effects of'seductive details' on macroprocessing and microprocessing in adults and children. *Cognition and Instruction*, *6*(1), 41–57. doi:10.12071532690xci0601_2

Gideon, L. (2012). Handbook of Survey Methodology for the Social Sciences. In L. Gideon (Ed.), *Handbook of Survey Methodology for the Social Sciences*. Springer New York. doi:10.1007/978-1-4614-3876-2

Gilles, J., Detroz, P., & Blais, J. (2011). An international online survey of the practices and perceptions of higher education professors with respect to the assessment of learning in the classroom. *Assessment & Evaluation in Higher Education*, *36*(6), 719–733. doi:10.1080/02602938.2010.484880

Girard, D., & Trim, J. L. M. (Eds.). (1998). *Learning and teaching modern languages for communication: Final report of the project group (activities 1982/87)*. Council of Europe.

Graneheim, U. H., & Lundman, B. (2004). Qualitative content analysis in nursing research: Concepts, procedures, and measures to achieve trustworthiness. *Nurse Education Today*, *24*(2), 105–112. doi:10.1016/j.nedt.2003.10.001 PMID:14769454

Greene, H., & Crespi, C. (2012). The value of student created videos in the college classroom-an exploratory study in marketing and accounting. *The International Journal of the Arts in Society*, *5*(1), 213–283.

Guragain, N. (2016). E-*learning benefits and applications.*

Haghshenas, M., Khademi, M., & Kabir, H. (2012). E-learning and authoring tools: At a glance. *International Journal of Research & Reviews in Applied Sciences*, *10*(2), 259–263.

Hall, L., Hume, C., & Tazzyman, S. (2016). Five Degrees of happiness: Effective Smiley Face Likert scales for evaluating with children. *Proceedings of IDC 2016 - The 15th International Conference on Interaction Design and Children*, (pp. 311–321). ACM. 10.1145/2930674.2930719

Harp, S. F., & Mayer, R. E. (1997). The role of interest in learning from scientific text and illustrations: On the distinction between emotional interest and cognitive interest. *Journal of Educational Psychology*, *89*(1), 92–102. doi:10.1037/0022-0663.89.1.92

Harp, S. F., & Mayer, R. E. (1998). How seductive details do their damage: A theory of cognitive interest in science learning. *Journal of Educational Psychology*, *90*(3), 414–434. doi:10.1037/0022-0663.90.3.414

Hartshorn, K. J., & Mcmurry, B. L. (2020). The effects of the COVID-19 pandemic on ESL learners and TESOL practitioners in the United States. *International Journal of TESOL Studies*, *2*(2), 140–156. doi:10.46451/ijts.2020.09.11

Hawley, R., & Allen, C. (2018). Student-generated video creation for assessment: Can it transform assessment within Higher Education? *International Journal for Transformative Research*, *5*(1), 1–11. doi:10.2478/ijtr-2018-0001

Hazaymeh, W. A. (2021). EFL students' perceptions of online distance learning for enhancing English language learning during Covid-19 pandemic. *International Journal of Instruction*, *14*(3), 501–518. doi:10.29333/iji.2021.14329a

Helsper, E. J., & Enyon, R. (2010). Digital natives: Where is the evidence? *British Educational Research Journal*, *36*(3), 503–520. doi:10.1080/01411920902989227

Henry, L., & Winfield, J. (2010). Working memory and educational achievement in children with intellectual disabilities. *Journal of Intellectual Disability Research*, *54*(4), 354–365. doi:10.1111/j.1365-2788.2010.01264.x PMID:20236191

Herrington, J., & Parker, J. (2013). Emerging technologies as cognitive tools for authentic learning. *British Journal of Educational Technology*, *4*(4), 607–615. doi:10.1111/bjet.12048

Hsu, M. H. (2006). *The effects of dramatic activities on reading comprehension of senior high school EFL students in Taiwan* [Unpublished doctoral dissertation, College of Graduate Studies Texas A & M University-Kingsville].

Hughes, R. (2002). *Teaching and researching speaking*. Pearson Education.

Hulstijn, J. H. (2007). The shaky ground beneath the CEFR: Quantitative and qualitative dimensions of language proficiency. *Modern Language Journal*, *91*(4), 663–667. doi:10.1111/j.1540-4781.2007.00627_5.x

Humphries, T., Kushalnagar, P., Mathur, G., Napoli, D. J., Padden, C., & Rathmann, C. (2014). Ensuring language acquisition for deaf children: What linguists can do. *Language*, *90*(2), e31–e52. doi:10.1353/lan.2014.0036

Janisch, C., Liu, X., & Akrof, A. (2007). Implementing alternative assessment: Opportunities and obstacles. *The Educational Forum*, *71*(3), 221–230. doi:10.1080/00131720709335007

Jennex, M. E. (2005). *Case Studies in Knowledge Management. Idea Group Publishing: Hersley. Johnson, L. et al. (2010). 2010 Horizon Report: K-* (12th ed.). The New Media Consortium.

Jewitt, C. (2003). Re-thinking assessment: Multimodality, literacy and computer-mediated learning. *Assessment in Education: Principles, Policy & Practice*, *10*(1), 83–102. doi:10.1080/09695940301698

Jewitt, C. (2012). Multimodal methods for researching digital technologies. In S. Price, C. Jewitt, & B. Brown (Eds.), *The Sage handbook of digital technology research* (pp. 250–265). Sage.

Jiang, J. (2018). *Millennials stand out for their technology use, but older generations.* Pew Research Center. https://www.pewresearch.org/fact-tank/2019/09/09/us-generations-technology-use/

Jonassen, D., & Grabowski, B. (1993). *Handbook of individual differences, learning and instruction*. LEA.

Jones, E.R. (2022). *Implications of SCORM and emerging e-learning standards on engineering education*. GSW.

Jong, M. S. Y. (2015). Does online game-based learning work in formal education at school? A case study of VISOLE. *Curriculum Journal*, *26*(2), 249–267. doi:10.1080/09585176.2015.1018915

Jorm, C., Roberts, C., Gordon, C., Nisbet, G., & Roper, L. (2019). Time for university educators to embrace student videography. *Cambridge Journal of Education*, *49*(6), 673–693. doi:10.1080/0305764X.2019.1590528

Kapounová, J. (2007). *Approaches to the evaluation of eLearning*. E-learning and distance learning.

Karataş, T. Ö., & Tuncer, H. (2020). Sustaining language skills development of pre-service EFL teachers despite the COVID-19 interruption: A case of emergency distance education. *Sustainability (Basel)*, *12*(19), 1–34. doi:10.3390u12198188

Kattoua, T., Al-Lozi, M., & Alrowwad, A. A. (2016). A review of literature on e-learning systems in higher education. *International Journal of Business Management and Economic Research*, *7*(5), 754–762.

Keller, C., & Cernerud, L. (2002). Students' perception of e-learning in university education. *Learning, Media and Technology*, *27*(1), 55–67.

Keller, J. M. (2010). The Arcs Model of Motivational Design. In *Motivational Design for Learning and Performance* (pp. 43–74). Springer US. doi:10.1007/978-1-4419-1250-3_3

Khademi, M., Haghshenas, M., & Kabir, H. (2011, September). A review on authoring tools. In *Proceedings of the 5th International Conference on Distance Learning and Education, IPCSIT* (*Vol. 12,* pp. 40-44). IEEE.

Kirovska-Simjanoska, D. (2019). Digital vs in-person learning environment in ESP classrooms: Let the students decide. *SEEU Review*, *14*(1), 36–68. doi:10.2478eeur-2019-0004

Kirschner, P. A., & De Bruyckere, P. (2017). The myths of the digital native and the multitasker. *Teaching and Teacher Education*, *67*, 135–142. doi:10.1016/j.tate.2017.06.001

Kleinheksel, A. J., Rockich-Winston, N., Tawfik, H., & Wyatt, T. R. (2020). Demystifying content analysis. *American Journal of Pharmaceutical Education*, *84*(1), 127–137. doi:10.5688/ajpe7113 PMID:32292185

Koch, M., Luck, K. V., Schwarzer, J., & Draheim, S. (2018). The novelty effect in large display deployments - Experiences and lessons-learned for evaluating prototypes. *16th European Conference on Computer-Supported Cooperative Work*, (pp. 1-19). Nancy, France. 10.18420/ecscw2018_3

Kuama, S., & Intharaksa, U. (2016). Is online learning suitable for all English language students? *PASAA*, *52*, 53–82.

Lan, Y.-J., Hsiao, I. Y. T., & Shih, M.-F. (2018). Effective Learning Design of Game-Based 3D Virtual Language Learning Environments for Special Education Students. *Journal of Educational Technology & Society*, *21*(3), 213–227. https://www.jstor.org/stable/26458519?seq=1#metadata_info_tab_contents

LaRose, R., Gregg, J., & Eastin, M. (1998). Audio graphic tele-courses for the Web: An experiment. *Journal of Computer-Mediated Communication*, *4*(2), 0. doi:10.1111/j.1083-6101.1998.tb00093.x

Lee, A. R., & Bailey, D. R. (2020). Learning from experience in the midst of covid-19: Benefits, challenges, and strategies in online teaching. *Call-Ej, 21*(2), 176-196. http://callej.org/journal/21-2/Bailey-Lee2020.pdf

Lemieux, A., Burkholder, C., & Ribiero, J. (2019). Pedagogies of empathy-building: Canadian and Azorean perspectives of film-viewing in higher education. In G. Barton & S. Garvis (Eds.), *Compassion and empathy in educational contexts* (pp. 271–288). Palgrave MacMillan. doi:10.1007/978-3-030-18925-9_14

Letina, A. (2015). Application of traditional and alternative assessment in science and social studies teaching. *Croatian Journal of Education*, *17*(1), 137–152. doi:10.15516/cje.v17i0.1496

Li, B. (2011). Design and implementation of Web-based laboratory management system in colleges and universities. *2011 3rd International Conference on Computer Research and Development*, (pp. 468-471). IEEE. 10.1109/ICCRD.2011.5764176

Liaw, S.-S., Huang, H.-M., & Chen, G.-D. (2007). Surveying instructor and learner attitudes toward E-learning. *Computers & Education*, *49*(4), 1066–1080. doi:10.1016/j.compedu.2006.01.001

Li, C.-L., Chen, Y.-H., & Li, H.-Y. (2018). Technical College Students' ARCS Learning Motivation on Hospitality English Vocabulary. *International Journal of Human Resource Studies*, *8*(1), 189. doi:10.5296/ijhrs.v8i1.12370

Li, E. (2016). The study on higher vocational English O2O teaching experiment from the perspective of MOOC. *Journal of HUBEI Correspondence University*, *29*, 136–137.

Lightle, K. (2011). More than just the technology. *Science Scope*, *34*(9), 6–9. PMID:21980630

Lindstrom, R. L. (1994). *Business Week guide to multimedia presentations*. New York: Osborne McGraw-Hill.

Lipps, R. (2018). *Beyond the Bitrate: Ensuring Campus Video Success* [Paper presentation]. Media and Learning Conference Leuven.

Liu, Z. (2012). Construction and application of scenarios in college EFL learning. *International Forum of Teaching and Studies, 8*(2), 32-40.

Liu, M., Moore, Z., Graham, L., & Lee, S. (2002). A look at the research on computer-based technology use in second language learning. *Journal of Research on Technology in Education, 34*(3), 250–273. doi:10.1080/15391523.2002.10782348

MacEntee, K., Burkholder, C., & Schwab-Cartas, J. (2016). *What's a cellpilms? Integrating mobile technology into participatory visual activism and activims*. Sense.

MacKenzie, W. I. Jr, & Scherer, F. R. (2019). Millennial research on fleek: Suggestions for improving generational research design. *The Journal of Social Psychology*, *159*(2), 119–124. doi:10.1080/00224545.2019.1572967 PMID:31002294

Magin, D. J., & Reizes, J. A. (1990). Computer simulation of laboratory experiments: An unrealized potential. *Computers & Education*, *14*(3), 263–270. doi:10.1016/0360-1315(90)90009-V

Margaryan, A., Littlejohn, A., & Vojt, G. (2011). Are digital natives a myth or reality? University students' use of digital technologies. *Computers & Education*, *56*(2), 429–440. doi:10.1016/j.compedu.2010.09.004

Marschark, M., & Hauser, P. C. (2008). Cognitive underpinnings of learning by deaf and hard-of-hearing students: Differences, diversity, and directions. In *Deaf cognition: Foundations and outcomes* (pp. 3–23). Oxford University Press. doi:10.1093/acprof:oso/9780195368673.003.0001

Martin, S. S., Chebak, A., & Barka, N. (2015). Development of renewable energy laboratory based on integration of wind, solar and biodiesel energies through a virtual and physical environment. *2015 3rd International Renewable and Sustainable Energy Conference (IRSEC),* (pp. 1-8). IEEE. 10.1109/IRSEC.2015.7455086

Masters, G. N. (2013). Reforming educational assessment: Imperatives, principles and challenges. Camberwel: Australian Council for Educational Research.

Masud, M. A. H., & Huang, X. (2012, May). A novel approach for adopting cloud-based e-learning system. In *2012 IEEE/ACIS 11th International Conference on Computer and Information Science* (pp. 37-42). IEEE. 10.1109/ICIS.2012.10

Maxammatkulova, I. N. (2021). Teaching Speaking in English Lessons in Elementary School: Problems and Solutions. *Academic research in educational sciences, 2*(7), 95-98.

Mayberry, R. I. (2007). When timing is everything: Age of first-language acquisition effects on second-language learning. *Applied Psycholinguistics, 28*(3), 537–549. doi:10.1017/S0142716407070294

Mayer, R. E. (1997). Multimedia learning: Are we asking the right questions? *Educational Psychologist, 32*(1), 1–19. doi:10.120715326985ep3201_1

Mayer, R. E. (2001). *Multimedia learning*. Cambridge University Press. doi:10.1017/CBO9781139164603

Mayer, R. E., & Anderson, R. B. (1991). Animations need narrations: An experimental test of a dual-coding hypothesis. *Journal of Educational Psychology, 83*(4), 484–490. doi:10.1037/0022-0663.83.4.484

Mayer, R. E., & Anderson, R. B. (1992). The instructive animation: Helping students build connections between words and pictures in multimedia learning. *Journal of Educational Psychology, 84*(4), 444–452. doi:10.1037/0022-0663.84.4.444

Mayer, R. E., Heiser, J., & Lonn, S. (2001). Cognitive constraints on multimedia learning: When presenting more material results in less understanding. *Journal of Educational Psychology, 93*(1), 187–198. doi:10.1037/0022-0663.93.1.187

Mayer, R. E., & Moreno, R. (1998). A split-attention effect in multimedia learning: Evidence for dual processing systems in working memory. *Journal of Educational Psychology, 90*(2), 312–320. doi:10.1037/0022-0663.90.2.312

Mayer, R. E., Steinhoff, K., Bower, G., & Mars, R. (1995). A generative theory of textbook design: Using annotated illustrations to foster meaningful learning of science text. *Educational Technology Research and Development, 43*(1), 31–41. doi:10.1007/BF02300480

Mayer, R., & Mayer, R. E. (Eds.). (2005). *The Cambridge handbook of multimedia learning* (pp. 1–16). Cambridge university press. doi:10.1017/CBO9780511816819

McLaren, S. V. (2007). An international overview of assessment issues in technology education: Disentangling the influences, confusion and complexities. *Design and Technology Education: An International Journal, 12*(2), 10–24.

McNiff, J., & Whitehead, J. (2005). *Action research for teachers: a practical guide* (1st ed.). David Fulton Publishers. https://www.routledge.com/Action-Research-for-Teachers-A-Practical-Guide/McNiff/p/book/9781843123217

Megat-Abdul-Rahim, P. T., Idris, S. L., Rahman, Z. I. A., Ya Shaq, M. S., & Nasir, N. F. (2021). Approaching listening and speaking skills using online to facilitate interactive learning from students' perspectives. [AJUE]. *Asian Journal of University Education, 17*(2), 203–214. doi:10.24191/ajue.v17i2.13400

Memić-Fišić, I., & Bijedić, N. (2017). Teaching materials for ESL distance learning. *Explorations in English Language and Linguistics, 5*(1), 40-54. https://hrcak.srce.hr/216834

Merizow, J. (1981). A critical theory of adult learning and education. *Adult Education, 32*(1), 3–24. doi:10.1177/074171368103200101

Miccoli, L. (2003). English through drama for oral skills development. *ELT Journal, 57*(2), 122–129. doi:10.1093/elt/57.2.122

Ministry of Education Tertiary Education Science and Technology. (2017). *Salient Features Inclusive Education for Children and Youth with Special Needs in Mauritius Concept to Reality Policy Framework and Strategy Document*. METEST. https://education.govmu.org/Documents/educationsector/Documents/Special Education Needs/Salient Features Startegy Doc (1).pdf

Mirici, İ. H. (2015). Contemporary ELT practices across Europe and in Turkey. *International Journal of Language Academy, 3*(4), 1–8. doi:10.18033/ijla.333

Misfeldt, M. (2015). Scenario Based Education as a Framework for Understanding Students Engagement and Learning in a Project Management Simulation Game. *Electronic Journal of e-Learning, 13*(3), 181–191. www.ejel.org

Mitchell, C. (2014). Digital Media and the knowledge-producing practices of young people in the age of AIDS. In K. Sandford, T. Rogers, & M. Kendrick, Cultural Studies and Transdisciplinarity in Education (Vol. 1, pp. 81-93). Springer. doi:10.1007/978-981-4451-03-1_6

Mitchell, C., Burkholder, C., Magubane, S., & Saioojee, S. (2019). Ethically significant moments in stirring up memories. In K. Pithouse-Morgan, D. Pillay, & C. Mitchell (Eds.), *Memory mosaics: Researching teacher professional learning through artful memory-work* (pp. 175–192). Springer. doi:10.1007/978-3-319-97106-3_10

Mitchell, J. (2021). Affective shifts: Mood, emotion and well-being. *Synthese, 199*(5-6), 11793–11820. doi:10.100711229-021-03312-3

Moreno, R., & Mayer, R. E. (1999). Cognitive principles of multimedia learning: The role of modality and contiguity. *Journal of Educational Psychology, 91*(2), 358–368. doi:10.1037/0022-0663.91.2.358

Mounika, K., & Tahamarana, S. (2018). Teaching Speaking Skills Online: Prospects and Possibilities. Eltai Tirupathi, *Annual International Conference,* (pp. 1-6). IEEE.

Mousavi, S. Y., Low, R., & Sweller, J. (1995). Reducing cognitive load by mixing auditory and visual presentation modes. *Journal of Educational Psychology, 87*(2), 319–334. doi:10.1037/0022-0663.87.2.319

Muanjayanah, A. (2004). *The implementation of communication language*. Bumi Aksara.

Musti, K. S. S. (2020a). Management Information Systems for Higher Education Institutions: Challenges and Opportunities. In Quality Management Implementation in Higher Education: Practices, Models, and Case Studies (pp. 110-131). IGI Global, doi:10.4018/978-1-5225-9829-9.ch006

Musti, K. S. S. (2015). An effective approach for teaching database course, International Journal of Learning. *Teaching and Educational Research*, *12*(1), 53–63.

Musti, K. S. S. (2020b). Quantification of Demand Response in Smart Grids. *IEEE International Conference INDISCON*, (pp. 278-282). IEEE. 10.1109/INDISCON50162.2020.00063

Musti, K. S., & Van der Merwe, M. (2022). A Novel MS Excel Tool for Multi-Criteria Decision Analysis in Energy Systems. In N. Jain, J. Maherchandani, N. Agrawal, & T. Gupta (Eds.), *Optimal Planning of Smart Grid With Renewable Energy Resources* (pp. 83–109). IGI Global. doi:10.4018/978-1-6684-4012-4.ch003

Naidu, S. (2010). Using scenario-based learning to promote situated learning and develop professional knowledge. In E. P. Errington (Ed.), *Preparing graduates for the professions using scenario- based learning* (pp. 39–49). Post Pressed.

Naidu, S., Menon, M., Gunawardena, C., Lekamge, D., & Karunanayaka, S. (2007). *How scenario-based learning can engender reflective practice in distance education.* Lawrence Erlbaum Associates, Publishers New Jersey.

Nakatani, Y. (2006). Developing an oral communication strategy inventory. *Modern Language Journal*, *90*(1), 151–168. doi:10.1111/j.1540-4781.2006.00390.x

Nasab, G. F. (2015). Alternative versus traditional assessment. *Journal of Applied Linguistics and Language Research*, *2*(6), 165–178.

Nedic, Z., & Nafalski, A. (2015). Development of an online renewable energy laboratory. *Proceedings of 2015 12th International Conference on Remote Engineering and Virtual Instrumentation (REV)*, (pp. 136-139). IEEE. 10.1109/REV.2015.7087279

Nepsha, F., Shubin, N., Andrievsky, A., & Golovin, A. (2021). Development of Energy Management System Based on a Digital Platform. 2021 Ural-Siberian Smart Energy Conference (USSEC), (pp. 120-124). IEEE. 10.1109/USSEC53120.2021.9655765

New London Group. (1996). A pedagogy of multiliteracies: Designing social futures. *Harvard Educational Review*, *66*(1), 60–92. doi:10.17763/haer.66.1.17370n67v22j160u

North, B. (2014). *The CEFR in practice.* Cambridge University Press.

Nusser, L., Heydrich, J., Carstensen, C. H., Artelt, C., & Weinert, S. (2016). Validity of Survey Data of Students with Special Educational Needs— Results From the National Educational Panel Study. In H. Blossfeld, J. Von Maurice, r M. Baye, & J. Skopek (Eds.), Methodological Issues of Longitudinal Surveys (pp. 251–266). Springer Fachmedien Wiesbaden. doi:10.1007/978-3-658-11994-2_15

Oblinger, D. G., & Hawkins, B. L. (2005). The Myth about E-Learning. *EDUCAUSE Review*.

OECD. (2005). E-learning in tertiary education [Online]. OECD. http://www.cumex.org.

Orús, C., Barlés, M. J., Belanche, D., Casaló, L., Fraj, E., & Gurrea, R. (2016). The effects of learner-generated videos for YouTube on learning outcomes and satisfaction. *Computers & Education*, *95*, 254–269. doi:10.1016/j.compedu.2016.01.007

Pace, D. (2011). Assessment in History: The case for"decoding" the discipline. *The Journal of Scholarship of Teaching and Learning*, *11*(3), 107–119.

Park, I., & Hannafin, M. J. (1993). Empirically-based guidelines for the design of interactive multimedia. *Educational Technology Research and Development*, *41*(3), 63–85. doi:10.1007/BF02297358

Parlakkılıç, A. (2014). Rapid E-Learning and Desktop Virtualization In Education. *International Conference on Computer Science, Computer Engineering, and Social Media*, Thessaloniki, Greece.

Pekrun, R., Goetz, T., Frenzel, A. C., Barchfeld, P., & Perry, R. P. (2011). Measuring emotions in students' learning and performance: The Achievement Emotions Questionnaire (AEQ). *Contemporary Educational Psychology*, *36*(1), 36–48. doi:10.1016/j.cedpsych.2010.10.002

Pereira, J., Echeazarra, L., Sanz-Santamaría, S., & Gutiérrez, J. (2014). Student-generated online videos to develop cross-curricular and curricular competencies in nursing studies. *Computers in Human Behavior*, *31*, 580–590. doi:10.1016/j.chb.2013.06.011

Pernice, R. (2003). Writing-in-role: Helping students explore emotional dimensions. In E. Errington (Ed.), *Developing scenario based learning: Practical insights for tertiary educators* (pp. 145–153). Dunmore Press.

Phongsirikul, M. (2018). Traditional and alternative assessments in ELT: Students' and teachers' perceptions. *Reflections: The SoL Journal*, *25*(1), 61–84. https://so05.tci-thaijo.org/index.php/reflections/article/view/136267

Pickering, S. J. (2006). Working Memory and Education. In *Working Memory and Education*. Elsevier. doi:10.1016/B978-012554465-8/50011-9

Pirhonen, J., & Rasi, P. (2017). Student-generated instructional videos facilitate learning through positive emotions. *Journal of Biological Education*, *51*(3), 215–227. doi:10.1080/00219266.2016.1200647

Plass, J. L., Chun, D. M., Mayer, R. E., & Leutner, D. (1998). Supporting visual and verbal learning preferences in a second-language multimedia learning environment. *Journal of Educational Psychology*, *90*(1), 25–36. doi:10.1037/0022-0663.90.1.25

Pop, A. (2020). Alternatives in assessment: Student-generated videos and online written case presentations in medical English. *The 15th International Conference on Virtual Learning ICVL 2020*. Bucharest. https://www.researchgate.net/publication/352090551_Alternatives_in_Assessment_Student-generated_Videos_and_Online_Written_Case_presentations_in_Medical_English

Postareff, L., Virtanen, V., Katajavuori, N., & Lindblom-Ylänne, S. (2012). Academics' conceptions of assessment and their assessment practices. *Studies in Educational Evaluation*, *38*(3-4), 84–92. doi:10.1016/j.stueduc.2012.06.003

Prensky, M. (2001a). Digital natives, digital immigrants, part 1. *On the Horizon*, *9*(5), 1–6. doi:10.1108/10748120110424816

Prensky, M. (2001b). Digital natives, digital immigrants Part 2: Do they really think differently? *On the Horizon*, *9*(6), 1–6. doi:10.1108/10748120110424843

Prieto-Araujo, E., Cheah-Mañé, M., Villafafila-Robles, R., Gomis-Bellmunt, O., & Junyent-Ferré, A. (2013). Development of a laboratory platform for testing new solutions to integrate renewable energy sources in power systems. *2013 15th European Conference on Power Electronics and Applications (EPE),* (pp. 1-10). IEEE. 10.1109/EPE.2013.6634674

Purpura, J. E. (2004). *Assessing grammar*. Cambridge University Press. doi:10.1017/CBO9780511733086

Rajputh, R., Rajabalee, Y., Soni, J., & Koheeallee, N. (2016). Interactive Materials Development using the Rapid e- Learning Method - Examples from the Field. *Proceedings of the Commonwealth of Learning PCF8 Conference*. Oasis. https://oasis.col.org/bitstream/handle/11599/

Ramkhelawan, R. & Musti. K. (2019). *Power system load flow analysis using Microsoft Excel–Version 2*. Spreadsheets in Education 12.1.

Rapport, M. D., Alderson, R. M., Kofler, M. J., Sarver, D. E., Bolden, J., & Sims, V. (2008). Working Memory Deficits in Boys with Attention-deficit/Hyperactivity Disorder (ADHD): The Contribution of Central Executive and Subsystem Processes. *Journal of Abnormal Child Psychology*, *36*(6), 825–837. doi:10.100710802-008-9215-y PMID:18317920

Rawlusyk, P. E. (2018). Assessment in higher education and student learning. *Journal of Instructional Pedagogies*, *21*, 1–34.

Reeve, J. (1989). The interest-enjoyment distinction in intrinsic motivation. *Motivation and Emotion*, *13*(2), 83–103. doi:10.1007/BF00992956

Refat, N., Kassim, H., Rahman, M. A., & Razali, R. (2020). Measuring student motivation on the use of a mobile assisted grammar learning tool. *PLoS One*, *15*(8), e0236862. doi:10.1371/journal.pone.0236862 PMID:32857762

Renée, D. (2022). Link and Maria Gallardo-Williams, We Should Keep Developing Digital Laboratory Resources in the Postpandemic Era. *Journal of Chemical Education*, *99*(2), 519–520. doi:10.1021/acs.jchemed.1c01197

Ringkjøb, H.-K., Haugan, P. M., & Solbrekke, I. M. (2018). A review of modelling tools for energy and electricity systems with large shares of variable renewables. *Renewable & Sustainable Energy Reviews*, *96*, 440–459. doi:10.1016/j.rser.2018.08.002

Rossi, P. G. (2009). Ambiente di apprendimento con elementi di artificial intelligence. JE-LKS. *Journal of E-Learning and Knowledge Society*, *5*(1), 65–75.

Ross, J., Curwood, J. S., & Bell, A. (2020). A multimodal assessment framework for higher education. *E-Learning and Digital Media*, *17*(4), 290–306. doi:10.1177/2042753020927201

Rughoobur-Seetah, S., & Hosanoo, Z. A. (2021). An evaluation of the impact of confinement on the quality of e-learning in higher education institutions. *Quality Assurance in Education*, *29*(4), 422–444. doi:10.1108/QAE-03-2021-0043

Ryan, B. (2013). A walk down the red carpet: Students as producers digital video-based knowledge. *International Journal of Technology Enhanced Learning*, *5*(1), 24–41. doi:10.1504/IJTEL.2013.055950

Ryan, R. M., & Deci, E. L. (2000). Self-determination theory and the facilitation of intrinsic motivation, social development, and well-being. *The American Psychologist*, *55*(1), 68–78. doi:10.1037/0003-066X.55.1.68 PMID:11392867

Sabatini, J., Bennett, R. E., & Deane, P. (2011). *Four years of cognitively based assessment of, for, and as learning (CBAL): Learning about through course assessment (TCA)* [Symposium presentation]. Invitational research symposium on through-course summative assessments, Atlanta, GA, United States.https://www.ets.org/Media/Research/pdf/TCSA_Symposium_Final_Paper_Sabatini.pd

Sadati, S. M. H., & Mitchell, C. (2021). Narrative imagination and social change: Instructors in agricultural colleges in Ethiopia address sexual and gender-based violence. *Educational Research for Social Change*, *10*(2), 124–141. doi:10.17159/2221-4070/2021/v10i2a8

Sáenz, J., Chacón, J., De La Torre, L., Visioli, A., & Dormido, S. (2015). Open and Low-Cost Virtual and Remote Labs on Control Engineering. *IEEE Access: Practical Innovations, Open Solutions*, *3*, 805–814. doi:10.1109/ACCESS.2015.2442613

Samsuri, N. N., Nadzri, F. A., & Rom, K. B. M. (2014). A Study on the student's perspective on the effectiveness of using elearning. *Procedia: Social and Behavioral Sciences*, *123*, 139–144. doi:10.1016/j.sbspro.2014.01.1407

Sang, Y., Liu, P., & Liao, L. (2020). Experimental Design of the Mechanical Design Course in Distance Education. 2020 IEEE 2nd International Conference on Computer Science and Educational Informatization (CSEI), (pp. 248-251). IEEE. 10.1109/CSEI50228.2020.9142512

Sastry Musti, K. S., Iileka, H., & Shidhika, F. (2020). Industry 4.0-Based Enterprise Information System for Demand-Side Management and Energy Efficiency. In Novel Approaches to Information Systems Design (pp. 137-163). IGI Global, doi:10.4018/978-1-7998-2975-1.ch007

Sastry, M. & Riaz, A. (2009). The design and development of a virtual laboratory for power system modelling and load flow analysis to promote innovative learning. *International Journal of Innovation and Learning, 6*(2), 178-191. doi:10.1504/IJIL.2009.022812

Sastry, M. K. S. (2007). Development of an academic information system for effective education management. *International Journal of Management Education*, *1*(3), 276–286.

Schofield, L., Baker, K., Vo, D., Pham, T., Lindsay, L., & Han, B. (2017). How does the option of video assessment impact on student choice and grades? In S. Nash, & L. M. Patston (eds.), Spaces and Pedagogies: New Zealand Tertiary Learning and Teaching Conference 2017 Proceedings (pp. 67-78). Auckland, New Zealand: ePress, Unitec Institute of Technology.

Şeker, M. (2016). Scenario-Based Instruction Design as a Tool to Promote Self-Regulated Language Learning Strategies. *SAGE Open*, *6*(4), 1–11. doi:10.1177/2158244016684175

Shaaban, S. S. A. (2020). TEFL professors' e-learning experiences during the Covid-19 pandemic. *European Journal of Foreign Language Teaching*, *5*(1), 82–97. doi:10.46827/ejfl.v5i1.3202

Shah, N., & Abraham, S. (2009). Digital natives with a cause?A knowledge survey and framework. The Centre for Internet and Society, San Francisco:Hivos Knowledge Program

Snowball, J. D., & McKenna, S. (2017). Student-generated content: An approach to harnessing the power of diversity in higher education. *Teaching in Higher Education*, *22*(5), 604–618. doi:10.1080/13562517.2016.1273205

Sorin, R., Errington, E., Ireland, L., Nickson, A., & Caltabiano, M. (2012). Embedding graduate attributes through scenario-based learning. *J. NUS Teach. Acad.*, *2*, 192–205.

Sorrentino, P. (2018). The mystery of the digital natives' existence: Questioning the validity of the Prenskian metaphor. *First Monday*, *23*(10). doi:10.5210/fm.v23i10.9434

Stahre Wästberg, B., Eriksson, T., Karlsson, G., Sunnerstam, M., Axelsson, M., & Billger, M. (2019). Design considerations for virtual laboratories: A comparative study of two virtual laboratories for learning about gas solubility and colour appearance. *Education and Information Technologies*, *24*(3), 2059–2080. doi:10.100710639-018-09857-0

Stange, M., Barry, A., Smyth, J., & Olson, K. (2018). Effects of Smiley Face Scales on Visual Processing of Satisfaction Questions in Web Surveys. *Social Science Computer Review*, *36*(6), 756–766. doi:10.1177/0894439316674166

Starr, L. J., & Mitchell, C. (2020). Cellphilming as a feminist tool. In D. Clover, S. Dzulkifli, H. Gelderman, & K. Sanford (Eds.), *Feminist adult educator's guide to aesthetic, creative and disruptive strategies in museums and communities* (pp. 119–128). University of Victoria Gender Justice, Creative Pedagogies and Arts- Based Research Group., https://onlineacademiccommunity.uvic.ca/comarts/

Strauss, W., & Howe, N. (1991). *Generations*. Harper Perennial.

Strauss, W., & Howe, N. (1997). *The fourth turning: An American prophecy—What the cycles of history tell us about America's next rendezvous with destiny*. Broadway Books.

Summers, J. J., Waigandt, A., & Whittaker, T. A. (2005). A comparison of student achievement and satisfaction in an online versus a traditional face-to-face statistics class. *Innovative Higher Education, 29*(3), 233–250. doi:10.100710755-005-1938-x

Swanson, H. L., Zheng, X., & Jerman, O. (2009). Working Memory, Short-Term Memory, and Reading Disabilities. *Journal of Learning Disabilities, 42*(3), 260–287. doi:10.1177/0022219409331958 PMID:19255286

Sweller, J. (1999). Instructional Design in Technical Areas. Australian Education Review, 43. PCS Data Processing. Inc. USA.

Sweller, J. (2003). Evolution of human cognitive architecture. *Psychology of Learning and Motivation, 43*, 216–266. doi:10.1016/S0079-7421(03)01015-6

Sweller, J., & Chandler, P. (1994). Why some material is difficult to learn. *Cognition and Instruction, 12*(3), 185–233. doi:10.12071532690xci1203_1

Sweller, J., Chandler, P., Tierney, P., & Cooper, M. (1990). Cognitive load as a factor in the structuring of technical material. *Journal of Experimental Psychology. General, 119*(2), 176–192. doi:10.1037/0096-3445.119.2.176

Sze, P. M. (2006). Developing students' listening and speaking skills through ELT podcasts. *Education Journal, 34*(2), 115–134.

Tabbers, H. K., Martens, R. L., & van Merriënboer, J. J. (2000). *Multimedia instructions and cognitive load theory: Split-attention and modality effects.* In *National Convention of the Association for Educational Communications and Technology*, Long Beach, CA.

Taber, K. S. (2018). The Use of Cronbach's Alpha When Developing and Reporting Research Instruments in Science Education. *Research in Science Education, 48*(6), 1273–1296. doi:10.100711165-016-9602-2

Tanyeli, N. (2009). The efficiency of online English language instruction on students' reading skills. *Procedia: Social and Behavioral Sciences, 1*(1), 564–567. doi:10.1016/j.sbspro.2009.01.102

Tao, Y. H., Yeh, C. R., & Sun, S. I. (2006). Improving training needs assessment processes via theInternet: System design and qualitative study. *Internet Research, 16*(4), 427–449. doi:10.1108/10662240610690043

Tapscott, D. (1998). *Growing up digital: the rise of the net generation.* McGraw-Hill.

Taraldsen, L. H., Haara, F. O., Lysne, M. S., Jensen, P. R., & Jenssen, E. S. (2020). *A review on use of escape rooms in education – touching the void.* Education Inquiry. doi:10.1080/20004508.2020.1860284

Tarmizi, R. A., & Sweller, J. (1988). Guidance during mathematical problem solving. *Journal of Educational Psychology, 80*(4), 424–436. doi:10.1037/0022-0663.80.4.424

Tarone, E. (1977). Conscious communication strategies in interlanguage: A progress report. In H. D. Brown, C. A. Yorio, & R. C. Crymes (Eds.), *On TESOL 77* (pp. 194–203). TESOL.

Tarone, E. (1980). Communication strategies, foreigner talk, and repair in interlanguage. *Language Learning*, *30*(4), 417–431. doi:10.1111/j.1467-1770.1980.tb00326.x

Taslibeyaz, E. (2020). The effect of scenario-based interactive videos on English learning. *Interactive Learning Environments*, *28*(7), 808–820. doi:10.1080/10494820.2018.1552870

Toepoel, V., Vermeeren, B., & Metin, B. (2019). Smileys, Stars, Hearts, Buttons, Tiles or Grids: Influence of Response Format on Substantive Response, Questionnaire Experience and Response Time: *Sage, 142*(1), 57–74. doi:10.1177/0759106319834665

Twigg, C. (2002). Quality, cost and access: the case for redesign. In M. S. Pittinsky (Ed.), *The Wired Tower* (pp. 111–143). Prentice-Hall.

UNESCO. (2015). *Global citizenship education: Preparing learners for the challenges of the twenty-first century.* UNESCO. https://en.unesco.org/news/global-citizenship-education-preparing-learners-challenges-twenty-first-century-0

Veldkamp, A., van de Grint, L., Knippels, M.-C. P. J., & van Joolingen, W. R. (2020). Escape education: A systematic review on escape rooms in education. *Educational Research Review*, *31*, 100364. doi:10.1016/j.edurev.2020.100364

Veletsianos, G. (2011). Designing opportunities for transformation with emerging technologies. *Educational Technology*, *51*(2), 41–46.

Venable, M. (2011). *The 7 Cs of effective communication in your online course*. Online College.org.

Wajiuhullah, A., Ashraf, S., & Majad, S. (2018). Development of Number Concepts in Students with Intellectual Disability by using Digital Game based Learning. *The Journal of Educational Research*, *21*(1), 122–129. https://www.bbc.co.uk/bitesiz/ks1/maths

Wang, S., Liu, J., & Fu, W. (2015). A study on the content-based college ESP instruction under the background of MOOC era. *China Educational Technology*, 98-120.

Wang, X., Chen, W., Qiu, H., Eldurssi, A., Xie, F., & Shen, J. (2020). A Survey on the E-learning platforms used during COVID-19. *2020 11th IEEE Annual Information Technology, Electronics and Mobile Communication Conference (IEMCON)*, (pp. 0808-0814). 10.1109/IEMCON51383.2020.9284840

Ward, M., & Sweller, J. (1990). Structuring effective worked examples. *Cognition and Instruction*, *7*(1), 1–39. doi:10.12071532690xci0701_1

Warschauer, M. (2000). *CALL for the 21st Century*. IATEFL and ESADE Conference, Barcelona, Spain. http://www.gse.uci.edu/markw/cyberspace.html

Warschauer, M., & Meskill, C. (2000). Technology and second language teaching and learning. UCI. https://education.uci.edu/markw-tslt.html

Watts, H. S. (1985). When Teachers Are Researchers, Teaching Improves. *Journal of Staff Development*, 6.

Welsh, E. T., Wanberg, C. R., Brown, E. G., & Simmering, M. J. (2003). E-learning: Emerging uses, empiricalresults and future directions. *International Journal of Training and Development, 2003*(7), 245–258. doi:10.1046/j.1360-3736.2003.00184.x

Wentling, T. L., Waight, C., Gallagher, J., La Fleur, J., Wang, C., & Kanfer, A. (2000). E-learning - a review of literature. *Knowledge and Learning Systems Group NCSA, 9*, 1–73.

Willis, D., & Willis, J. (2007). *Doing Task-based Teaching*. Oxford University Press.

Wojton, H., Snavely, J., & Mary, J. (2016). *Introduction to Survey Design*. Institute for Defense Analyses. https://www.jstor.org/stable/resrep22713

World Health Organization [WHO]. (2020a). *Novel Coronavirus (2019-nCoV) SITUATION REPORT-1*. WHO. https://www.who.int/docs/default-source/coronaviruse/situation-reports/20200121- sitrep-1-2019-ncov.pdf?sfvrsn=20a99c10_4

World Health Organization [WHO]. (2020b). *Novel Coronavirus (2019-nCoV) SITUATION REPORT-22*. WHO. https://www.who.int/docs/default-source/coronaviruse/situation-reports/20200211- sitrep-22-ncov.pdf?sfvrsn=fb6d49b1_2

World Health Organization [WHO]. (2021). *WHO Coronavirus (COVID-19) Dashboard*. WHO. https://covid19.who.int/

Yearta, L., & Kelly, K. (2021). Digital storytelling to enhance social studies content knowledge, explore multiple perspectives, and advocate for social justice. In L. Hass & J. Tussey (Eds.), *Connecting disciplinary literacy and digital storytelling in K-12 education* (pp. 235–256). IGI Global. doi:10.4018/978-1-7998-5770-9.ch012

Yi, Y. (2008). Relay writing in an adolescent online community. *Journal of Adolescent & Adult Literacy, 51*(8), 670–680. https://www.jstor.org/stable/40012404. doi:10.1598/JAAL.51.8.6

Yüce, E. (2022). The immediate reactions of EFL learners towards total digitalization at higher education during the Covid-19 pandemic. *Kuramsal Eğitimbilim Dergisi [Journal of Theoretical Educational Science], 15*(1), 1-15.

Yüce, E. (2019). Possible problems in online foreign language teaching at a university context. *International Journal of Curriculum and Instruction, 11*(2), 75–86.

Yuen, T. (2021). Low Cost Simulation Lab for Teaching Control Theory Concepts, advances in intelligent systems and computing (Vol. 1314). Springer. doi:10.1007/978-3-030-67209-6_22

Zhuang, Y. L. (2014). *A Research of the Application of Visual Simulation Technology in College English Teaching*. Paper presented at the Advanced Materials Research. Scientific Net. 10.4028/www.scientific.net/AMR.1044-1045.1565

Zur, O., & Zur, A. (2011). *On digital immigrants and digital natives: How the digital divide affects families, educational institutions, and the workplace?* Zur Institute - Online Publication. http://www.zurinstitute.com/digital_divide.html

Related References

To continue our tradition of advancing academic research, we have compiled a list of recommended IGI Global readings. These references will provide additional information and guidance to further enrich your knowledge and assist you with your own research and future publications.

Aburezeq, I. M., & Dweikat, F. F. (2017). Cloud Applications in Language Teaching: Examining Pre-Service Teachers' Expertise, Perceptions and Integration. *International Journal of Distance Education Technologies, 15*(4), 39–60. doi:10.4018/IJDET.2017100103

Acharjya, B., & Das, S. (2022). Adoption of E-Learning During the COVID-19 Pandemic: The Moderating Role of Age and Gender. *International Journal of Web-Based Learning and Teaching Technologies, 17*(2), 1–14. https://doi.org/10.4018/IJWLTT.20220301.oa4

Adams, J. L., & Thomas, S. K. (2022). Non-Linear Curriculum Experiences for Student Learning and Work Design: What Is the Maximum Potential of a Chat Bot? In S. Ramlall, T. Cross, & M. Love (Eds.), *Handbook of Research on Future of Work and Education: Implications for Curriculum Delivery and Work Design* (pp. 299–306). IGI Global. https://doi.org/10.4018/978-1-7998-8275-6.ch018

Adera, B. (2017). Supporting Language and Literacy Development for English Language Learners. In J. Keengwe (Ed.), *Handbook of Research on Promoting Cross-Cultural Competence and Social Justice in Teacher Education* (pp. 339–354). Hershey, PA: IGI Global. doi:10.4018/978-1-5225-0897-7.ch018

Ahamer, G. (2017). Quality Assurance for a Developmental "Global Studies" (GS) Curriculum. In I. Management Association (Ed.), Educational Leadership and Administration: Concepts, Methodologies, Tools, and Applications (pp. 438-477). Hershey, PA: IGI Global. https://doi.org/ doi:10.4018/978-1-5225-1624-8.ch023

Ahamer, G. (2017). Quality Assurance for a Developmental "Global Studies" (GS) Curriculum. In I. Management Association (Ed.), Educational Leadership and Administration: Concepts, Methodologies, Tools, and Applications (pp. 438-477). Hershey, PA: IGI Global. https://doi.org/ doi:10.4018/978-1-5225-1624-8.ch023

Akayoğlu, S., & Seferoğlu, G. (2019). An Analysis of Negotiation of Meaning Functions of Advanced EFL Learners in Second Life: Negotiation of Meaning in Second Life. In M. Kruk (Ed.), *Assessing the Effectiveness of Virtual Technologies in Foreign and Second Language Instruction* (pp. 61–85). IGI Global. https://doi.org/10.4018/978-1-5225-7286-2.ch003

Akella, N. R. (2022). Unravelling the Web of Qualitative Dissertation Writing!: A Student Reflects. In A. Zimmerman (Ed.), *Methodological Innovations in Research and Academic Writing* (pp. 260–282). IGI Global. https://doi.org/10.4018/978-1-7998-8283-1.ch014

Alegre de la Rosa, O. M., & Angulo, L. M. (2017). Social Inclusion and Intercultural Values in a School of Education. In S. Mukerji & P. Tripathi (Eds.), *Handbook of Research on Administration, Policy, and Leadership in Higher Education* (pp. 518–531). Hershey, PA: IGI Global. doi:10.4018/978-1-5225-0672-0.ch020

Alexander, C. (2019). Using Gamification Strategies to Cultivate and Measure Professional Educator Dispositions. *International Journal of Game-Based Learning*, *9*(1), 15–29. https://doi.org/10.4018/IJGBL.2019010102

Anderson, K. M. (2017). Preparing Teachers in the Age of Equity and Inclusion. In I. Management Association (Ed.), Medical Education and Ethics: Concepts, Methodologies, Tools, and Applications (pp. 1532-1554). Hershey, PA: IGI Global. doi:10.4018/978-1-5225-0978-3.ch069

Awdziej, M. (2017). Case Study as a Teaching Method in Marketing. In D. Latusek (Ed.), *Case Studies as a Teaching Tool in Management Education* (pp. 244–263). Hershey, PA: IGI Global. doi:10.4018/978-1-5225-0770-3.ch013

Bakos, J. (2019). Sociolinguistic Factors Influencing English Language Learning. In N. Erdogan & M. Wei (Eds.), *Applied Linguistics for Teachers of Culturally and Linguistically Diverse Learners* (pp. 403–424). IGI Global. https://doi.org/10.4018/978-1-5225-8467-4.ch017

Banas, J. R., & York, C. S. (2017). Pre-Service Teachers' Motivation to Use Technology and the Impact of Authentic Learning Exercises. In L. Tomei (Ed.), *Exploring the New Era of Technology-Infused Education* (pp. 121–140). Hershey, PA: IGI Global. doi:10.4018/978-1-5225-1709-2.ch008

Barton, T. P. (2021). Empowering Educator Allyship by Exploring Racial Trauma and the Disengagement of Black Students. In C. Reneau & M. Villarreal (Eds.), *Handbook of Research on Leading Higher Education Transformation With Social Justice, Equity, and Inclusion* (pp. 186–197). IGI Global. https://doi.org/10.4018/978-1-7998-7152-1.ch013

Benhima, M. (2021). Moroccan English Department Student Attitudes Towards the Use of Distance Education During COVID-19: Moulay Ismail University as a Case Study. *International Journal of Information and Communication Technology Education, 17*(3), 105–122. https://doi.org/10.4018/IJICTE.20210701.oa7

Beycioglu, K., & Wildy, H. (2017). Principal Preparation: The Case of Novice Principals in Turkey. In I. Management Association (Ed.), Educational Leadership and Administration: Concepts, Methodologies, Tools, and Applications (pp. 1152-1169). Hershey, PA: IGI Global. https://doi.org/ doi:10.4018/978-1-5225-1624-8.ch054

Bharwani, S., & Musunuri, D. (2018). Reflection as a Process From Theory to Practice. In M. Khosrow-Pour, D.B.A. (Ed.), Encyclopedia of Information Science and Technology, Fourth Edition (pp. 1529-1539). Hershey, PA: IGI Global. doi:10.4018/978-1-5225-2255-3.ch132

Bhushan, A., Garza, K. B., Perumal, O., Das, S. K., Feola, D. J., Farrell, D., & Birnbaum, A. (2022). Lessons Learned From the COVID-19 Pandemic and the Implications for Pharmaceutical Graduate Education and Research. In C. Ford & K. Garza (Eds.), *Handbook of Research on Updating and Innovating Health Professions Education: Post-Pandemic Perspectives* (pp. 324–345). IGI Global. https://doi.org/10.4018/978-1-7998-7623-6.ch014

Bintz, W., Ciecierski, L. M., & Royan, E. (2021). Using Picture Books With Instructional Strategies to Address New Challenges and Teach Literacy Skills in a Digital World. In L. Haas & J. Tussey (Eds.), *Connecting Disciplinary Literacy and Digital Storytelling in K-12 Education* (pp. 38–58). IGI Global. https://doi.org/10.4018/978-1-7998-5770-9.ch003

Bohjanen, S. L., Cameron-Standerford, A., & Meidl, T. D. (2018). Capacity Building Pedagogy for Diverse Learners. In J. Keengwe (Ed.), *Handbook of Research on Pedagogical Models for Next-Generation Teaching and Learning* (pp. 195–212). Hershey, PA: IGI Global. doi:10.4018/978-1-5225-3873-8.ch011

Brewer, J. C. (2018). Measuring Text Readability Using Reading Level. In M. Khosrow-Pour, D.B.A. (Ed.), Encyclopedia of Information Science and Technology, Fourth Edition (pp. 1499-1507). Hershey, PA: IGI Global. doi:10.4018/978-1-5225-2255-3.ch129

Brookbanks, B. C. (2022). Student Perspectives on Business Education in the USA: Current Attitudes and Necessary Changes in an Age of Disruption. In A. Zhuplev & R. Koepp (Eds.), *Global Trends, Dynamics, and Imperatives for Strategic Development in Business Education in an Age of Disruption* (pp. 214–231). IGI Global. doi:10.4018/978-1-7998-7548-2.ch011

Brown, L. V., Dari, T., & Spencer, N. (2019). Addressing the Impact of Trauma in High Poverty Elementary Schools: An Ecological Model for School Counseling. In K. Daniels & K. Billingsley (Eds.), *Creating Caring and Supportive Educational Environments for Meaningful Learning* (pp. 135–153). IGI Global. https://doi.org/10.4018/978-1-5225-5748-7.ch008

Brown, S. L. (2017). A Case Study of Strategic Leadership and Research in Practice: Principal Preparation Programs that Work – An Educational Administration Perspective of Best Practices for Master's Degree Programs for Principal Preparation. In V. Wang (Ed.), *Encyclopedia of Strategic Leadership and Management* (pp. 1226–1244). Hershey, PA: IGI Global. doi:10.4018/978-1-5225-1049-9.ch086

Brzozowski, M., & Ferster, I. (2017). Educational Management Leadership: High School Principal's Management Style and Parental Involvement in School Management in Israel. In V. Potocan, M. Üngan, & Z. Nedelko (Eds.), *Handbook of Research on Managerial Solutions in Non-Profit Organizations* (pp. 55–74). Hershey, PA: IGI Global. doi:10.4018/978-1-5225-0731-4.ch003

Cahapay, M. B. (2020). Delphi Technique in the Development of Emerging Contents in High School Science Curriculum. *International Journal of Curriculum Development and Learning Measurement, 1*(2), 1–9. https://doi.org/10.4018/IJCDLM.2020070101

Camacho, L. F., & Leon Guerrero, A. E. (2022). Indigenous Student Experience in Higher Education: Implementation of Culturally Sensitive Support. In P. Pangelinan & T. McVey (Eds.), *Learning and Reconciliation Through Indigenous Education in Oceania* (pp. 254–266). IGI Global. https://doi.org/10.4018/978-1-7998-7736-3.ch016

Cannaday, J. (2017). The Masking Effect: Hidden Gifts and Disabilities of 2e Students. In P. Dickenson, P. Keough, & J. Courduff (Eds.), *Preparing Pre-Service Teachers for the Inclusive Classroom* (pp. 220–231). Hershey, PA: IGI Global. doi:10.4018/978-1-5225-1753-5.ch011

Cederquist, S., Fishman, B., & Teasley, S. D. (2022). What's Missing From the College Transcript?: How Employers Make Sense of Student Skills. In Y. Huang (Ed.), *Handbook of Research on Credential Innovations for Inclusive Pathways to Professions* (pp. 234–253). IGI Global. https://doi.org/10.4018/978-1-7998-3820-3.ch012

Cockrell, P., & Gibson, T. (2019). The Untold Stories of Black and Brown Student Experiences in Historically White Fraternities and Sororities. In P. Hoffman-Miller, M. James, & D. Hermond (Eds.), *African American Suburbanization and the Consequential Loss of Identity* (pp. 153–171). IGI Global. https://doi.org/10.4018/978-1-5225-7835-2.ch009

Cohen, M. (2022). Leveraging Content Creation to Boost Student Engagement. In T. Driscoll III, (Ed.), *Designing Effective Distance and Blended Learning Environments in K-12* (pp. 223–239). IGI Global. https://doi.org/10.4018/978-1-7998-6829-3.ch013

Contreras, E. C., & Contreras, I. I. (2018). Development of Communication Skills through Auditory Training Software in Special Education. In M. Khosrow-Pour, D.B.A. (Ed.), Encyclopedia of Information Science and Technology, Fourth Edition (pp. 2431-2441). Hershey, PA: IGI Global. doi:10.4018/978-1-5225-2255-3.ch212

Cooke, L., Schugar, J., Schugar, H., Penny, C., & Bruning, H. (2020). Can Everyone Code?: Preparing Teachers to Teach Computer Languages as a Literacy. In J. Mitchell & E. Vaughn (Eds.), *Participatory Literacy Practices for P-12 Classrooms in the Digital Age* (pp. 163–183). IGI Global. https://doi.org/10.4018/978-1-7998-0000-2.ch009

Cooley, D., & Whitten, E. (2017). Special Education Leadership and the Implementation of Response to Intervention. In F. Topor (Ed.), *Handbook of Research on Individualism and Identity in the Globalized Digital Age* (pp. 265–286). Hershey, PA: IGI Global. doi:10.4018/978-1-5225-0522-8.ch012

Cosner, S., Tozer, S., & Zavitkovsky, P. (2017). Enacting a Cycle of Inquiry Capstone Research Project in Doctoral-Level Leadership Preparation. In I. Management Association (Ed.), Educational Leadership and Administration: Concepts, Methodologies, Tools, and Applications (pp. 1460-1481). Hershey, PA: IGI Global. doi:10.4018/978-1-5225-1624-8.ch067

Crawford, C. M. (2018). Instructional Real World Community Engagement. In M. Khosrow-Pour, D.B.A. (Ed.), Encyclopedia of Information Science and Technology, Fourth Edition (pp. 1474-1486). Hershey, PA: IGI Global. doi:10.4018/978-1-5225-2255-3.ch127

Crosby-Cooper, T., & Pacis, D. (2017). Implementing Effective Student Support Teams. In P. Dickenson, P. Keough, & J. Courduff (Eds.), *Preparing Pre-Service Teachers for the Inclusive Classroom* (pp. 248–262). Hershey, PA: IGI Global. doi:10.4018/978-1-5225-1753-5.ch013

Curran, C. M., & Hawbaker, B. W. (2017). Cultivating Communities of Inclusive Practice: Professional Development for Educators – Research and Practice. In C. Curran & A. Petersen (Eds.), *Handbook of Research on Classroom Diversity and Inclusive Education Practice* (pp. 120–153). Hershey, PA: IGI Global. doi:10.4018/978-1-5225-2520-2.ch006

Dass, S., & Dabbagh, N. (2018). Faculty Adoption of 3D Avatar-Based Virtual World Learning Environments: An Exploratory Case Study. In I. Management Association (Ed.), Technology Adoption and Social Issues: Concepts, Methodologies, Tools, and Applications (pp. 1000-1033). Hershey, PA: IGI Global. https://doi.org/ doi:10.4018/978-1-5225-5201-7.ch045

Davison, A. M., & Scholl, K. G. (2017). Inclusive Recreation as Part of the IEP Process. In C. Curran & A. Petersen (Eds.), *Handbook of Research on Classroom Diversity and Inclusive Education Practice* (pp. 311–330). Hershey, PA: IGI Global. doi:10.4018/978-1-5225-2520-2.ch013

DeCoito, I. (2018). Addressing Digital Competencies, Curriculum Development, and Instructional Design in Science Teacher Education. In M. Khosrow-Pour, D.B.A. (Ed.), Encyclopedia of Information Science and Technology, Fourth Edition (pp. 1420-1431). Hershey, PA: IGI Global. https://doi.org/ doi:10.4018/978-1-5225-2255-3.ch122

DeCoito, I., & Richardson, T. (2017). Beyond Angry Birds™: Using Web-Based Tools to Engage Learners and Promote Inquiry in STEM Learning. In I. Levin & D. Tsybulsky (Eds.), *Digital Tools and Solutions for Inquiry-Based STEM Learning* (pp. 166–196). Hershey, PA: IGI Global. doi:10.4018/978-1-5225-2525-7.ch007

Delmas, P. M. (2017). Research-Based Leadership for Next-Generation Leaders. In R. Styron Jr & J. Styron (Eds.), *Comprehensive Problem-Solving and Skill Development for Next-Generation Leaders* (pp. 1–39). Hershey, PA: IGI Global. doi:10.4018/978-1-5225-1968-3.ch001

Demiray, U., & Ekren, G. (2018). Administrative-Related Evaluation for Distance Education Institutions in Turkey. In K. Buyuk, S. Kocdar, & A. Bozkurt (Eds.), *Administrative Leadership in Open and Distance Learning Programs* (pp. 263–288). Hershey, PA: IGI Global. doi:10.4018/978-1-5225-2645-2.ch011

Dickenson, P. (2017). What do we Know and Where Can We Grow?: Teachers Preparation for the Inclusive Classroom. In P. Dickenson, P. Keough, & J. Courduff (Eds.), *Preparing Pre-Service Teachers for the Inclusive Classroom* (pp. 1–22). Hershey, PA: IGI Global. doi:10.4018/978-1-5225-1753-5.ch001

Ding, Q., & Zhu, H. (2021). Flipping the Classroom in STEM Education. In J. Keengwe (Ed.), *Handbook of Research on Innovations in Non-Traditional Educational Practices* (pp. 155–173). IGI Global. https://doi.org/10.4018/978-1-7998-4360-3.ch008

Dixon, T., & Christison, M. (2021). Teaching English Grammar in a Hybrid Academic ESL Course: A Mixed Methods Study. In K. Kelch, P. Byun, S. Safavi, & S. Cervantes (Eds.), *CALL Theory Applications for Online TESOL Education* (pp. 229–251). IGI Global. https://doi.org/10.4018/978-1-7998-6609-1.ch010

Donne, V., & Hansen, M. (2017). Teachers' Use of Assistive Technologies in Education. In L. Tomei (Ed.), *Exploring the New Era of Technology-Infused Education* (pp. 86–101). Hershey, PA: IGI Global. doi:10.4018/978-1-5225-1709-2.ch006

Donne, V., & Hansen, M. A. (2018). Business and Technology Educators: Practices for Inclusion. In I. Management Association (Ed.), Business Education and Ethics: Concepts, Methodologies, Tools, and Applications (pp. 471-484). Hershey, PA: IGI Global. https://doi.org/ doi:10.4018/978-1-5225-3153-1.ch026

Dos Santos, L. M. (2022). Completing Student-Teaching Internships Online: Instructional Changes During the COVID-19 Pandemic. In M. Alaali (Ed.), *Assessing University Governance and Policies in Relation to the COVID-19 Pandemic* (pp. 106–127). IGI Global. https://doi.org/10.4018/978-1-7998-8279-4.ch007

Dreon, O., Shettel, J., & Bower, K. M. (2017). Preparing Next Generation Elementary Teachers for the Tools of Tomorrow. In M. Grassetti & S. Brookby (Eds.), *Advancing Next-Generation Teacher Education through Digital Tools and Applications* (pp. 143–159). Hershey, PA: IGI Global. doi:10.4018/978-1-5225-0965-3.ch008

Durak, H. Y., & Güyer, T. (2018). Design and Development of an Instructional Program for Teaching Programming Processes to Gifted Students Using Scratch. In J. Cannaday (Ed.), *Curriculum Development for Gifted Education Programs* (pp. 61–99). Hershey, PA: IGI Global. doi:10.4018/978-1-5225-3041-1.ch004

Egorkina, E., Ivanov, M., & Valyavskiy, A. Y. (2018). Students' Research Competence Formation of the Quality of Open and Distance Learning. In V. Mkrttchian & L. Belyanina (Eds.), *Handbook of Research on Students' Research Competence in Modern Educational Contexts* (pp. 364–384). Hershey, PA: IGI Global. doi:10.4018/978-1-5225-3485-3.ch019

Ekren, G., Karataş, S., & Demiray, U. (2017). Understanding of Leadership in Distance Education Management. In I. Management Association (Ed.), Educational Leadership and Administration: Concepts, Methodologies, Tools, and Applications (pp. 34-50). Hershey, PA: IGI Global. https://doi.org/ doi:10.4018/978-1-5225-1624-8.ch003

Elmore, W. M., Young, J. K., Harris, S., & Mason, D. (2017). The Relationship between Individual Student Attributes and Online Course Completion. In K. Shelton & K. Pedersen (Eds.), *Handbook of Research on Building, Growing, and Sustaining Quality E-Learning Programs* (pp. 151–173). Hershey, PA: IGI Global. doi:10.4018/978-1-5225-0877-9.ch008

Ercegovac, I. R., Alfirević, N., & Koludrović, M. (2017). School Principals' Communication and Co-Operation Assessment: The Croatian Experience. In I. Management Association (Ed.), Educational Leadership and Administration: Concepts, Methodologies, Tools, and Applications (pp. 1568-1589). Hershey, PA: IGI Global. https://doi.org/ doi:10.4018/978-1-5225-1624-8.ch072

Everhart, D., & Seymour, D. M. (2017). Challenges and Opportunities in the Currency of Higher Education. In K. Rasmussen, P. Northrup, & R. Colson (Eds.), *Handbook of Research on Competency-Based Education in University Settings* (pp. 41–65). Hershey, PA: IGI Global. doi:10.4018/978-1-5225-0932-5.ch003

Farmer, L. S. (2017). Managing Portable Technologies for Special Education. In V. Wang (Ed.), *Encyclopedia of Strategic Leadership and Management* (pp. 977–987). Hershey, PA: IGI Global. doi:10.4018/978-1-5225-1049-9.ch068

Farmer, L. S. (2018). Optimizing OERs for Optimal ICT Literacy in Higher Education. In J. Keengwe (Ed.), *Handbook of Research on Mobile Technology, Constructivism, and Meaningful Learning* (pp. 366–390). Hershey, PA: IGI Global. doi:10.4018/978-1-5225-3949-0.ch020

Ferguson, B. T. (2019). Supporting Affective Development of Children With Disabilities Through Moral Dilemmas. In S. Ikuta (Ed.), *Handmade Teaching Materials for Students With Disabilities* (pp. 253–275). IGI Global. doi:10.4018/978-1-5225-6240-5.ch011

Fındık, L. Y. (2017). Self-Assessment of Principals Based on Leadership in Complexity. In I. Management Association (Ed.), Educational Leadership and Administration: Concepts, Methodologies, Tools, and Applications (pp. 978-991). Hershey, PA: IGI Global. https://doi.org/ doi:10.4018/978-1-5225-1624-8.ch047

Flor, A. G., & Gonzalez-Flor, B. (2018). Dysfunctional Digital Demeanors: Tales From (and Policy Implications of) eLearning's Dark Side. In I. Management Association (Ed.), The Dark Web: Breakthroughs in Research and Practice (pp. 37-50). Hershey, PA: IGI Global. https://doi.org/ doi:10.4018/978-1-5225-3163-0.ch003

Floyd, K. K., & Shambaugh, N. (2017). Instructional Design for Simulations in Special Education Virtual Learning Spaces. In T. Kidd & L. Morris Jr., (Eds.), *Handbook of Research on Instructional Systems and Educational Technology* (pp. 202–215). Hershey, PA: IGI Global. doi:10.4018/978-1-5225-2399-4.ch018

Freeland, S. F. (2020). Community Schools: Improving Academic Achievement Through Meaningful Engagement. In R. Kronick (Ed.), *Emerging Perspectives on Community Schools and the Engaged University* (pp. 132–144). IGI Global. https://doi.org/10.4018/978-1-7998-0280-8.ch008

Ghanbarzadeh, R., & Ghapanchi, A. H. (2019). Applied Areas of Three Dimensional Virtual Worlds in Learning and Teaching: A Review of Higher Education. In I. Management Association (Ed.), *Virtual Reality in Education: Breakthroughs in Research and Practice* (pp. 172-192). IGI Global. https://doi.org/10.4018/978-1-5225-8179-6.ch008

Giovannini, J. M. (2017). Technology Integration in Preservice Teacher Education Programs: Research-based Recommendations. In M. Grassetti & S. Brookby (Eds.), *Advancing Next-Generation Teacher Education through Digital Tools and Applications* (pp. 82–102). Hershey, PA: IGI Global. doi:10.4018/978-1-5225-0965-3.ch005

Good, S., & Clarke, V. B. (2017). An Integral Analysis of One Urban School System's Efforts to Support Student-Centered Teaching. In J. Keengwe & G. Onchwari (Eds.), *Handbook of Research on Learner-Centered Pedagogy in Teacher Education and Professional Development* (pp. 45–68). Hershey, PA: IGI Global. doi:10.4018/978-1-5225-0892-2.ch003

Guetzoian, E. (2022). Gamification Strategies for Higher Education Student Worker Training. In C. Lane (Ed.), *Handbook of Research on Acquiring 21st Century Literacy Skills Through Game-Based Learning* (pp. 164–179). IGI Global. https://doi.org/10.4018/978-1-7998-7271-9.ch009

Hamidi, F., Owuor, P. M., Hynie, M., Baljko, M., & McGrath, S. (2017). Potentials of Digital Assistive Technology and Special Education in Kenya. In C. Ayo & V. Mbarika (Eds.), *Sustainable ICT Adoption and Integration for Socio-Economic Development* (pp. 125–151). Hershey, PA: IGI Global. doi:10.4018/978-1-5225-2565-3.ch006

Hamim, T., Benabbou, F., & Sael, N. (2022). Student Profile Modeling Using Boosting Algorithms. *International Journal of Web-Based Learning and Teaching Technologies, 17*(5), 1–13. https://doi.org/10.4018/IJWLTT.20220901.oa4

Henderson, L. K. (2017). Meltdown at Fukushima: Global Catastrophic Events, Visual Literacy, and Art Education. In R. Shin (Ed.), *Convergence of Contemporary Art, Visual Culture, and Global Civic Engagement* (pp. 80–99). Hershey, PA: IGI Global. doi:10.4018/978-1-5225-1665-1.ch005

Hudgins, T., & Holland, J. L. (2018). Digital Badges: Tracking Knowledge Acquisition Within an Innovation Framework. In I. Management Association (Ed.), Wearable Technologies: Concepts, Methodologies, Tools, and Applications (pp. 1118-1132). Hershey, PA: IGI Global. https://doi.org/ doi:10.4018/978-1-5225-5484-4.ch051

Hwang, R., Lin, H., Sun, J. C., & Wu, J. (2019). Improving Learning Achievement in Science Education for Elementary School Students via Blended Learning. *International Journal of Online Pedagogy and Course Design*, *9*(2), 44–62. https://doi.org/10.4018/IJOPCD.2019040104

Jančec, L., & Vodopivec, J. L. (2019). The Implicit Pedagogy and the Hidden Curriculum in Postmodern Education. In J. Vodopivec, L. Jančec, & T. Štemberger (Eds.), *Implicit Pedagogy for Optimized Learning in Contemporary Education* (pp. 41–59). IGI Global. https://doi.org/10.4018/978-1-5225-5799-9.ch003

Janus, M., & Siddiqua, A. (2018). Challenges for Children With Special Health Needs at the Time of Transition to School. In I. Management Association (Ed.), Autism Spectrum Disorders: Breakthroughs in Research and Practice (pp. 339-371). Hershey, PA: IGI Global. doi:10.4018/978-1-5225-3827-1.ch018

Jesus, R. A. (2018). Screencasts and Learning Styles. In M. Khosrow-Pour, D.B.A. (Ed.), Encyclopedia of Information Science and Technology, Fourth Edition (pp. 1548-1558). Hershey, PA: IGI Global. doi:10.4018/978-1-5225-2255-3.ch134

John, G., Francis, N., & Santhakumar, A. B. (2022). Student Engagement: Past, Present, and Future. In S. Ramlall, T. Cross, & M. Love (Eds.), *Handbook of Research on Future of Work and Education: Implications for Curriculum Delivery and Work Design* (pp. 329–341). IGI Global. https://doi.org/10.4018/978-1-7998-8275-6.ch020

Karpinski, A. C., D'Agostino, J. V., Williams, A. K., Highland, S. A., & Mellott, J. A. (2018). The Relationship Between Online Formative Assessment and State Test Scores Using Multilevel Modeling. In M. Khosrow-Pour, D.B.A. (Ed.), Encyclopedia of Information Science and Technology, Fourth Edition (pp. 5183-5192). Hershey, PA: IGI Global. doi:10.4018/978-1-5225-2255-3.ch450

Kats, Y. (2017). Educational Leadership and Integrated Support for Students with Autism Spectrum Disorders. In I. Management Association (Ed.), Educational Leadership and Administration: Concepts, Methodologies, Tools, and Applications (pp. 101-114). Hershey, PA: IGI Global. https://doi.org/ doi:10.4018/978-1-5225-1624-8.ch007

Kaya, G., & Altun, A. (2018). Educational Ontology Development. In M. Khosrow-Pour, D.B.A. (Ed.), Encyclopedia of Information Science and Technology, Fourth Edition (pp. 1441-1450). Hershey, PA: IGI Global. doi:10.4018/978-1-5225-2255-3.ch124

Keough, P. D., & Pacis, D. (2017). Best Practices Implementing Special Education Curriculum and Common Core State Standards using UDL. In P. Dickenson, P. Keough, & J. Courduff (Eds.), *Preparing Pre-Service Teachers for the Inclusive Classroom* (pp. 107–123). Hershey, PA: IGI Global. doi:10.4018/978-1-5225-1753-5.ch006

Kilburn, M., Henckell, M., & Starrett, D. (2018). Factors Contributing to the Effectiveness of Online Students and Instructors. In M. Khosrow-Pour, D.B.A. (Ed.), Encyclopedia of Information Science and Technology, Fourth Edition (pp. 1451-1462). Hershey, PA: IGI Global. doi:10.4018/978-1-5225-2255-3.ch125

Koban Koç, D. (2021). Gender and Language: A Sociolinguistic Analysis of Second Language Writing. In E. Hancı-Azizoglu & N. Kavaklı (Eds.), *Futuristic and Linguistic Perspectives on Teaching Writing to Second Language Students* (pp. 161–177). IGI Global. https://doi.org/10.4018/978-1-7998-6508-7.ch010

Konecny, L. T. (2017). Hybrid, Online, and Flipped Classrooms in Health Science: Enhanced Learning Environments. In I. Management Association (Ed.), Flipped Instruction: Breakthroughs in Research and Practice (pp. 355-370). Hershey, PA: IGI Global. https://doi.org/ doi:10.4018/978-1-5225-1803-7.ch020

Kupietz, K. D. (2021). Gaming and Simulation in Public Education: Teaching Others to Help Themselves and Their Neighbors. In N. Drumhiller, T. Wilkin, & K. Srba (Eds.), *Simulation and Game-Based Learning in Emergency and Disaster Management* (pp. 41–62). IGI Global. https://doi.org/10.4018/978-1-7998-4087-9.ch003

Kwee, C. T. (2022). Assessing the International Student Enrolment Strategies in Australian Universities: A Case Study During the COVID-19 Pandemic. In M. Alaali (Ed.), *Assessing University Governance and Policies in Relation to the COVID-19 Pandemic* (pp. 162–188). IGI Global. https://doi.org/10.4018/978-1-7998-8279-4.ch010

Lauricella, S., & McArthur, F. A. (2022). Taking a Student-Centred Approach to Alternative Digital Credentials: Multiple Pathways Toward the Acquisition of Microcredentials. In D. Piedra (Ed.), *Innovations in the Design and Application of Alternative Digital Credentials* (pp. 57–69). IGI Global. https://doi.org/10.4018/978-1-7998-7697-7.ch003

Llamas, M. F. (2019). Intercultural Awareness in Teaching English for Early Childhood: A Film-Based Approach. In E. Domínguez Romero, J. Bobkina, & S. Stefanova (Eds.), *Teaching Literature and Language Through Multimodal Texts* (pp. 54–68). IGI Global. https://doi.org/10.4018/978-1-5225-5796-8.ch004

Lokhtina, I., & Kkese, E. T. (2022). Reflecting and Adapting to an Academic Workplace Before and After the Lockdown in Greek-Speaking Cyprus: Opportunities and Challenges. In A. Zhuplev & R. Koepp (Eds.), *Global Trends, Dynamics, and Imperatives for Strategic Development in Business Education in an Age of Disruption* (pp. 126–148). IGI Global. https://doi.org/10.4018/978-1-7998-7548-2.ch007

Lovell, K. L. (2017). Development and Evaluation of Neuroscience Computer-Based Modules for Medical Students: Instructional Design Principles and Effectiveness. In J. Stefaniak (Ed.), *Advancing Medical Education Through Strategic Instructional Design* (pp. 262–276). Hershey, PA: IGI Global. doi:10.4018/978-1-5225-2098-6.ch013

Maher, D. (2019). The Use of Course Management Systems in Pre-Service Teacher Education. In J. Keengwe (Ed.), *Handbook of Research on Blended Learning Pedagogies and Professional Development in Higher Education* (pp. 196–213). IGI Global. https://doi.org/10.4018/978-1-5225-5557-5.ch011

Makewa, L. N. (2019). Teacher Technology Competence Base. In L. Makewa, B. Ngussa, & J. Kuboja (Eds.), *Technology-Supported Teaching and Research Methods for Educators* (pp. 247–267). IGI Global. https://doi.org/10.4018/978-1-5225-5915-3.ch014

Mallett, C. A. (2022). School Resource (Police) Officers in Schools: Impact on Campus Safety, Student Discipline, and Learning. In G. Crews (Ed.), *Impact of School Shootings on Classroom Culture, Curriculum, and Learning* (pp. 53–70). IGI Global. https://doi.org/10.4018/978-1-7998-5200-1.ch004

Marinho, J. E., Freitas, I. R., Leão, I. B., Pacheco, L. O., Gonçalves, M. P., Castro, M. J., Silva, P. D., & Moreira, R. J. (2022). Project-Based Learning Application in Higher Education: Student Experiences and Perspectives. In A. Alves & N. van Hattum-Janssen (Eds.), *Training Engineering Students for Modern Technological Advancement* (pp. 146–164). IGI Global. https://doi.org/10.4018/978-1-7998-8816-1.ch007

McCleskey, J. A., & Melton, R. M. (2022). Rolling With the Flow: Online Faculty and Student Presence in a Post-COVID-19 World. In S. Ramlall, T. Cross, & M. Love (Eds.), *Handbook of Research on Future of Work and Education: Implications for Curriculum Delivery and Work Design* (pp. 307–328). IGI Global. https://doi.org/10.4018/978-1-7998-8275-6.ch019

McCormack, V. F., Stauffer, M., Fishley, K., Hohenbrink, J., Mascazine, J. R., & Zigler, T. (2018). Designing a Dual Licensure Path for Middle Childhood and Special Education Teacher Candidates. In D. Polly, M. Putman, T. Petty, & A. Good (Eds.), *Innovative Practices in Teacher Preparation and Graduate-Level Teacher Education Programs* (pp. 21–36). Hershey, PA: IGI Global. doi:10.4018/978-1-5225-3068-8.ch002

McDaniel, R. (2017). Strategic Leadership in Instructional Design: Applying the Principles of Instructional Design through the Lens of Strategic Leadership to Distance Education. In V. Wang (Ed.), *Encyclopedia of Strategic Leadership and Management* (pp. 1570–1584). Hershey, PA: IGI Global. doi:10.4018/978-1-5225-1049-9.ch109

McKinney, R. E., Halli-Tierney, A. D., Gold, A. E., Allen, R. S., & Carroll, D. G. (2022). Interprofessional Education: Using Standardized Cases in Face-to-Face and Remote Learning Settings. In C. Ford & K. Garza (Eds.), *Handbook of Research on Updating and Innovating Health Professions Education: Post-Pandemic Perspectives* (pp. 24–42). IGI Global. https://doi.org/10.4018/978-1-7998-7623-6.ch002

Meintjes, H. H. (2021). Learner Views of a Facebook Page as a Supportive Digital Pedagogical Tool at a Public South African School in a Grade 12 Business Studies Class. *International Journal of Smart Education and Urban Society*, *12*(2), 32–45. https://doi.org/10.4018/IJSEUS.2021040104

Melero-García, F. (2022). Training Bilingual Interpreters in Healthcare Settings: Student Perceptions of Online Learning. In J. LeLoup & P. Swanson (Eds.), *Handbook of Research on Effective Online Language Teaching in a Disruptive Environment* (pp. 288–310). IGI Global. https://doi.org/10.4018/978-1-7998-7720-2.ch015

Meletiadou, E. (2022). The Use of Peer Assessment as an Inclusive Learning Strategy in Higher Education Institutions: Enhancing Student Writing Skills and Motivation. In E. Meletiadou (Ed.), *Handbook of Research on Policies and Practices for Assessing Inclusive Teaching and Learning* (pp. 1–26). IGI Global. https://doi.org/10.4018/978-1-7998-8579-5.ch001

Memon, R. N., Ahmad, R., & Salim, S. S. (2018). Critical Issues in Requirements Engineering Education. In I. Management Association (Ed.), Computer Systems and Software Engineering: Concepts, Methodologies, Tools, and Applications (pp. 1953-1976). Hershey, PA: IGI Global. doi:10.4018/978-1-5225-3923-0.ch081

Mendenhall, R. (2017). Western Governors University: CBE Innovator and National Model. In K. Rasmussen, P. Northrup, & R. Colson (Eds.), *Handbook of Research on Competency-Based Education in University Settings* (pp. 379–400). Hershey, PA: IGI Global. doi:10.4018/978-1-5225-0932-5.ch019

Mense, E. G., Griggs, D. M., & Shanks, J. N. (2018). School Leaders in a Time of Accountability and Data Use: Preparing Our Future School Leaders in Leadership Preparation Programs. In E. Mense & M. Crain-Dorough (Eds.), *Data Leadership for K-12 Schools in a Time of Accountability* (pp. 235–259). Hershey, PA: IGI Global. doi:10.4018/978-1-5225-3188-3.ch012

Mense, E. G., Griggs, D. M., & Shanks, J. N. (2018). School Leaders in a Time of Accountability and Data Use: Preparing Our Future School Leaders in Leadership Preparation Programs. In E. Mense & M. Crain-Dorough (Eds.), *Data Leadership for K-12 Schools in a Time of Accountability* (pp. 235–259). Hershey, PA: IGI Global. doi:10.4018/978-1-5225-3188-3.ch012

Mestry, R., & Naicker, S. R. (2017). Exploring Distributive Leadership in South African Public Primary Schools in the Soweto Region. In I. Management Association (Ed.), Educational Leadership and Administration: Concepts, Methodologies, Tools, and Applications (pp. 1041-1064). Hershey, PA: IGI Global. doi:10.4018/978-1-5225-1624-8.ch050

Monaghan, C. H., & Boboc, M. (2017). (Re) Defining Leadership in Higher Education in the U.S. In V. Wang (Ed.), *Encyclopedia of Strategic Leadership and Management* (pp. 567–579). Hershey, PA: IGI Global. doi:10.4018/978-1-5225-1049-9.ch040

Morall, M. B. (2021). Reimagining Mobile Phones: Multiple Literacies and Digital Media Compositions. In C. Moran (Eds.), *Affordances and Constraints of Mobile Phone Use in English Language Arts Classrooms* (pp. 41-53). IGI Global. https://doi.org/10.4018/978-1-7998-5805-8.ch003

Mthethwa, V. (2022). Student Governance and the Academic Minefield During COVID-19 Lockdown in South Africa. In M. Alaali (Ed.), *Assessing University Governance and Policies in Relation to the COVID-19 Pandemic* (pp. 255–276). IGI Global. https://doi.org/10.4018/978-1-7998-8279-4.ch015

Muthee, J. M., & Murungi, C. G. (2018). Relationship Among Intelligence, Achievement Motivation, Type of School, and Academic Performance of Kenyan Urban Primary School Pupils. In M. Khosrow-Pour, D.B.A. (Ed.), Encyclopedia of Information Science and Technology, Fourth Edition (pp. 1540-1547). Hershey, PA: IGI Global. https://doi.org/ doi:10.4018/978-1-5225-2255-3.ch133

Naranjo, J. (2018). Meeting the Need for Inclusive Educators Online: Teacher Education in Inclusive Special Education and Dual-Certification. In D. Polly, M. Putman, T. Petty, & A. Good (Eds.), *Innovative Practices in Teacher Preparation and Graduate-Level Teacher Education Programs* (pp. 106–122). Hershey, PA: IGI Global. doi:10.4018/978-1-5225-3068-8.ch007

Nkabinde, Z. P. (2017). Multiculturalism in Special Education: Perspectives of Minority Children in Urban Schools. In J. Keengwe (Ed.), *Handbook of Research on Promoting Cross-Cultural Competence and Social Justice in Teacher Education* (pp. 382–397). Hershey, PA: IGI Global. doi:10.4018/978-1-5225-0897-7.ch020

Nkabinde, Z. P. (2018). Online Instruction: Is the Quality the Same as Face-to-Face Instruction? In J. Keengwe (Ed.), *Handbook of Research on Digital Content, Mobile Learning, and Technology Integration Models in Teacher Education* (pp. 300–314). Hershey, PA: IGI Global. doi:10.4018/978-1-5225-2953-8.ch016

Nugroho, A., & Albusaidi, S. S. (2022). Internationalization of Higher Education: The Methodological Critiques on the Research Related to Study Overseas and International Experience. In H. Magd & S. Kunjumuhammed (Eds.), *Global Perspectives on Quality Assurance and Accreditation in Higher Education Institutions* (pp. 75–89). IGI Global. https://doi.org/10.4018/978-1-7998-8085-1.ch005

Nulty, Z., & West, S. G. (2022). Student Engagement and Supporting Students With Accommodations. In P. Bull & G. Patterson (Eds.), *Redefining Teacher Education and Teacher Preparation Programs in the Post-COVID-19 Era* (pp. 99–116). IGI Global. https://doi.org/10.4018/978-1-7998-8298-5.ch006

O'Connor, J. R. Jr, & Jackson, K. N. (2017). The Use of iPad® Devices and "Apps" for ASD Students in Special Education and Speech Therapy. In Y. Kats (Ed.), *Supporting the Education of Children with Autism Spectrum Disorders* (pp. 267–283). Hershey, PA: IGI Global. doi:10.4018/978-1-5225-0816-8.ch014

Okolie, U. C., & Yasin, A. M. (2017). TVET in Developing Nations and Human Development. In U. Okolie & A. Yasin (Eds.), *Technical Education and Vocational Training in Developing Nations* (pp. 1–25). Hershey, PA: IGI Global. doi:10.4018/978-1-5225-1811-2.ch001

Pack, A., & Barrett, A. (2021). A Review of Virtual Reality and English for Academic Purposes: Understanding Where to Start. *International Journal of Computer-Assisted Language Learning and Teaching, 11*(1), 72–80. https://doi.org/10.4018/IJCALLT.2021010105

Pashollari, E. (2019). Building Sustainability Through Environmental Education: Education for Sustainable Development. In L. Wilson, & C. Stevenson (Eds.), *Building Sustainability Through Environmental Education* (pp. 72-88). IGI Global. https://doi.org/10.4018/978-1-5225-7727-0.ch004

Paulson, E. N. (2017). Adapting and Advocating for an Online EdD Program in Changing Times and "Sacred" Cultures. In I. Management Association (Ed.), Educational Leadership and Administration: Concepts, Methodologies, Tools, and Applications (pp. 1849-1876). Hershey, PA: IGI Global. https://doi.org/doi:10.4018/978-1-5225-1624-8.ch085

Petersen, A. J., Elser, C. F., Al Nassir, M. N., Stakey, J., & Everson, K. (2017). The Year of Teaching Inclusively: Building an Elementary Classroom for All Students. In C. Curran & A. Petersen (Eds.), *Handbook of Research on Classroom Diversity and Inclusive Education Practice* (pp. 332–348). Hershey, PA: IGI Global. doi:10.4018/978-1-5225-2520-2.ch014

Pfannenstiel, K. H., & Sanders, J. (2017). Characteristics and Instructional Strategies for Students With Mathematical Difficulties: In the Inclusive Classroom. In C. Curran & A. Petersen (Eds.), *Handbook of Research on Classroom Diversity and Inclusive Education Practice* (pp. 250–281). Hershey, PA: IGI Global. doi:10.4018/978-1-5225-2520-2.ch011

Phan, A. N. (2022). Quality Assurance of Higher Education From the Glonacal Agency Heuristic: An Example From Vietnam. In H. Magd & S. Kunjumuhammed (Eds.), *Global Perspectives on Quality Assurance and Accreditation in Higher Education Institutions* (pp. 136–155). IGI Global. https://doi.org/10.4018/978-1-7998-8085-1.ch008

Preast, J. L., Bowman, N., & Rose, C. A. (2017). Creating Inclusive Classroom Communities Through Social and Emotional Learning to Reduce Social Marginalization Among Students. In C. Curran & A. Petersen (Eds.), *Handbook of Research on Classroom Diversity and Inclusive Education Practice* (pp. 183–200). Hershey, PA: IGI Global. doi:10.4018/978-1-5225-2520-2.ch008

Randolph, K. M., & Brady, M. P. (2018). Evolution of Covert Coaching as an Evidence-Based Practice in Professional Development and Preparation of Teachers. In V. Bryan, A. Musgrove, & J. Powers (Eds.), *Handbook of Research on Human Development in the Digital Age* (pp. 281–299). Hershey, PA: IGI Global. doi:10.4018/978-1-5225-2838-8.ch013

Rell, A. B., Puig, R. A., Roll, F., Valles, V., Espinoza, M., & Duque, A. L. (2017). Addressing Cultural Diversity and Global Competence: The Dual Language Framework. In L. Leavitt, S. Wisdom, & K. Leavitt (Eds.), *Cultural Awareness and Competency Development in Higher Education* (pp. 111–131). Hershey, PA: IGI Global. doi:10.4018/978-1-5225-2145-7.ch007

Richards, M., & Guzman, I. R. (2020). Academic Assessment of Critical Thinking in Distance Education Information Technology Programs. In I. Management Association (Ed.), *Learning and Performance Assessment: Concepts, Methodologies, Tools, and Applications* (pp. 1-19). IGI Global. https://doi.org/10.4018/978-1-7998-0420-8.ch001

Riel, J., Lawless, K. A., & Brown, S. W. (2017). Defining and Designing Responsive Online Professional Development (ROPD): A Framework to Support Curriculum Implementation. In T. Kidd & L. Morris Jr., (Eds.), *Handbook of Research on Instructional Systems and Educational Technology* (pp. 104–115). Hershey, PA: IGI Global. doi:10.4018/978-1-5225-2399-4.ch010

Roberts, C. (2017). Advancing Women Leaders in Academe: Creating a Culture of Inclusion. In S. Mukerji & P. Tripathi (Eds.), *Handbook of Research on Administration, Policy, and Leadership in Higher Education* (pp. 256–273). Hershey, PA: IGI Global. doi:10.4018/978-1-5225-0672-0.ch012

Rodgers, W. J., Kennedy, M. J., Alves, K. D., & Romig, J. E. (2017). A Multimedia Tool for Teacher Education and Professional Development. In C. Martin & D. Polly (Eds.), *Handbook of Research on Teacher Education and Professional Development* (pp. 285–296). Hershey, PA: IGI Global. doi:10.4018/978-1-5225-1067-3.ch015

Romanowski, M. H. (2017). Qatar's Educational Reform: Critical Issues Facing Principals. In I. Management Association (Ed.), Educational Leadership and Administration: Concepts, Methodologies, Tools, and Applications (pp. 1758-1773). Hershey, PA: IGI Global. https://doi.org/ doi:10.4018/978-1-5225-1624-8.ch080

Ruffin, T. R., Hawkins, D. P., & Lee, D. I. (2018). Increasing Student Engagement and Participation Through Course Methodology. In M. Khosrow-Pour, D.B.A. (Ed.), Encyclopedia of Information Science and Technology, Fourth Edition (pp. 1463-1473). Hershey, PA: IGI Global. doi:10.4018/978-1-5225-2255-3.ch126

Sabina, L. L., Curry, K. A., Harris, E. L., Krumm, B. L., & Vencill, V. (2017). Assessing the Performance of a Cohort-Based Model Using Domestic and International Practices. In I. Management Association (Ed.), Educational Leadership and Administration: Concepts, Methodologies, Tools, and Applications(pp. 913-929). Hershey, PA: IGI Global. https://doi.org/ doi:10.4018/978-1-5225-1624-8.ch044

Samkian, A., Pascarella, J., & Slayton, J. (2022). Towards an Anti-Racist, Culturally Responsive, and LGBTQ+ Inclusive Education: Developing Critically-Conscious Educational Leaders. In E. Cain-Sanschagrin, R. Filback, & J. Crawford (Eds.), *Cases on Academic Program Redesign for Greater Racial and Social Justice* (pp. 150–175). IGI Global. https://doi.org/10.4018/978-1-7998-8463-7.ch007

Santamaría, A. P., Webber, M., & Santamaría, L. J. (2017). Effective School Leadership for Māori Achievement: Building Capacity through Indigenous, National, and International Cross-Cultural Collaboration. In I. Management Association (Ed.), Educational Leadership and Administration: Concepts, Methodologies, Tools, and Applications (pp. 1547-1567). Hershey, PA: IGI Global. https://doi.org/ doi:10.4018/978-1-5225-1624-8.ch071

Santamaría, L. J. (2017). Culturally Responsive Educational Leadership in Cross-Cultural International Contexts. In I. Management Association (Ed.), Educational Leadership and Administration: Concepts, Methodologies, Tools, and Applications (pp. 1380-1400). Hershey, PA: IGI Global. https://doi.org/ doi:10.4018/978-1-5225-1624-8.ch064

Segredo, M. R., Cistone, P. J., & Reio, T. G. (2017). Relationships Between Emotional Intelligence, Leadership Style, and School Culture. *International Journal of Adult Vocational Education and Technology*, *8*(3), 25–43. doi:10.4018/IJAVET.2017070103

Shalev, N. (2017). Empathy and Leadership From the Organizational Perspective. In Z. Nedelko & M. Brzozowski (Eds.), *Exploring the Influence of Personal Values and Cultures in the Workplace* (pp. 348–363). Hershey, PA: IGI Global. doi:10.4018/978-1-5225-2480-9.ch018

Siamak, M., Fathi, S., & Isfandyari-Moghaddam, A. (2018). Assessment and Measurement of Education Programs of Information Literacy. In R. Bhardwaj (Ed.), *Digitizing the Modern Library and the Transition From Print to Electronic* (pp. 164–192). Hershey, PA: IGI Global. doi:10.4018/978-1-5225-2119-8.ch007

Siu, K. W., & García, G. J. (2017). Disruptive Technologies and Education: Is There Any Disruption After All? In I. Management Association (Ed.), Educational Leadership and Administration: Concepts, Methodologies, Tools, and Applications (pp. 757-778). Hershey, PA: IGI Global. https://doi.org/ doi:10.4018/978-1-5225-1624-8.ch037

Slagter van Tryon, P. J. (2017). The Nurse Educator's Role in Designing Instruction and Instructional Strategies for Academic and Clinical Settings. In J. Stefaniak (Ed.), *Advancing Medical Education Through Strategic Instructional Design* (pp. 133–149). Hershey, PA: IGI Global. doi:10.4018/978-1-5225-2098-6.ch006

Slattery, C. A. (2018). Literacy Intervention and the Differentiated Plan of Instruction. In *Developing Effective Literacy Intervention Strategies: Emerging Research and Opportunities* (pp. 41–62). Hershey, PA: IGI Global. doi:10.4018/978-1-5225-5007-5.ch003

Smith, A. R. (2017). Ensuring Quality: The Faculty Role in Online Higher Education. In K. Shelton & K. Pedersen (Eds.), *Handbook of Research on Building, Growing, and Sustaining Quality E-Learning Programs* (pp. 210–231). Hershey, PA: IGI Global. doi:10.4018/978-1-5225-0877-9.ch011

Souders, T. M. (2017). Understanding Your Learner: Conducting a Learner Analysis. In J. Stefaniak (Ed.), *Advancing Medical Education Through Strategic Instructional Design* (pp. 1–29). Hershey, PA: IGI Global. doi:10.4018/978-1-5225-2098-6.ch001

Spring, K. J., Graham, C. R., & Ikahihifo, T. B. (2018). Learner Engagement in Blended Learning. In M. Khosrow-Pour, D.B.A. (Ed.), Encyclopedia of Information Science and Technology, Fourth Edition (pp. 1487-1498). Hershey, PA: IGI Global. doi:10.4018/978-1-5225-2255-3.ch128

Storey, V. A., Anthony, A. K., & Wahid, P. (2017). Gender-Based Leadership Barriers: Advancement of Female Faculty to Leadership Positions in Higher Education. In V. Wang (Ed.), *Encyclopedia of Strategic Leadership and Management* (pp. 244–258). Hershey, PA: IGI Global. doi:10.4018/978-1-5225-1049-9.ch018

Stottlemyer, D. (2018). Develop a Teaching Model Plan for a Differentiated Learning Approach. In *Differentiated Instructional Design for Multicultural Environments: Emerging Research and Opportunities* (pp. 106–130). Hershey, PA: IGI Global. doi:10.4018/978-1-5225-5106-5.ch005

Stottlemyer, D. (2018). Developing a Multicultural Environment. In *Differentiated Instructional Design for Multicultural Environments: Emerging Research and Opportunities* (pp. 1–27). Hershey, PA: IGI Global. doi:10.4018/978-1-5225-5106-5.ch001

Swagerty, T. (2022). Digital Access to Culturally Relevant Curricula: The Impact on the Native and Indigenous Student. In E. Reeves & C. McIntyre (Eds.), *Multidisciplinary Perspectives on Diversity and Equity in a Virtual World* (pp. 99–113). IGI Global. https://doi.org/10.4018/978-1-7998-8028-8.ch006

Swami, B. N., Gobona, T., & Tsimako, J. J. (2017). Academic Leadership: A Case Study of the University of Botswana. In N. Baporikar (Ed.), *Innovation and Shifting Perspectives in Management Education* (pp. 1–32). Hershey, PA: IGI Global. doi:10.4018/978-1-5225-1019-2.ch001

Swanson, K. W., & Collins, G. (2018). Designing Engaging Instruction for the Adult Learners. In M. Khosrow-Pour, D.B.A. (Ed.), Encyclopedia of Information Science and Technology, Fourth Edition (pp. 1432-1440). Hershey, PA: IGI Global. doi:10.4018/978-1-5225-2255-3.ch123

Swartz, B. A., Lynch, J. M., & Lynch, S. D. (2018). Embedding Elementary Teacher Education Coursework in Local Classrooms: Examples in Mathematics and Special Education. In D. Polly, M. Putman, T. Petty, & A. Good (Eds.), *Innovative Practices in Teacher Preparation and Graduate-Level Teacher Education Programs* (pp. 262–292). Hershey, PA: IGI Global. doi:10.4018/978-1-5225-3068-8.ch015

Taliadorou, N., & Pashiardis, P. (2017). Emotional Intelligence and Political Skill Really Matter in Educational Leadership. In I. Management Association (Ed.), Educational Leadership and Administration: Concepts, Methodologies, Tools, and Applications (pp. 1274-1303). Hershey, PA: IGI Global. https://doi.org/doi:10.4018/978-1-5225-1624-8.ch060

Tandoh, K. A., & Ebe-Arthur, J. E. (2018). Effective Educational Leadership in the Digital Age: An Examination of Professional Qualities and Best Practices. In J. Keengwe (Ed.), *Handbook of Research on Digital Content, Mobile Learning, and Technology Integration Models in Teacher Education* (pp. 244–265). Hershey, PA: IGI Global. doi:10.4018/978-1-5225-2953-8.ch013

Tobin, M. T. (2018). Multimodal Literacy. In M. Khosrow-Pour, D.B.A. (Ed.), Encyclopedia of Information Science and Technology, Fourth Edition (pp. 1508-1516). Hershey, PA: IGI Global. doi:10.4018/978-1-5225-2255-3.ch130

Torres, K. M., Arrastia-Chisholm, M. C., & Tackett, S. (2019). A Phenomenological Study of Pre-Service Teachers' Perceptions of Completing ESOL Field Placements. *International Journal of Teacher Education and Professional Development, 2*(2), 85–101. https://doi.org/10.4018/IJTEPD.2019070106

Torres, M. C., Salamanca, Y. N., Cely, J. P., & Aguilar, J. L. (2020). All We Need is a Boost! Using Multimodal Tools and the Translanguaging Strategy: Strengthening Speaking in the EFL Classroom. *International Journal of Computer-Assisted Language Learning and Teaching, 10*(3), 28–47. doi:10.4018/IJCALLT.2020070103

Torres, M. L., & Ramos, V. J. (2018). Music Therapy: A Pedagogical Alternative for ASD and ID Students in Regular Classrooms. In P. Epler (Ed.), *Instructional Strategies in General Education and Putting the Individuals With Disabilities Act (IDEA) Into Practice* (pp. 222–244). Hershey, PA: IGI Global. doi:10.4018/978-1-5225-3111-1.ch008

Toulassi, B. (2017). Educational Administration and Leadership in Francophone Africa: 5 Dynamics to Change Education. In S. Mukerji & P. Tripathi (Eds.), *Handbook of Research on Administration, Policy, and Leadership in Higher Education* (pp. 20–45). Hershey, PA: IGI Global. doi:10.4018/978-1-5225-0672-0.ch002

Umair, S., & Sharif, M. M. (2018). Predicting Students Grades Using Artificial Neural Networks and Support Vector Machine. In M. Khosrow-Pour, D.B.A. (Ed.), Encyclopedia of Information Science and Technology, Fourth Edition (pp. 5169-5182). Hershey, PA: IGI Global. doi:10.4018/978-1-5225-2255-3.ch449

Vettraino, L., Castello, V., Guspini, M., & Guglielman, E. (2018). Self-Awareness and Motivation Contrasting ESL and NEET Using the SAVE System. In M. Khosrow-Pour, D.B.A. (Ed.), Encyclopedia of Information Science and Technology, Fourth Edition (pp. 1559-1568). Hershey, PA: IGI Global. doi:10.4018/978-1-5225-2255-3.ch135

Wiemelt, J. (2017). Critical Bilingual Leadership for Emergent Bilingual Students. In I. Management Association (Ed.), Educational Leadership and Administration: Concepts, Methodologies, Tools, and Applications (pp. 1606-1631). Hershey, PA: IGI Global. doi:10.4018/978-1-5225-1624-8.ch074

Wolf, F., Seyfarth, F. C., & Pflaum, E. (2018). Scalable Capacity-Building for Geographically Dispersed Learners: Designing the MOOC "Sustainable Energy in Small Island Developing States (SIDS)". In U. Pandey & V. Indrakanti (Eds.), *Open and Distance Learning Initiatives for Sustainable Development* (pp. 58–83). Hershey, PA: IGI Global. doi:10.4018/978-1-5225-2621-6.ch003

Woodley, X. M., Mucundanyi, G., & Lockard, M. (2017). Designing Counter-Narratives: Constructing Culturally Responsive Curriculum Online. *International Journal of Online Pedagogy and Course Design*, *7*(1), 43–56. doi:10.4018/IJOPCD.2017010104

Yell, M. L., & Christle, C. A. (2017). The Foundation of Inclusion in Federal Legislation and Litigation. In C. Curran & A. Petersen (Eds.), *Handbook of Research on Classroom Diversity and Inclusive Education Practice* (pp. 27–52). Hershey, PA: IGI Global. doi:10.4018/978-1-5225-2520-2.ch002

Zinner, L. (2019). Fostering Academic Citizenship With a Shared Leadership Approach. In C. Zhu & M. Zayim-Kurtay (Eds.), *University Governance and Academic Leadership in the EU and China* (pp. 99–117). IGI Global. https://doi.org/10.4018/978-1-5225-7441-5.ch007

About the Contributors

Mohammad Santally is a Professor of Education Technology at the University of Mauritius. His research interests are learning design, open educational resources, and innovative pedagogies to improve learning outcomes in online contexts. He is currently interested in exploring AI in Education given his background in ICTs. He has served at top positions at the University of Mauritius, and has worked as consultant in e-elearning for international organisations.

Yousra Banoor Rajabalee is an eLearning specialist. She has specialized herself in educational technologies and computer-based instructional design. She is a Lecturer in Education Technology at the Mauritius Institute of Education & Member of the Pole of Research on Innovative Pedagogies, Technologies and Practices in Education at the University of Mauritius.

***

C.V. Suresh Babu, is a pioneer in content development. A true entrepreneur, he founded Anniyappa Publications, a company that is highly active in publishing books related to Computer Science and Management. Dr. C.V. Suresh Babu has also ventured into SB Institute, a center for knowledge transfer. He holds a Ph.D. in Engineering Education from the National Institute of Technical Teachers Training & Research in Chennai, along with seven master's degrees in various disciplines such as Engineering, Computer Applications, Management, Commerce, Economics, Psychology, Law, and Education. Additionally, he has UGC-NET/SET qualifications in the fields of Computer Science, Management, Commerce, and Education. Currently, Dr. C.V. Suresh Babu is a Professor in the Department of Information Technology at the School of Computing Science, Hindustan Institute of Technology and Science (Hindustan University) in Padur, Chennai, Tamil Nadu, India.

Ashvin Beetul is a Visual Communication Designer and Part Time Lecturer in Multimedia related modules, with a 20-year extensive industry experience in the field along with advertising and marketing. He is also a PhD candidate with significant interest in the immersive environment as Augmented/Virtual/Mixed Reality (VR/AR/MR) in the field of education.

Tahani R. Bsharat is a Ph. D. Researcher pursuing a Ph. D. at Faculty of Major Language Studies, Universiti Sains Islam, Malaysia. Bsharat's research interest are learning pedagogy, education curriculum, development teaching experience pedagogy, collaborative learning, educational evaluation, and e-learning teaching materials.

Zeynep Çetin Köroğlu has been working as an Associate Professor Doctor at the English Language Teaching Department of Aksaray University, Turkey. Her academic background mainly consists of English Language Teaching. She graduated from Gazi University and got her MA degree. Then, she started her Ph.D. at the same university and completed it in 2015. She is especially interested in intercultural communication, language teachers' education, ICT implementations in language pedagogy, and language assessment. She published numerous book chapters and articles related to her research interests. Orcid ID: 0000-0002-9456-8910

Islam Ismail is a Ph. D. researcher in English Language Education. Ismail does research in writing mistakes, learning during COVID-19, integration technology in education, curriculum development, and honing teachers' teaching quality in ESL classrooms.

Linda Van Laren is an Honorary Lecturer in the School of Education at the University of KwaZulu-Natal in South Africa. Her disciplinary expertise lies in the area of mathematics education. Her research interests include assessment in mathematics, multicultural and anti-racist education integration of HIV and AIDS education across disciplines and Self-study methodology. She has used a variety of arts-inspired methods, including digital animation, in collaborative self-study research projects.

Claudia Mitchell is a Distinguished James McGill Professor, McGill University where she is the Director of the Particpatory Cultures Lab, and an Honorary Professor in the School of Education, University of KwaZulu-Natal. Her research addresses issues of social justice, participatory methodologies, girlhood studies and teacher education. She is the Editor-in-Chief of Girlhood Studies: An Interdisciplinary Journal.

Harmony Musiyarira is a professor who holds a PhD in Engineering degree from the University of the Witwatersrand, a Master's Degree in Manufacturing Systems and Operations Management, and an Honours degree in Metallurgical Engineering. Harmony is the Executive Dean of the Faculty of Engineering and the Built Environment at Namibia University of Science and Technology (NUST) and is the former Head of the Department of Mining and Process Engineering. He previously managed Refractory High-Temperature materials, Earthenware, and Sanitaryware ceramic production plants for a formerly Anglo-American Corporation. Prof Musiyarira was the project leader in developing the Mineral Beneficiation Strategy for Namibia and was instrumental in developing the Namibian Sector Growth Strategy for Coloured Gemstones. He was a member of the Intergovernmental Forum (IGF) project team on Mining, Metals, Minerals, and Sustainable Development that carried out the Mineral Policy Framework Assessment for Namibia. Harmony has proven to establish successful collaboration networks and consultancy projects with the local industry, government, and leading international research institutions. He is a PhD external examiner for the University of Queensland in Australia, the University of Johannesburg, and the Witwatersrand. Harmony is the conference chairperson for the Sustainable Development in the Minerals Industry (SDIMI) conference to be held in Namibia in September 2022. He is the President of the Society of Mining Professors (SOMP). His teaching and research interests are in Minerals Processing, Mine and process waste treatment and management, and Cleaner Production application in the minerals industry.

K.S. Sastry Musti is presently with Namibia University of Science and Technology, Windhoek, Namibia. He has than 30 years of professional experience. He obtained his BTech in Electrical Engineering from JNTU, Kakinada (A.P.) in 1990, MTech and PhD from NIT, Warangal in the years 1996 and 2002 respectively. Some of his earlier employments include University of the West Indies, St Augustine, Trinidad, ESIGELEC, Rouen, France and Sophia University, Tokyo, Japan. His research interests include Power and Energy Systems, Information Systems and Engineering Education.

Dorothy Cooshna-Naik, Ph.D., is a senior lecturer in visual communication at the Centre for Innovative and Lifelong Learning (CILL) of the University of Mauritius. Her first degree is in Applied Arts. She holds her M.A. from the University of Strasbourg, France and her Ph.D. from the University of KwaZulu-Natal, Durban, South Africa. Her research interest focuses on areas such as visual communication, computer mediated communication and pedagogies, alternative modes of assessment, multimedia learning and multimodal learning experiences and how emerging technologies and pedagogies can be leveraged to support and sustain teaching and learning at all level of education. In parallel, she has worked on several locally and internationally funded research projects.

Fariza Puteh-Behak currently works at the Faculty of Major Languages Studies, USIM I Universiti Sains Islam Malaysia. Fariza does research on multiliteracies, socio-cultural learning and indigenous education.

Jack Whitehead is a Visiting Professor at the University of Cumbria. He is a former president of the British Educational Research Association and Distinguished Scholar in Residence at Westminster College, Utah. He is a Visiting Professor at Ningxia University in China and an Extraordinary Professor of Community Based Educational Research at North-West University, South Africa. He is a member of the editorial board of the Educational Journal of Living Theories (). Since 1973 his research programme has focused on the creation of the living educational theories that individuals use to improve their practice and explain their educational influences in their workplaces.

Erkan Yüce is an Associate Professor at the Faculty of Education of Aksaray University. He received his Ph.D. degree in English Language Teaching from Hacettepe University Graduate School of Educational Sciences in 2018. English Language Teaching, the CEFR, Curriculum and Instruction, language program evaluation, and CBI are among his fields of interest. His recent research appeared in journals such as Adult Learning, Journal on Efficiency and Responsibility in Education and Science (ERIES Journal), and Novitas-ROYAL Journal.

Index

A

Acoustic Awareness 75
Active Learning 5, 31, 44, 47, 80
Alternative Assessment 27-28, 30, 44, 49-50
Authentic Learning 27, 31, 44-45, 49
Authoring tool 55, 139, 149-151, 153, 177-178

B

benefits and drawbacks of e-learning 1, 5

C

CEFR 95-97, 99, 101, 106, 110-112, 114
CEFR Companion Volume 95-97, 99, 106, 111
CEFR-CV 96-98, 101-104, 106-110, 114
Covid-19 8, 45, 59, 79, 88, 90, 95-98, 103-105, 110-114, 116, 138

D

Deaf 54-56, 72-73, 75
Deaf and Hard of Hearing (DHH) 54-55
Digital Multimodal Text 29
digital platforms 115-121, 124, 126-128, 130-135

E

Educational Technology 12, 16, 25-26, 47, 49, 53-54, 72-73, 93, 111
EFL learners 76, 78, 82, 84, 95, 110-111, 113-114
eLearning 8-9, 139-142, 147-158, 161-162, 164, 168-170, 178, 181
engineering education 46, 115, 135, 170
English language speaking skills 76, 89, 99, 103, 110
escape classrooms 129-130, 132-134
Evaluation approach 139, 158

F

fidelity 128, 130-132
Foreign language speaking skills 104

H

Hard of Hearing 54-55, 75

I

Inclusive Education 72, 74

L

learning and assessment 116, 128, 130, 132, 134
Learning Design 13, 15, 73
learning platforms 1, 4, 88, 157
LiveCode 54-55, 60, 62-64, 70-71

M

MS-Excel 119, 121-125, 129, 131-132, 134-135

Multimedia learning 11-17, 21, 24-26, 174, 181-182

N

New Literacy Practices 44

O

online learning 4, 7-8, 11, 88, 90-91, 98, 104, 109-111, 158

P

Phonological Awareness 75
Phonological Coding 75
Publishing formats 171

Q

Quality Assurance 139, 141, 154-158, 164-166, 169-170, 181

R

Rapid e-learning 115-119, 121-126, 128-134, 139, 141, 147, 169, 171-182
Rapid eLearning 147-148, 154-155, 158, 169
Rapid Game Development 54-55, 59

S

Scenario- based language learning 76, 78
Scenario Based Learning 77, 91-92, 94
SCORM 149-150, 156-157, 170, 177
SEN Schools 55, 75
SEN Teachers or Educators 75
SPEAK model 163-164
Special Education Needs (SEN) 54-55
Split-attention effect 11, 13, 16-19, 22-25
Storyboarding 39
Student Agency 43
Student engagement 117
Students as Producers 31-32, 52
Synchronisation 18

T

transactions and collaboration 96-98, 101-103, 108-109

www.ingramcontent.com/pod-product-compliance
Lightning Source LLC
LaVergne TN
LVHW080650011026
849160LV00014B/1376